Shakespeare's Essays

For my mother,
Gee Gee Platt (aka Gram)

Shakespeare's Essays

Sampling Montaigne from Hamlet *to* The Tempest

Peter G. Platt

EDINBURGH
University Press

Edinburgh University Press is one of the leading university presses in the UK. We publish academic books and journals in our selected subject areas across the humanities and social sciences, combining cutting-edge scholarship with high editorial and production values to produce academic works of lasting importance. For more information visit our website: edinburghuniversitypress.com

© Peter G. Platt, 2020, 2022

Edinburgh University Press Ltd
The Tun – Holyrood Road
12(2f) Jackson's Entry
Edinburgh EH8 8PJ

First published in hardback by Edinburgh University Press 2020

Typeset in 10.5/13 Adobe Sabon by
IDSUK (DataConnection) Ltd

A CIP record for this book is available from the British Library

ISBN 978 1 4744 6340 9 (hardback)
ISBN 978 1 4744 6341 6 (paperback)
ISBN 978 1 4744 6342 3 (webready PDF)
ISBN 978 1 4744 6343 0 (epub)

The right of Peter G. Platt to be identified as the author of this work has been asserted in accordance with the Copyright, Designs and Patents Act 1988, and the Copyright and Related Rights Regulations 2003 (SI No. 2498).

Contents

Acknowledgements		vi
Texts and Titles		ix
	Introduction: 'Were my mind settled, I would not essay but resolve myself'	1
1.	Knowing and Being in Montaigne and Shakespeare	24
2.	'A little thing doth divert and turn us': Fictions, Mourning, and Playing in 'Of Diverting or Diversion' and *Hamlet*	45
3.	Mingled Yarns and Hybrid Worlds: 'We Taste Nothing Purely', *Measure for Measure,* and *All's Well That Ends Well*	77
4.	'We are both father and mother together in this generation': Physical and Intellectual Creations in 'Of the Affection of Fathers to Their Children' and *King Lear*	109
5.	Custom, Otherness, and the Fictions of Mastery: 'Of the Caniballes' and *The Tempest*	129
Epilogue: Shakespeare before the *Essays*		154
Works Cited		169
Index		185

Acknowledgements

This book came into being as the result of two conversations. First, my Columbia colleague Jean Howard convinced me to break my Shakespeare and Montaigne project into two: an edited selection of John Florio's 1603 English translation of the *Essays* and a scholarly monograph on the Montaigne–Shakespeare connection. I am very grateful to Jean for that early pep talk. Second, upon learning that Stephen Greenblatt was simultaneously starting to work on a Florio edition, I asked him if he wanted to combine our efforts. Thankfully, he agreed, and working with him on what became *Shakespeare's Montaigne* (New York Review Books, 2014) was a true delight, personally and intellectually. This book, then, is a companion volume of sorts to our Florio edition.

Barnard Provost Linda Bell has provided crucial institutional support throughout this project. Butler Library at Columbia, Wollman Library (now the Milstein Center) at Barnard, Doe Library at the University of California, Berkeley, and the San Francisco Public Library (including its affiliation with the amazing Link+ catalogue) have provided me with essential resources. The Mechanics' Institute Library in San Francisco has, for over twenty years, been my scholarly home away from home; most of this book was written there, and I am grateful to my officemate at Mechanics', Bill Littmann, for his advice, patience and (mostly) good jokes. Thanks to Michelle Houston of Edinburgh University Press for believing in this project and helping me to see it through to publication and to Camilla Rockwood for superlative copy-editing.

I am very thankful for twenty-five years of teaching Barnard and Columbia students, who have kept me learning about and essaying Montaigne and Shakespeare. Thank you as well to the graduate teaching assistants who have helped me with my Shakespeare classes and who manage to be both outstanding scholars and teachers: John

Bird, Gabriel Bloomfield, Jessica Forbes, John Kuhn, Alexander Lash, Bernadette Myers, Seth Williams, and Kevin Windhauser. Thanks yet again to former graduate students (and now tenured titans) Alan Farmer, Zack Lesser, Doug Pfeiffer, Ben Robinson, Tiffany Werth, and Adam Zucker for making me proud and making me smarter.

My Columbia colleagues have been incredibly supportive during this project: thanks to Julie Crawford, Kathy Eden, Molly Murray, and especially Jim Shapiro and Alan Stewart. Barnard's 'Renaissance wing' is essential to my scholarly and general happiness: I am grateful to Rachel Eisendrath, Achsah Guibbory, Kim Hall, and Anne Prescott. Liz Auran, Jim Basker, Chris Baswell, Yvette Christiansë, Pam Cobrin, Pat Denison, Lisa Gordis, Saskia Hamilton, Jennie Kassanoff, Sarah Pasadino, Rio Santisteban-Edwards, Wendy Schor-Haim, Timea Szell, and Margaret Vandenburg have helped keep me sane. Bill Sharpe heroically read several versions of this entire book and, crucially, after one memorable run and gyro, helped me figure out its title. Outside of the English Department, my Barnard life has been enriched by Anne Boyman, Marisa Buzzeo, Lisa Hollibaugh, Brian Larkin, Dina Merrer, Nancy Worman, Bill Worthen, Hana Worthen, and especially Peter Connor. Beyond Barnard and Columbia, I send thanks to Joel Altman, Leonard Barkan, Piers Brown, Bradin Cormack, Jeff Dolven, David Kastan, and Pashmina Murthy. Branching out into the world of Montaigne Studies has introduced me to some wonderful colleagues who have provided me with a new scholarly community: Lars Engle, Saul Frampton, Patrick Gray, John O'Brien, Phillip Usher, and especially Will Hamlin have made my academic life much more fulfilling. Finally, thanks to Andrew Auchincloss, Judith Boies, Mark Bridges, Cabot Brown, Robert Christman, Howard Fishman, Peter Freedberger, David Gendelman, Ken Joye, John Kurtz, Philippe Lambert, Charles Louderback, Murdock Martin, Richard Michaelis, Anna Murphy, George Olive, Mark Ouweleen, Bill Rappel, Antonio Rossi, Julintip Thirasilpa, Todd West, and Matt Wolf for providing levity and wisdom at just the right moments.

My family continues to be my anchor. Thanks to dad and brother Geoff for patiently listening to and encouraging me. My wife, Nancy – herself a translator – has been extremely helpful in my forays into Florio; her love and support have been constant and sustaining. I trust that our son, Jordy – despite our too frequent separations – has no doubts about 'that singular and loving affection which in my soul I bare unto him'. This book is for my mom, who taught me how to write better, to obsess over editing, to love books – inside and out. I can no other answer make but thanks, and thanks, and ever thanks.

Part of Chapter 3 appeared as '"The Web of our Life is of a Mingled Yarn": Mixed Worlds and Kinds in Montaigne's "We Taste Nothing Purely" and Shakespeare's *All's Well That Ends Well*', in *Shakespeare and Montaigne*, ed. Lars Engle, Patrick Gray, and William M. Hamlin (Edinburgh: Edinburgh University Press, 2021). I thank the Press for permission to include that material here.

Texts and Titles

I adopt Will Hamlin's spelling protocols in his *Montaigne's English Journey* for the texts of Montaigne: *Essayes* for references to Florio's translation, *Essais* for references to French editions, and *Essays* for general references to the book.

Introduction: 'Were my mind settled, I would not essay but resolve myself'

Why do critics and audiences feel that there is something 'different' about the plays that Shakespeare wrote after 1603? Scholars have for years focused on Shakespeare's later works as 'Jacobean' because of James I's accession to the throne in 1603. The plays – in the darkness of their comedy and in the general pessimism of the largely tragic period that followed – have been seen to mirror the despair and unease of an England that had lost its queen and had been plunged into the uncertainty that is inevitably part of a transition in power. More recently it has been argued that other crucial factors coincided with the change in regime. Shakespeare's interest in judicial rhetoric, the personnel changes in his own acting company, and his performances at court – all these helped shape such diverse and troubling plays as *Measure for Measure*, *King Lear*, and *The Tempest*.[1]

But 1603 was also the year in which John Florio published his widely read translation of Montaigne's essays, which Shakespeare undoubtedly knew and used as he constructed phrases, speeches, and perhaps the thematic universe of whole plays.[2]

In this book I contend that Shakespeare's reading of Montaigne is an under-recognised driving force in the development of his later work, from the choice of specific words to the employment of whole patterns of thought. Montaigne and Shakespeare share similar approaches to ideas of knowing, being, and aesthetic form, what John O'Brien has called 'an esthetics of *non finito* and an ontology of incompleteness'.[3] Theirs is a world of doubt, contingency, uncertainty, and mutability – in which receptivity to new ideas and new, more 'open' methods of literary composition feature strongly. Both authors dedicate themselves to exploring instabilities of self, knowledge, and form in disjunctive ways that stress interruption, fracture, and unexpected alternatives to conventional wisdom.

This quest to probe the instabilities of self, knowing, and world takes, for both writers, the form of 'essays'. Although writing in a different genre, Shakespeare *essays* the *Essais*. For as a contemporary dictionary – Randall Cotgrave's *A Dictionarie of the French and English Tongves* (1611) – tells us, 'essayer' could mean 'To *essay*; try, proue, *tast*, attempt; *take a tast*, make a tryall of; *to feele before hand*.'[4] So, while Montaigne's essays created a major literary genre and gave a name to intellectual questing in prose form, Shakespeare's own 'essays' – his trials of ideas, forms, and even specific words on a Montaignian model – have gone relatively unremarked. This book will not reveal a prose Shakespeare, but it will show how, after reading Montaigne, as translated by Florio in 1603, Shakespeare made the tentative, provisional, sceptical essaying of ideas an integral part of his plays. 'Shakespeare's essays' are both prose and poetry. On the one hand, they are the edition of Florio that he knew so well, and on the other hand, they are the plays that he wrote exploring concepts and approaches that Montaigne had singled out for attention.

In arguing for a Montaignian Shakespeare, I am not dismissing the extensive work done on the Jacobean context of the later plays, and I am not introducing the topic for the first time. But I believe that we need to take more seriously the words of Friedrich Nietzsche, who in 1876 called Shakespeare Montaigne's 'best reader'.[5] By reading Montaigne and Florio as Shakespeare must have, with an eye keen for vivid details and telling phrases, and a mind attuned to challenging ideas and gnawing doubts, we can become better readers ourselves. Shakespeare's Montaigne is not always easy to grasp, but he is almost always 'there'. Once we begin to catch on to the characteristics of his subtle, shifting form, we meet him repeatedly in Shakespeare's later plays.[6]

Florio's translation of Montaigne made a substantial impression when it was first published, as I will show in a moment. But surprisingly no one connected Montaigne explicitly to Shakespeare for more than a century and a half. Indeed, it was not until 1780 that a Shakespeare scholar noticed, at least in print, that Shakespeare had read Montaigne at all.[7] In that year Edward Capell's *Notes and Various Readings to Shakespeare* noted the now-famous verbal echoes of Montaigne's 'Of the Caniballes' (1.31, 1.30 in Florio) in Gonzalo's speech about a pastoral utopia in *The Tempest*. Thus began a debate over Shakespeare's 'debt to Montaigne' that has waxed and waned over the centuries.[8] Because that debt might be seen to question Shakespeare's own creativity, it has at times echoed the authorship debate in its intensity.

The existence of the debate is remarkable in itself, since Shakespeare's contemporaries in the dramatic and literary worlds of early modern

England would not have found it at all strange to think of Shakespeare as a reader of Montaigne, since they were often his readers as well. If early modern publishers can be counted as the earliest audiences for the books they ushered into the world, then Edward Blount may have been among the first to make the Montaigne–Shakespeare connection: he published both the Florio Montaigne in 1603 and the Shakespeare First Folio in 1623.[9]

More certainly, in an important poem at the beginning of Volume I of Florio's translation, Florio's brother-in-law and poet extraordinaire Samuel Daniel revealed himself a perceptive reader of Montaigne's ideas on custom, praising '*Prince* Montaigne *(if he be not more)*' for, among other reasons, having

> made such bolde sallies out upon
> Custome, *the mightie tyrant of the earth*,
> *In whose* Seraglio *of subjection*
> *We all seeme bred-up, from our tender birth.*[10]

What Daniel shows us is that Florio / Montaigne is challenging his audience in provocative ways, asking them to consider why they think and act as they do.

The playwright John Marston made ample use of Florio's translation, especially in his *The Dutch Courtesan* (1605), as did John Webster in *The White Devil* (1611–12).[11] In Ben Jonson's *Volpone* (1607), Lady Politic Would-Be suggests that the English routinely used Montaigne's essays for their own writing.[12] Discussing the Italian writer Giambattista Guarini (1538–1612) and especially his *Il pastor fido*, Lady Politic explains that

> All our English writers,
> I meane such, as are happy in the Italian,
> Will deigne to steal out of this Author, mainely;
> Almost as much, as from Montagnie. (3.4)

Jonson's character says what everyone seems to have known – that Montaigne was the first choice for prospective stealers and borrowers.

Yet it was not until 1780 and Capell's note that anyone noticed that Shakespeare had 'deigne[d] to steal out of ... Montagnie'. Capell's observation of the similarities between Gonzalo's discussion of an ideal commonwealth in 2.1 of *The Tempest* and a passage from Montaigne's 'Of the Caniballes' deserves quoting in full:

> This speech, and one that comes after it, prove the writer's acquaintance with one he has not been trac'd in by any, annotator or editor; for thus old Montaigne, speaking of the Indian discovery and of the new people's

manners: 'C'est une Nation, diray-je a Platon, en laquelle il n'y a a aucune esperance de trafiq, nulle cognoissance de Lettres, nulle science de nombres, nul nom de magistrat, ny de superiorité politique, nul usage de service, de richesse, ou de pauvreté, nulls contracts, nulls successions, nulls partages, nulls occupations qu'oysives, nul respect de parenté que commun, nulls vestments, nulle agriculture, nul metal, nul usage de vin ou de bled. Les paroles mesmes, qui signifient le mensonge, la trahison, la dissumulation, l'avarice, l'envie, la detraction, le pardon, inouyes.' – *Essais de Montaigne*, vol. i, p. 270, Bruxelles, 1659. The person who shall compare this passage with the translations of it that were extant in Shakespeare's time will see reason to think he read it in French.[13]

'Old Montaigne' – but, explicitly, not John Florio – and Shakespeare were linked for the first time.[14] Ten years later, Edmund Malone – in a rather harsh take-down of Capell – was the first to link Shakespeare and *Florio's* Montaigne:

> Our author has here closely followed a passage in Montaigne's ESSAIES, translated by John Florio, folio, 1603: 'It is a nation, (would I answer Plato,) that hath *no kind of trafficke, no knowledge of letters*. . . . The very words that import lying, falsehood, *treason,* dissimulations, covetousness, envie, detraction and pardon, were never heard amongst them.' The passage was pointed out by Mr. Capell, who knew so little of his author as to suppose that Shakspeare [sic] had the original French before him, though he has almost literally followed Florio's translation.[15]

So Shakespeare and Montaigne are linked in 1780, Shakespeare and Florio in 1790.

In the *Essays*, the crucial passage comes as Montaigne – speaking of Brazilian Indians near Rio de Janeiro, where Nicolas Durand de Villegagnon had established a colony by 1555 – wrote, in Florio's translation,

> It is a nation, would I answer *Plato*, that hath no kind of traffic, no knowledge of letters, no intelligence of numbers, no name of magistrate, nor of politic superiority; no use of service, of riches, or of poverty; no contracts, no successions, no dividences, no occupation but idle; no respect of kindred, but common; no apparel but natural; no manuring of lands, no use of wine, corn, or metal.[16]

When Shakespeare's Gonzalo discusses his model commonwealth with the remnants of the Neapolitan court, he steals from 'Montagnie':

> Had I plantation of this isle my lord . . .,
> I' the commonwealth I would by contraries
> Execute all things. For no kind of traffic

> Would I admit; no name of magistrate;
> Letters should not be known; riches, poverty,
> And use of service, none; contract, succession,
> Bourn, bound of land, tilth, vineyard, none;
> No use of metal, corn, or wine, or oil;
> No occupation; all men idle, all;
> And women too – but innocent and pure;
> No sovereignty . . .
> All things in common nature should produce
> Without sweat or endeavor. Treason, felony,
> Sword, pike, knife, gun, or need of any engine,
> Would I not have; but nature should bring forth,
> Of it own kind all foison, all abundance,
> To feed my innocent people. (2.1.142; 147–56, 159–64)

I will return to the exact language of – and the variety of perspectives on the 'cannibals' in – the two texts when I discuss *The Tempest* in Chapter 5. But this is obviously a crucial moment in the Montaigne–Shakespeare nexus, and most scholars have shared Robert Ellrodt's conclusion about the relationship between the two passages: 'certainty is afforded by the recurrence of such phrases as "no kinde of traffike", "no name of magistrate", etc.'[17]

Following on from Capell, the nineteenth century saw the beginning of a debate about the extent of Shakespeare's debt to Montaigne, and the origins of this discussion are quite compelling because they reveal readers going beyond verbal echoes and thinking about literary and philosophical connections between the two writers. In 1838, Sir Frederic Madden claimed that the now-infamous copy of the 1603 *Essayes*, bearing Shakespeare's autograph, was authentic and confirmed that 'this book was consulted by Shakspere [sic] in the composition of his plays'.[18] In the same year, John Sterling not only concurred with the notion that Montaigne influenced Shakespeare but also claimed that 'The Prince of Denmark is very nearly a Montaigne.'[19] As Jean-François Chappuit notes, by this time, 'La polémique à propos de l'influence possible de Montaigne sur Shakespeare était lancée.'[20]

If Capell's note is the foundational moment, and 'the polemic was launched' in 1838, it was not long afterward that the debate began to pick up steam.[21] In 1846, the French scholar Philarète Chasles claimed that 'once on the track of the studies and tastes of Shakespeare, we find Montaigne at every corner, in *Hamlet*, in *Othello*, in *Coriolanus*'.[22] German scholars of the nineteenth century pushed the connection into the polemical,[23] and one of them, Jacob Feis, notably claimed that Hamlet not only was, as Sterling had it in 1838, 'a Montaigne' but was an embodied refutation of Montaigne's philosophy, which 'preached the rights of nature whilst yet clinging to dogmatic tenets . . . from the narrow cells of a superstitious Christianity'.[24]

Major works without such a strong agenda appeared in 1902 and 1909, by Elizabeth R. Hooker and J. M. Robertson respectively.[25] Hooker performed an exhaustive exploration of links between Shakespeare and both Montaigne's ideas and Florio's language, while Robertson made the case that the *Essays* helped both to provide Shakespeare's 'culture-evolution' and to form his 'mental history'.[26] Shakespeare drew on Montaigne for *Hamlet*, left him behind for a while, and then, 'after his period of pessimism[,] view[ed] life in a spirit which could be expressed in terms of Montaigne's philosophy'.[27] Robertson famously concluded that Shakespeare's debt to Montaigne ultimately was so great that it altered his own sense of Shakespeare's originality: Shakespeare is 'differentiated from other men not by his inventive and strictly "creative" faculty, but by his unparalleled plasticity and receptivity and responsiveness'.[28] For Robertson, then, Shakespeare essayed – and assayed – the *Essays* for his best ideas.

Dissent came very quickly. As early as 1904 – following the first edition of Robertson's book and Hooker's long article – J. Churlton Collins almost entirely dismissed the connection: 'It may be said at once that of all the parallel passages adduced there is not one, except that from *The Tempest*, which may not resolve itself into mere coincidence.'[29] The great Montaigne scholar Pierre Villey was even more certain of the lack of evidence, and weighed in with a famous claim: 'Cents zéros additionnes ensemble ne font toujours que zéro.'[30] In Villey's view, a hundred zeroes still add up to zero.

Then, in 1925, George Coffin Taylor launched a counterattack. *Shakspere's Debt to Montaigne* is still the most valuable book in presenting parallels between Shakespeare and Florio's Montaigne. It notes overlaps in 'vocabulary, phrases, short and long passages, and, after a fashion . . . also in thought'.[31] Taylor divides the key passages into three groups:

> First, that . . . group of passages in the Florio Montaigne and in the plays of Shakspere written during 1603 and after, so similar in phraseology as practically to preclude all possibility of doubt. Second, another group of passages and phrases in the Florio Montaigne and in Shakespeare's plays written during and after 1603, which, though not so strikingly similar in phraseology as to preclude all doubt, are yet similar enough to make one feel that the Shakspere passage could not have taken on its final form unless Shakspere had made the acquaintance of the Montaigne passage. Third, a list of approximately seven hundred and fifty words and phrases from the Florio Montaigne used also by

Shakspere, but never in any composition of his antedating 1603 – many of them, if one may judge from the Oxford Dictionary, never used by anyone before 1603.[32]

In an early review of Taylor's book, T. S. Eliot was particularly impressed by the third list, consisting of 'words and phrases numerous enough to create a presumption that Shakespeare picked them up from Florio'.[33] Eliot also praised Taylor for focusing on parallel words rather than on thoughts:

> And in bringing more clearly to light this verbal influence Mr. Taylor supplies a corrective in the invariable human impulse to look for mystery and excitement. For certainly it was not the influence of one philosopher on another. . . . Montaigne is just the sort of writer to provide a stimulant to a poet; for what the poet looks for in his reading is not a philosophy – not a doctrine or even a consistent point of view which he endeavours to *understand* – but a point of departure. The attitude of a craftsman like Shakespeare – whose business was to write plays, not to think – is very different from that of the philosopher or even the literary critic.
>
> Not that Montaigne did not influence Shakespeare in ways which we can never know. Mr. Taylor does not deny the existence of some deeper influence than an influence of vocabulary. But he refrains – and for this abstention must be given all praise – from attempting to plumb these depths.[34]

For Eliot, in essaying Montaigne, Shakespeare found a 'stimulant' for his poetry and maybe 'some deeper influence'. For its important collection of verbal echoes – and tantalising hints at intellectual parallels – Taylor's book is the one that must be confronted by all who wish to deny the Montaigne–Florio connection to Shakespeare.

And there have been potent rebuttals. In an essay as painstaking in its collection of data as was Taylor's book, Alice Harmon asked in 1942, 'How Great was Shakespeare's Debt to Montaigne?'[35] Harmon documents classical sources for all of the major parallels outlined by Taylor and others, and sees classical commonplaces – rather than shared ideas and language – as the link: 'Certainly, Shakespeare could have had from the popular commonplaces from the classics the type of material which he shares with Montaigne – in many instances indeed he could have found there the specific sentences and similitudes which occur with similar wording in Florio and the plays.'[36] Harmon misses the forest for the trees here, in addition to missing the occasions when Shakespeare and Montaigne (via Florio) depart from the very commonplaces she so assiduously lines up.[37]

Margaret Hodgen was less dogmatic in her 1952 essay, 'Montaigne and Shakespeare Again', which attempted to show that the ideas in both Montaigne's 'Of the Caniballes' and Shakespeare's *The Tempest* – the ground zero of the Montaigne–Shakespeare connection – were available in the 'anthropological' texts of the period.[38] She argues that 'this very ancient model was the one chosen by both men, not alone, as some have thought, because it embodied the ideas of the Golden Age and the Noble Savage, but because, with the use of these philosophical, moral, and historical ingredients, it included others of an equally ancient ethnological character'.[39] That said, she grudgingly recognised that 'it seems not unlikely that some indebtedness may have existed. . . . [T]he lines in *The Tempest* are still more like those in *Of the Caniballes* than any other formulation.'[40]

* * *

I will show in the pages that follow that the Montaigne–Shakespeare connection has roots that are deeper than – or at least different from – those of classical commonplaces (whether rhetorical, literary, or anthropological/ethnographic). It adds up to much more than Villey's 'zéros'.[41] This book builds on recent scholarship that has once again found the evidence for Montaigne's effect on Shakespeare to be too compelling to ignore. Arthur Kirsch has perceptively noted the links between Shakespeare's intellectual interests in *The Tempest* and 'Montaigne's thinking' as follows: 'inclusive; interrogative rather than programmatic; anti-sentimental but humane; tragicomic rather than only tragic or comic; incorporating adversities rather than italicizing them as subversive ironies'.[42] Kirsch's insights can be applied to other post-1603 plays as well.

Indeed, in recent years, 'Shakespeare's debt' has again become a critical focal point, especially in Anglo-American scholarship.[43] There were research seminars on Montaigne and Shakespeare both at the International Shakespeare World Congress in Valencia, Spain, in 2001 and at the Shakespeare Association of America's Annual Meeting in Bermuda in 2005, as well as a major conference on 'Shakespeare et Montaigne: Vers un Nouvel Humanisme' in France in 2003. Most recently, the Shakespeare Association of America's Annual Meeting in New Orleans in 2016 included a research seminar on 'Shakespeare and Montaigne'.[44] Hugh Grady has usefully connected the two writers in his *Shakespeare, Machiavelli, and Montaigne* (2002), and Peter Mack's *Reading and Rhetoric in Shakespeare and Montaigne* appeared in 2010. William Hamlin's superb *Montaigne's English Journey* (2013) focuses on the reception of Florio's Montaigne in Shakespeare's age, Robert Ellrodt's *Montaigne and Shakespeare: The Emergence of Modern Self Consciousness* (2015) explores the writers' shared intellectual terrain, and Warren Boutcher has seen Shakespeare as one of many important students in *The School of Montaigne* (2017).[45]

Scholars interested in the Montaigne–Shakespeare nexus have paid special attention to the way in which both writers look at human problems and experience from multiple perspectives. This kaleidoscopic exploration of human diversity has been attributed to Shakespeare before. John Keats in the nineteenth century focused on Shakespeare's 'negative capability'.[46] Jorge Luis Borges in the twentieth asserted Shakespeare's ability to be 'everything and nothing'.[47] If Montaigne did not influence Shakespeare's perspectivism — and he may have — he certainly shared it. Isaiah Berlin saw Montaigne as one of those thinkers who resisted 'magnetisation by either polar force', urging 'moderation in a disturbed situation' because he was one of those who could 'see, and cannot help seeing, many sides of a case ... who perceive that a humane cause promoted by means that are too ruthless is in danger of turning into its opposite'.[48] For it is Montaigne who claimed that 'I would have this worldes-frame to be my Schollers choise-booke: So many strange humours, sundry sects, varying judgements, diverse opinions, different lawes, and fantastical customs teach vs to judge rightly of ours, and instruct our judgement to acknowledge his [ie, its] imperfections and naturall weakenesse, which is no easie an apprentiship' ('Of the Institution and Education of Children [1.25], 75).

I argue, then, that Montaigne — especially in Florio's 1603 translation — was deeply important to both Shakespeare's thinking and the expression of his thought. Indeed, Jonathan Bate has recently claimed that 'it was this [Montaigne's] book, perhaps above all others, that shaped the mind of Shakespeare in the second half of his career'.[49]

Montaigne and Shakespeare shared an interest in multiplicity: a sense of perspectivism in their epistemology and a sense of a discontinuous self in their ontology. Because Montaigne and Shakespeare have so much in common, critics often end up distinguishing between the two writers on the basis of what Lars Engle has called 'a contrast in sensibility that accompanies the obvious difference in genre between the essay and the play'.[50] And this is the conclusion of Fred Parker, in his 'Shakespeare's Argument with Montaigne', who argues that there is a significant difference between the private essay and the 'populous' drama:

> There is no space in Shakespeare for the privileged viewpoint of the essayist, reflecting on experience, earthing the personal and particular in some large general commonplace or *sententia*. ... If there is one drama by Shakespeare which could lend itself to being read as an *essai*, it is *The Tempest*, the least populous of all the plays, and the only one where we know for sure that Shakespeare was thinking of Montaigne.[51]

Robert Ellrodt seeks to bridge this formal gap by linking Montaigne's essays both to Shakespeare's sonnets but even more to Shakespeare's soliloquies: 'It is through the evolution of the Shakespearean soliloquy that the evolution of subjectivity is best grasped. ... I think it certain that Shakespeare's acquaintance with the *Essays* increased his attention to the inner life and the necessity of self knowledge in the period from *Hamlet* to *King Lear*.'[52]

Indeed, as I have suggested earlier, even the generic difference may be over-stated. There is often a shared 'sensibility', and the difference in genre is more than made up for by a similarity in approach to form – O'Brien's 'esthetics of *non-finito*'. Furthermore, what Lawrence Kritzman has identified as 'the corrosive practice of the essay', which 'undermines the legislating power of absolute forms of knowledge since the multiplying of its points of reference confounds us', can be linked to Shakespeare's multivocal stagings. For Shakespeare's plays function similarly to Kritzman's sense of the essay as 'an exercise in approaching a horizon of possibilities'.[53] Although Shakespeare's thinking does not always line up with Montaigne's, their interest in alterity – other ways of being, knowing, writing – more often than not connects the two writers.

*   *   *

Pursuing these threads, I will, in the chapter that follows this Introduction, explore the two authors' relationship to scepticism and knowing on the one hand and to selfhood and being on the other. Chapters 2 to 5 then provide four case studies linking specific essays of Montaigne to specific post-1603 plays of Shakespeare, exploring ideas and connections that can be missed if the focus is merely on verbal echoes.

Chapter 2, the first case study, will pair 'Of Diverting and Diversion' (3.4) and *Hamlet*. *Hamlet* is a crucial text here both because it is, verbally and conceptually, the most Montaignian of Shakespeare's plays and because it is arguably too early to be included in the book. I will address the problem of the dates of the various versions – and especially the differences between the First Quarto (Q1) and the Second Quarto (Q2) – of *Hamlet* in this chapter. My central argument, after an exploration of the multiple versions of Shakespeare's play and of the Montaignian nature of the post-Q1 *Hamlet*, is that Shakespeare essays Montaigne's ambivalence towards diversions. At times Montaigne sees them as essential, even beautiful, and at other times highly misleading, illusory, and escapist. Shakespeare explores diversions through Hamlet's meditations, especially those on mourning and theatricality in the first two acts.[54]

Chapter 3 focuses on both authors' examination of the blended and hybrid nature of the world and compares 'We Taste Nothing Purely' (2.20) with Shakespeare's notoriously mixed, 'impure' problem plays, *Measure for Measure* and *All's Well That Ends Well*. Exploring play-worlds that are 'mingled yarns' of 'good and ill together', these plays blend comedy and tragedy as well; indeed, they seem to be dramatic elaborations on the opening sentence of Montaigne's essay: 'The weakness of our condition causeth that things in their natural simplicity and purity cannot fall into our use. The elements we enjoy are altered, metals likewise, yea gold must be empared with some other stuff to make it fit for our service' (56; 100).

In Chapter 4 I examine the connection between physical and intellectual creations in 'Of the Affection of Fathers to Their Children' (2.8) and *King Lear*. I will argue that Montaigne is at once more optimistic and more pessimistic about the love between parents and children than Shakespeare in *Lear*: he both argues for the natural bond between parents and their offspring and anatomises the treacheries and missed opportunities for achieving this bond that happen in the real world, beyond ideals. Further, the even greater connection between essay and play is the shared fascination with non-bodily creations. For Montaigne, 'Of the Affection' ultimately argues that 'what we engender by the mind, the fruits of our courage, sufficiency, or spirit, are brought forth by a far more noble part than the corporeal and more our own' (137; 232). For Shakespeare, *King Lear* provides a sustained meditation not only on filial impiety but on mental engenderings: those of 'fools and madmen' (3.4.75), 'noble philosopher[s]' (3.4.160), and the theatre itself.

Chapter 5, my final case study, examines the most famous of the links between Shakespeare and Montaigne. Even Montaigne–Shakespeare sceptics must acknowledge the presence of 'Of the Caniballes' in Gonzalo's speech in 2.1 of *The Tempest*. Scholars have not always agreed on just what work Shakespeare's use of Montaigne is doing, though the dominant view is something akin to Jonathan Bate's sense that Shakespeare has 'reversed Montaigne' – making complex and ironic what Montaigne had portrayed as simple and natural.[55] But I will argue that, whereas there are undoubtedly differences between Montaigne's cannibal and Shakespeare's Caliban, neither one is entirely 'simple' or 'natural'. I believe that Shakespeare is responding not to the singleness of Montaigne's cannibals but to their doubleness – not to their simplicity but to their complexity. And, like Montaigne's essay, *The Tempest* can be seen to anatomise what David Quint has called 'an ethics of yielding'.[56] Shakespeare may just be ringing changes on – rather than changing – Montaigne.

I finish the book with an Epilogue that explores what Shakespeare did with three major topics *before* he encountered Florio's translation of Montaigne: the mutability of the self; the multiplicity of truth claims and scepticism in a variety of forms; and the cultural other and outsider. Looking at Shakespeare's thinking about these issues before his encounter with the *Essays* reminds us that Montaigne gave Shakespeare the tools both to explore these ideas more deeply and to make them more prominent in his plays.

Method and Argument

This book seeks to combine the close reading for verbal echoes that characterises Robertson's and Taylor's studies with the exploration of shared ideas, especially of knowledge and the self, that are central to the books of Grady, Mack, Hamlin, and Ellrodt. Without abandoning Eliot's attention to 'words and phrases numerous enough to create a presumption that Shakespeare picked them up from Florio', I keep larger patterns – of thought, form, discourse – in mind.[57] Will Hamlin, too, has explored this tension between the specificity of Eliot's 'words and phrases' and the more expansive approach of something like Hugh Grady's 'discursive dynamics'.[58] Hamlin has cautioned – first in 2006 and most recently in his essay on 'Montaigne and Shakespeare' in the *Oxford Handbook of Montaigne* – against relying too much on strict verbal echoes and 'diachronic vectors of intellectual impact', preferring instead 'the weaker thesis of synchronic affinity'.[59]

Although Hamlin's 'weaker thesis' can lead to an impotent free-for-all of associations, this book argues that the greater danger is focusing too intently on verbal parallels and missing larger thematic and structural parallels that even more powerfully suggest the connection between Montaigne and Shakespeare.[60] In this way, we avoid 'scouring texts for potential source-trajectories that may deceive us into thinking we have found instances of indebtedness when in fact we have compromised our attention to both writers'.[61] Teasing out the Montaignian Shakespeare requires a 'scouring' not just of texts but also of contexts – ideas, patterns, forms.[62]

What I explore here, rather than a single thematic through-line, are connections and resonances that swirl throughout the essays and plays, especially those concerning the problems of knowing and being. By pairing specific plays with specific Montaignian essays – some of which have rarely or never been paired – I will show how these *Shakespearean* essays, his trials and samplings of Montaigne, are far from arbitrary but instead essential to the meanings of the plays.[63] Neither Montaigne nor Shakespeare rests with certainties, and both seem to share Montaigne's notion that 'Were my mind settled, I would not essay but resolve myself. It is still a prentise and a probationer.'[64] Shakespeare learned from his French collaborator how to essay and not to resolve. He grew to understand that essaying was a way of continuing his apprenticeship and his testing in and of life, a way to alternative possibilities.[65]

Montaigne's essays and Shakespeare's essaying plays share what Theodor Adorno called the essay form's para-doxical, heretical power: 'In opposition to the cliché of the 'understandable', the notion of truth as a network of causes and effects, the essay insists that a matter be considered, from the very first, in its whole complexity. . . . By transgressing the orthodoxy of thought, something becomes visible in the object which it is orthodoxy's secret purpose to keep invisible.'[66] As Montaigne claimed, 'Some writers there are, whose ende is but to relate the events. Mine, if I could attaine to it, should be to declare, what may come to passe . . .'[67] This focus on possibility, multiple selves, brave new worlds – what has not yet been but might still be – is at the heart of Montaigne's and Shakespeare's essays.[68]

Notes

1. For the Jacobean Shakespeare, see among others Longworth de Chambrun, *Giovanni Florio*; E. K. Chambers, *Shakespeare: A Survey*; John Dover Wilson, *The Essential Shakespeare: A Biographical Adventure*; Sisson, 'The Mythical Sorrows of Shakespeare'; R.W. Chambers, *Man's Unconquerable Mind*; and F. W. Wilson, *Elizabethan and Jacobean*. For Shakespeare and judicial rhetoric, see Skinner, *Forensic Shakespeare*. For the plays' being different as a result of Shakespeare's acting company and of Shakespeare's performances at court, see, respectively, Van Es, *Shakespeare in Company*, and Dutton, *Shakespeare, Court Dramatist*, esp. 267–90. Exploring Shakespeare's post-1603 connections in London – based on his relationship with his French Protestant landlords and their acquaintances – Charles Nicholl has brilliantly examined *The Lodger Shakespeare*.
2. See *Shakespeare's Montaigne*, ed. Greenblatt and Platt.
3. O'Brien, 'Montaigne and Antiquity', 69. Writing about Shakespeare's sonnets, Colin Burrow – in his 'Why Shakespeare is Not Michelangelo' – has called Shakespeare's approach to art an 'aesthetic of mobility: that beauty lies in change rather than chiselling' (20). On Shakespeare's form of possibility, see Palfrey, *Shakespeare's Possible Worlds*: 'Perhaps three things, all inevitably interdependent, most characterise Shakespearean form. First, the instinct to split and double all phenomena, such that everything is shadowed by alternatives it cannot escape; second, a feeling of the potentiality for life, and for the release of or into emotion, in *all* things, animate and inanimate, including instruments of his craft, objects used in it, and abstractions; third, a knowledge that every surface hides dimensions, and can be tented like a wound, or magnified into multiplicity, and that this spatial variety speaks equally of temporal extension, backward and forward in history, such that all phenomena contain their sources, their struggles, and their possible futures. We seem never to be given something – word, concept, emotion, institution – without being asked to imagine it otherwise, inside out, upside down, conjoined' (33).
4. See 'Essayer', in Cotgrave, *A Dictionarie of the French and English Tongues*. In his entry on '*Essai (genre)*' in the *Dictionnaire de Michel de Montaigne*,

ed. Desan, Philippe Desan notes that 'Une des premières définitions du mot <<essai>> fut donnée par La Croix du Maine dans sa *Bibliothèque française* (1584): <<ce titre ou inscription est fort modeste, car si on veut prendre ce mot d'*Essais*, pour coup d'Essai, ou apprentissage, cela est fort humble et rabaissé . . .>>. Il est en effet assez courant à cette époque de considérer la première publication d'un auteur un coup d'essai. . . L'expression <<coup d'essai>> est fréquente à la Renaissance' (341). Indeed, Cotgrave is very helpful here, too: 'Coup d'essay: The Maister-peece of a young workeman, or of one that's but newly come of his yeares; a beginning, entrance, onset, attempt; a flourish, or preamble, whereby a tast of a thing is giuen, or taken' (n.p.). So *coup d'essay* is a first attempt at a work – whether a book or something else made by a 'young workeman' – but it also possesses the humility that is associated with 'essay' generally: From its origins, it is an extremely modest ('fort modeste . . . fort humble') and self-diminishing ('rabaissé') form. That Shakespeare essays Montaigne's *Essais* – both of them tasting but neither of them hoping to master – is significant.

5. Nietzsche, 'Richard Wagner in Bayreuth', 207.
6. For recent surveys of the Montaigne–Shakespeare connection, see Mack, 'Montaigne and Shakespeare'; Burrow, 'Montaignian Moments'; and Hamlin, 'Montaigne and Shakespeare'. And I have been chastened by Warren Boutcher's questions, in his 'Montaigne in England and America', about just what 'influence' means when it comes to Montaigne's effect on early modern England and beyond: 'Is Montaigne's reception to be studied as "influence" on the part of the author or as "appropriation" on the part of readers? Is it still a matter of the afterlife, "fortunes", or posterity of the original text, which is more or less faithfully and richly interpreted by English readers and writers? Or is it an active process whose meaning and outcomes are shaped primarily by the agents and circumstances of reception?' (306). My sense of 'influence' is close to that of Tetsuo Anzai, in his *Shakespeare and Montaigne Reconsidered*: 'an influence [is] one that can be pointed out on the deeper, structural level of a work . . . perhaps a more appropriate term would be "resonance": that is, an intellectual response to the received impact, reinforced by vibration or reflection. To put it another way, we may well call it an actualization of inherent potentiality' (4–5).
7. Capell, *Notes and Various Readings to Shakespeare*, volume II, part IV, p. 63. There has been confusion about exactly when Capell's note on *The Tempest* and Montaigne's 'Of the Caniballes' originally appeared. Most scholars accept 1780 as the date, largely on the evidence put forward by George Coffin Taylor, 'The Date of Edward Capell's *Notes and Various Readings to Shakespeare, Volume II*'.
8. The phrase 'debt to Montaigne' alludes to the still-important book of George Coffin Taylor, *Shakspere's Debt to Montaigne*. Taylor consistently spells 'Shakespeare' as 'Shakspere'.
9. See Lesser, *Renaissance Drama and the Politics of Publication*.

10. Samuel Daniel, 'To my deere friend M. *Iohn Florio*, concerning *his translation of* Montaigne', in *The Essayes or Morall, Politike and Millitarie Discourses* (1603), sig. ¶r–v.
11. See Webster, *The White Devil*, ed. Robinson, *passim*.
12. See Hamlin, *Tragedy and Scepticism in Shakespeare's England*: 'Certainly Jonson and Marston were reading Montaigne shortly after Florio's translation appeared: Jonson owned a copy of the book, and Marston drew on it heavily as he composed *The Dutch Courtesan*' (72–3). For the definitive work on the subject, see Hamlin's *Montaigne's English Journey*.
13. Capell, *Notes and Various Readings to Shakespeare*, volume II, part IV, p. 63.
14. Shakespeare, *The Tempest*, 5.1.15, in *The Norton Shakespeare*, second edition. Unless otherwise noted, all further citations from the plays of Shakespeare are to this edition and are annotated within the text.
15. *The Plays and Poems of William Shakespeare*, ed. Malone, vol. 1, part 2, p. 38.
16. Montaigne, 'Of Cannibals' (1.30/31), in *Shakespeare's Montaigne*. Where available, quotations from Florio's Montaigne will come from this edition; citations will be included in the text and will list, first, this edition's page number and, second, the page number of the 1603 *Essayes* (61; 102).
17. Ellrodt, 'Self-Consciousness in Montaigne and Shakespeare', 37n3.
18. Madden, 'Observations on an Autograph of Shakspere, and the orthography of his Name', 116. Capell's linking of Shakespeare to Montaigne is known enough that Madden wants to dispel doubt that this is a post-1780 forgery: 'How or when this gentlemen [the father of the current owner, Reverend Edward Patteson] first became possessed of it, is not known; but it is very certain that previous to the year 1780, Mr. Patteson used to exhibit the volume to his friends as a curiosity, *on account of the autograph*' (114–15).
19. [Sterling], 'Art. IV', A review of 'Observations on an Autograph . . .', 321. See Ellrodt, 'Self-Consciousness in Montaigne and Shakespeare', esp. 38n2, for a history of the dispute over the Shakespeare autograph.
20. Chappuit, 'Avant-Propos', *Shakespeare et Montaigne*, ed. Maguin, 4.
21. Hugh Grady helpfully points out that the more intense and sustained interest of French and German scholars is not surprising because of 'the tendency of traditional French scholarship . . . to define the "system" of thinking within the works of major authors' and 'the Hegelian interest in German scholarship, with its traditions of cultural history and consequent attention to large scale cultural developments'. See his 'Afterword', 173.
22. *Journal des Débats*, 7 November 1846; repr. in his *L'Angleterre au seizième siècle* (1879), 136.
23. See Elze, *Essays on Shakespeare* and *Life of Shakespeare*; Stedefeld, *Hamlet*; and Feis, *Shakspere and Montaigne*.
24. Feis, 43, 90.
25. Hooker, 'The Relation of Shakespeare to Montaigne', and Robertson, *Montaigne and Shakespeare*. An earlier version of Robertson's book appeared as *Montaigne and Shakspere* in 1897.

26. Robertson, *Montaigne and Shakespeare*, 139 and 120.
27. Robertson, *Montaigne and Shakespeare*, 219. F. O. Matthiessien – drawing on Taylor's research and tables of words used by Shakespeare only after 1603 – tells a similar story with a different explanation: 'Shakespeare used these new words and phrases very often immediately after 1603, and then there is a gradual tapering off until *The Tempest*, where they again increase. This fact suggests an eager first reading that caused many phrases to stay half consciously in Shakespeare's memory for a period of years, and then a later return to the book which resulted in the passage on the ideal commonwealth' (*Translation*, 165).
28. Robertson, *Montaigne and Shakespeare*, 285. In her superb *John Florio*, Frances Yates claimed that, for Robertson, Shakespeare's debt to Montaigne 'seriously diminished his [Shakespeare's] stature' (243). This claim seems overstated, for Robertson concludes his essay on 'The Originality of Shakespeare' with a rather optimistic observation: 'It is none the less a stimulating and reconciling thought that the supremacy of the work of our greatest man of letters is largely the outcome of his untroubled willingness to adopt other men's plans and performance, wherever he could turn them to good account, he having the while no thought of becoming immortal by such means' (290–1).
29. Collins, *Studies in Shakespeare*, 280. Nonetheless, Collins makes insightful comparisons between the two writers: 'In each a subtle and restless wit delighting in nice distinctions, in paradox, in casuistry, sought naturally the themes which would call it into play, and afford it scope. To each, the riddles of life, the relation of reason to truth, of free will to necessity, of humanity to the divine, of fancy to fact, had the deepest attraction[;] and both accepted with perfect equanimity, for both were humorists, the absolute insolubility of the problems which fascinated them. In both there was a certain timidity of temper. Both abhorred dogmatism, and both, to all appearance, delighting in chafing its upholders. Their religious opinions and their attitude towards orthodoxy are exactly identical. Both are, practically, theistical agnostics, but both reverence, and for the same formal reasons, Christianity, the one as embodied in Roman Catholicism, the other as embodied in Protestantism' (295–6). When he tries to return to his more negative thesis, both his logic and his prose break down: 'The true nature of Shakespeare's indebtedness to Montaigne may be fairly estimated if we say what, we believe, may be said with truth, that had the Essays never appeared[,] there is nothing to warrant the assumption that what he has in common with Montaigne would not have been equally conspicuous' (296). It is hard to know how conspicuous 'what [Shakespeare] had in common with Montaigne' would be 'had the Essays never appeared'.
30. Villey, 'Montaigne et Shakespeare', in *A Book of Homage to Shakespeare*, 418. See also his 'Montaigne et les poètes dramatiques anglais du tempes de Shakespeare'.
31. Taylor, *Shakspere's Debt*, 5.
32. Taylor, *Shakspere's Debt*, 7–8.

33. T. S. Eliot, 'Shakespeare and Montaigne', 895.
34. Eliot, 'Shakespeare and Montaigne', 895. Montaigne as a 'stimulant' for Shakespeare's writing could echo the language of Robertson, who had claimed 'Montaigne is for Shakespeare the source of the stimulus' (*Montaigne and Shakespeare*, 87). Eliot had favourably reviewed Robertson's *The Problem of 'Hamlet'* in 1919, the first time Eliot famously declared Shakespeare's play an 'artistic failure' (See 'Hamlet and His Problems', 941.) Eliot's interest in Shakespeare's connection to Montaigne is evident here as well: 'We need a great many facts in his biography; and we should like to know whether, and when, and after or at the same time as what personal experience, he read Montaigne, II. xii., 'Apologie de Raimond Sebond'. We should have, finally, to know something which is by hypothesis unknowable, for we assume it to be an experience which, in the manner indicated, exceeded the facts. We should have to understand things which Shakespeare did not understand himself' (941). The review was expanded and published in *The Sacred Wood*.
35. Harmon, 'How Great was Shakespeare's Debt to Montaigne?' For more early scepticism towards Taylor's argument, see Frederic Page, 'Shakespeare and Florio'. In a still-valuable book published in German a few years after Harmon's essay, Hugo Friedrich in his *Montaigne* (1949) makes points about Montaigne that can be used to link the French author to Shakespeare (see Chapter 1 below). Nonetheless, he is a 'nexus skeptic': 'Contrary to prevailing opinion among the English, German, and French scholars of English, I am not convinced that this influence amounted to much. The only thing solidly established is that Shakespeare read the Florio translation. But the parallels of the ideal kind cited in the research in the main concerns commonplace things for which Montaigne only played the vehicle, or things that could also have come to Shakespeare from other sources' (405–6n292).
36. Harmon, 1007. See Taylor's spirited reply to Harmon in his 'Montaigne–Shakespeare and the Deadly Parallel': 'Practically every idea in the Renaissance is a commonplace. Literary *expressions* of the ideas, poetical and prose *patterns*, *architectonics*, are another matter' (336). Although a confirmed 'conservative' (262) in the Montaigne–Shakespeare source debate, Eleanor Prosser, in her 'Shakespeare, Montaigne, and the Rarer Action', added arguably only the second certain parallel of Florio's Montaigne in the work of Shakespeare: the links between Prospero's speech to Ariel on the 'rarer action' of virtue over vengeance in Act V of *The Tempest* (5.1.25–28) and Montaigne's 'Of Crueltie' (2.11). Agreeing with Harmon that 'coincidences in diction as well as in idea' must be 'unmistakable', Prosser argues persuasively for this connection as 'one more parallel passage that passes Miss Harmon's test' (261).
37. A classic example of her misreading involves Hamlet's bitter speech about the 'quintessence of dust', which arguably has its source in 2.12:

> **Ham.** . . . .this goodly frame the earth seems to me a sterile promontory, this most excellent canopy the air, look you, this brave o'erhanging firmament, this majestical roof fretted with golden fire,

why, it appeareth nothing to me but a foul and pestilent congregation of vapours. What piece of work is a man, how noble in reason, how infinite in faculties, in form and moving how express and admirable, in action how like an angel, in apprehension how like a god: the beauty of the world, the paragon of animals – and yet, to me, what is this quintessence of dust?' (2.2.289–98)

Compare Montaigne, trans. Florio: 'Who hath perswaded him, that this admirable mooving of heavens-vaults; that the eternal light of these lampes so fiercely rowling over his head; that the horror-moving and continuall motion of the infinite vaste Ocean, were established, and continue so manie ages for his commoditie and service? Is it possible to imagine any thing so rediculous, as this miserable and wretched creature, which is not so much as maister of himselfe, exposed and subject to offences of all things, and yet dareth call himselfe Maister and Emperour of this Vniverse?' (*Essayes*, II.12, 258).

Although Harmon dismisses the link as a commonplace description of 'the beauty and order of the universe as contemplated by the mind of man' (995), it is the shared cynical turn *against* 'the beauty and order of the universe' and the critique of 'this miserable and wretched creature', 'this quintessence of dust', that makes the connection compelling. See Chapter 2 below.

38. Hodgen, 'Montaigne and Shakespeare Again'.
39. Hodgen, 'Montaigne and Shakespeare Again', 42.
40. Hodgen, 'Montaigne and Shakespeare Again', 39. In a very helpful summary of the early decades of this debate, Hugh Grady insightfully notes that 'positivist skepticism over evidentiary questions produced a scholarly consensus that suspicions of a shared skeptical philosophy between Montaigne and Shakespeare were not viable professional discourse' ('Afterword', 171).
41. See also Jourdan, *The Sparrow and the Flea*: 'What distinguishes Shakespeare and Montaigne from many if not most of their contemporaries and elevates them to preeminence among humanists of all time is their passion for probing the truth and practicality of these *loci communes*. If Shakespeare read Montaigne, the evidence should not be that both used commonplaces but the direction and significance of their departure from them' (16).
42. Kirsch, 'Virtue, Vice, and Compassion in Montaigne and *The Tempest*', 338.
43. Grady attributes the change in Anglo-American interest in the 'linkage' to a shift away from the 'empiricist tradition, with its corrosive suspicions of generalizations and rational systematizing . . . that tended to preclude investigation of anything like a systematic Shakespearean "philosophy" or "system of thought"'. Because of 'the influence of the various forms of literary theory at work within English studies for the last twenty years or more . . . it is possible to venture non-empirical generalizations and hypotheses that also avoid the Hegelian and Cartesian assumptions which often accompanied such hypotheses in German and French literary studies respectively and which drew the fire of Anglo-American empiricists accordingly' ('Afterword', 173).

44. Papers from the 2001 and 2005 seminars appear in Bradshaw and Bishop (eds), *The Shakespearean International Yearbook* 6; Robert Ellrodt's paper from the 2001 seminar, 'Self-Consistency in Montaigne and Shakespeare', can be found in Clayton, Brock, and Forés (eds), *Shakespeare and the Mediterranean*. The papers from the 2003 conference are collected in Maguin (ed.), *Shakespeare et Montaigne*. Some of the papers from the 2016 SAA seminar appear in Engle, Gray, and Hamlin (eds), *Shakespeare and Montaigne*.
45. Grady, *Shakespeare, Machiavelli, and Montaigne*; Mack, *Reading and Rhetoric in Shakespeare and Montaigne*; Hamlin, *Montaigne's English Journey*; Ellrodt, *Montaigne and Shakespeare*; Boutcher, *The School of Montaigne: Volume II, The Reader-Writer*, 189–271. See also Jourdan's relatively early – and very hard to find – *The Sparrow and the Flea*, esp. 1–25.
46. Letter from John Keats to George and Tom Keats, 21 December 1817, in *The Letters of John Keats* 1:193–4. See also Hazlitt, *Table Talk*, Essay 5, 'On Genius and Common Sense' (1821): 'His genius consisted in the faculty of transforming himself at will into whatever he chose; his originality was the power of seeing every object from the exact point of view in which others would see it. He was the Proteus of the human intellect' (*The Collected Works of William Hazlitt*, 6: 42).
47. Borges, 'Everything and Nothing', in *Labyrinths*, 248–50.
48. Berlin, 'Fathers and Children', in *Russian Thinkers*, 297.
49. Bate, 'Montaigne and Shakespeare'.
50. Engle, 'Sovereign Cruelty in Montaigne and *King Lear*', 134.
51. Parker, 'Shakespeare's Argument with Montaigne', 18.
52. Ellrodt, *Montaigne and Shakespeare*, 73; 94. See also Levin, *The Question of Hamlet*: 'in retrospection, his [Shakespeare's] mentor is Montaigne; the soliloquies are like the *Essays* in balancing arguments with counter-arguments, in pursuing wayward ideas and unmasking stubborn illusions' (71), and Mack, *Reading and Rhetoric*: 'The soliloquy depicts thought which moves by statement, response and reflection, just as Montaigne's *Essais* do. Shakespeare portrays in Claudius's soliloquy something of the movement and changeability of the human mind, which Montaigne asserts as a general principle on the basis of collecting different examples and testing their implications against his introspection' (19).
53. Kritzman, *The Fabulous Imagination*, 5, 4.
54. Because of their respective approaches to the topic of succession (and *not* because of their respective engagements with Montaigne), Richard Dutton, in his *Shakespeare, Court Dramatist*, sees Q1 as an Elizabethan play and Q2 as a Jacobean one: 'Q2 (and indeed F) are both Jacobean texts, revised when the outcome of the succession was a fait accompli and it was possible to review events with some equanimity, whereas Q1 is an Elizabethan play, as fraught with anxieties about regime change as *Gorbuduc* or *King Leir*' (238–9).
55. Bate, *Shakespeare and Ovid*, 256.

56. Quint, *Montaigne and the Quality of Mercy*, 99.
57. Eliot, 'Shakespeare and Montaigne', 895. Julia Kristeva's 'notion of *intertextuality*', developed in an essay on Bakhtin's work on dialogism and the carnivalesque, is also relevant here: 'any text is constructed as a mosaic of quotations; any text is the absorption and transformation of another'. See her 'Word, Dialogue, and Novel' (1966/1969), in *Desire in Language*, 66. Montaigne's take on intertextuality comes in his 'Of the Institution and Education of Children' (1.26, 1.25 in Florio): 'The bees do heere and there sucke this, and cull that flower, but afterward they produce the hony, which is peculiarly their owne, then is it no more Thyme or Marjoram. So of peeces borrowed of others, he may lawfully alter, transforme, and confound them, to shape out of them a perfect peece of worke, altogether his owne' (71). For Montaigne and his source texts, so for Shakespeare and his, including Montaigne: Shakespeare can be seen to – *pace* Greene and Chettle – 'lawfully alter, transforme, and confound' Montaigne's essays because he ultimately 'shape[s] out of them a perfect peece of worke, altogether his owne'. See also Hartle, *Michel de Montaigne*, 75. On this process at work in Shakespeare's transforming Florio transforming Montaigne, see Boutcher, 'Butchering the Cannibals', in *Montaigne in Transit*, esp. 121. This altering, transforming, and confounding is part of what I am calling Shakespearean *essaying*.
58. Grady, *Shakespeare, Machiavelli, and Montaigne*, 29. See also de Gooyer, '"Their Senses I'll Restore"': '. . . admittedly, almost any other type of proposed connection other than verbal borrowing or generic development will probably remain (merely) annotative, or be so loose as to become plainly speculative. . . . [C]onnections other than verifiable borrowings are difficult to confirm, and when suggested they are always in danger of falling prey to charges of vagueness, or relying on some misty notion of *zeitgeist* or some thinly attenuated claim that cultural negotiations are (secretly) at work. Against such criticism there is little to be said, except that if we relate the two works in order to complicate or deepen our sense of the play, or as a way to nudge us out of the rut of the familiar transcendental and revisionist readings, we have done the play some service' (513).
59. See Hamlin, 'Montaigne and Shakespeare', 342. Earlier versions of his argument appear in 'The Shakespeare–Montaigne–Sextus Nexus', 29, and in *Montaigne's English Journey*, 110.
60. See, most recently, Burrow, 'Montaignian Moments', who argues persuasively for Shakespeare's 'reactive reading of discursive texts' based on a 'range of reactions which a discursive text might prompt – disagreement, the recognition of an underlying logical structure, chance overlaps with personal concerns, the provision of commonplaces or *sententiae*, or a provocation to thinking. . . . Shakespeare did not just read Montaigne from at least 1603, but reacted to him as Montaigne reacted to his own reading, with the kind of resistant eclecticism that comes of treating a book as akin to a person with whom you might argue' (248–9). For Burrow,

'Montaignian moments... punctuate the action in scenes in which characters reflect, joke, philosophize, explore the awkward misrelation between general principle and personal experience, and open out alternative perspectives on the main action' (250). See also Hamlin, 'The Shakespeare–Montaigne–Sextus Nexus': 'Neither Montaigne nor Shakespeare display much interest in systematic thinking; their most fundamental commonality may indeed be a blithe disregard for contradiction, a consuming and brilliant attention to the urgencies of the moment rather than to worries about overall intellectual cohesion. Vigorously pursuing the conversation is of paramount interest to both' (32).

61. Hamlin, 'Montaigne and Shakespeare', 342. See Hugh Grady's warning against getting 'bogged down in the technicalities of source-hunting and evidence' ('Afterword', 171). See also Hamlin's caution, in his 'The Shakespeare–Montaigne–Sextus Nexus', against leaning too hard on *influence* at all: '[B]ecause we cannot assume that our own electicisms correspond to those of readers four centuries ago, we are on safer ground if we concentrate on large-scale patterns and tendencies in the *Essays*, all the while remaining cautious about what "influence" might amount to for any specific early modern reader' (31). Serena Jourdan, in her *The Sparrow and the Flea*, also wished to look at the two writers while suspending the notion of influence: 'The aim of this study is to... determine whether a close, binary reading of Shakespeare and Montaigne without concern for influence and without necessity therefore to respect or speculate about chronologies can be valuably instructive' (v).

62. I have little doubt that using a method combining plagiarism software, such as WCopyfind, and the searchable database of Early English Books Online (EEBO) – both brilliantly deployed by Dennis McCarthy and June Schlueter in their *'A Brief Discourse of Rebellion and Rebels'* – would yield data that would build on Taylor's pioneering work, adding examples and 'confirm[ing] rarity' in a way that pre-digitised texts did not allow Taylor to do (12). I hope that work will be done. As I have said above, however, my goal is not only to rely on verbal echoes but also to move beyond them in an attempt to uncover other, deeper affinities between Montaigne and Shakespeare.

63. Colin Burrow, in his 'Montaignian Moments', underscores an important problem that I am trying to address here: 'literary criticism has historically not been well equipped with a vocabulary or a method for writing about relationships between two authors where thinking, rather than direct verbal borrowing, might be involved' (240). See also Frampton, '"To Be, or Not to Be": *Hamlet* Q1, Q2 and Montaigne', who asks, 'what are we finally to make of Shakespeare's "borrowings"? Are they purloining, graftings, rewritings?' (110).

64. Montaigne, 'Of Repenting' (3.2), 196; 483. The French clearly aligns essaying with learning and trying: 'Si mon ame pouvoit prendre pied, je m'essaierois pas, je resoudrois: elle est tousjours en apprentissage, et en

espreuve. See *Les Essais*, ed. Balsamo, et al., 845. For 'apprentissage', Cotgrave has 'A Prentiship'; for 'espreuve', clearly a synonymn for 'essay', he gives us 'A proofe, tryall, experiment, essay, attempt'. This passage, Eric Auerbach claims in *Mimesis*, 'explains the meaning of the title *Essais*, which might fittingly though not very gracefully be rendered as "Tests upon One's Self" or "Self-Try-Outs"' (292).

65. I argue that both writers are questing to find what a Montaigne scholar has recently called 'the possibility of their being otherwise' and a Shakespeare scholar has recently deemed 'dispatches from alternative futures'. See Guild, *Unsettling Montaigne*, 11, and Kiernan Ryan, *Shakespeare's Universality*, 25. For Montaigne and possibility, see Kritzman, *The Fabulous Imagination*: 'Montaigne . . . implies that the imagination can produce fantasies that can eventually be encountered in the world. . . . The exemplarity of the Montaignian imagination teaches us that we can transcend the dominant positivism of our current age by seeing things otherwise' (5, 26). For Shakespeare and possibility, see a related point by Simon Palfrey: 'His work is permissive, unjealous, open. Above all, his writing is generous, in the invitations and the trust that it affords to both actors and attenders; a trust that necessarily extends to his own creations, that they will remain open, and partially yielding, when the actors and attenders return, as they must' (41). Interestingly, for Aristotle, 'the subjects of our deliberation [in rhetoric] are such as seem to present us with alternative possibilities' (*Rhetoric* 1357a). See Aristotle, *Rhetoric*, in *The Complete Works of Aristotle*, ed. Barnes, 2: 2157.

66. Adorno, 'The Essay as Form', 162–3. He goes on to claim that '[the essay] counteracts that hardened primitiveness that always allies itself with reason's current form. Whereas science treats the difficulties and complexities of an antagonistic and monadologically split reality according to the expectation of this society by reducing them to simplifying models and then belatedly differentiates them with fabricated material, the essay shakes off the illusion of a simple, basically logical world that so perfectly suits the defense of the status quo. . . . Therefore the law of the innermost form of the essay is heresy' (171). See also Zalloua, 'Essaying Trouble': 'Montaigne's essaying aims at devalorizing his authority as a "sujet supposé savoir" by making his readers (co)responsible for the interpretive labor. . . . Essaying keeps our eyes focused on vulnerability as both an ontological category and a hermeneutic challenge, as a remainder and reminder of what lies beyond mastery, beyond the control of philosophy's sovereign subject, and as an opportunity to trouble closure, to complicate, scrutinize, and multiple [sic] its meanings' (172).

67. Michel de Montaigne, 'Of the Force of Imagination' (1.20/1.21), *The Essayes*, trans. Florio, 45. Drawing on this Montaignian key-text as well as many others, Ann Hartle, in her *Michel de Montaigne*, has claimed that Montaigne's 'skeptical moment' is 'a moment of openness to the possible rather than a suspension of judgment', as it would be in ancient,

Pyrrhonian scepticism. 'Montaigne incorporates the skeptical moment into the dialectical movement of his thought: the moment of openness to the possible allows him to find the strange in the familiar' (3).

68. David Carroll Simon, in his *Light without Heat*, has recently identified a Montaignian approach that, I argue, would resonate with Shakespeare: 'Montaigne's critique falls not on any particular source of knowledge but rather on an attitude of zealous adherence – to precedence, doctrine, cause, or any chosen object of attention. Montaigne looks to tradition all the time, but without the premise that it delivers a verdict. He suspends the assumption that ancient sources have more to tell us than we can tell ourselves, even about the very messages he calls on them to transmit' (56). For Hugh Grady, in his 'Afterword', Shakespeare and Montaigne share 'an abhorrence of the reification of absolutizing, instrumental rationality; insight into the resistance of the world's complexities to the schemas of subjects-who-are-supposed-to-know; a keen sense of the limitations and delusions of desire-driven alienated subjectivity and yet an insistence on feeling, interiority, and the subjective as aspects of adequate knowledge' (179). See also Rossiter: Crucial to Shakespeare's thinking 'was the scepticism of Montaigne, which by probing into the unsteadiness and varyingness of purely human standards, set men's minds to the discovery of what in this mutable world *was* enduring and stable and the same from generation to generation' (*Angel with Horns*, 187).

Chapter 1

Knowing and Being in Montaigne and Shakespeare

Plato hath (in my seeming) loved this manner of Philosophying, Dialogue wise in good ernest, that thereby he might more decently place in sundrie mouths the diversitie and variation of his owne conceits. *Diversly to treate of matters, is as good and better as to treat them conformably*; that is to say, more copiously and more profitably.

(Montaigne, 'An Apologie of Raymond Sebond' [2.12])[1]

Central to an exploration of Shakespeare's essaying of Montaigne is an examination of their epistemology and ontology, their approaches to knowing and being. As Ayesha Ramachandran would have it, the world 'is also the most frequently repeated and powerfully suggestive analogue for the self, offering an external parallel for the endless variety and vast spaces within. The wonder with which Montaigne encounters *le moi* is the same wonder with which he encounters *le monde*.'[2] These discursive fields – of knowledge and the world on the one hand and of the self on the other – will swirl in and out of Shakespeare's words, as they do Montaigne's.[3]

For these two authors shared, at the very least, an interest in multiplicity: a sense of perspectivism in their epistemology and a sense of a discontinuous self in their ontology: 'And there is as much difference found between us and our selves, as there is between ourselves and others. . . . *Esteem it a great matter, to play but one man*,' as Montaigne says.[4] In anatomising their approaches to knowledge and the self, I will explore the sceptical background that shaped Montaigne's thinking and that Shakespeare essays; the multiplicity and theatricality of being that lie at the heart of the ontological explorations of both authors; and finally the current literary-critical and philosophical interest in these writers' approaches to knowledge and selfhood. The intellectual world of

Montaigne and Shakespeare is a world of doubt, contingency, uncertainty, and mutability – a world that is at once early modern and (post-)modern.[5]

Montaigne, Shakespeare, and Ancient Scepticism

Whether or not their scepticism was identical, Montaigne and Shakespeare shared a sceptical approach to truth and knowledge. But what did 'scepticism' mean for these two authors? It did not mean, as we might think today, 'a series of doubts concerning traditional religious beliefs' but instead was a philosophical system with roots in ancient Greece.[6] The first Latin edition of Sextus Empiricus's *Sexti Philosophi Pyrrhoniarum hypotyposeon libri III* (known both as the *Hypotyposes* and as the *Outlines of Pyrrhonism*), probably written in the late second century AD, was translated and published in Geneva by Henri Estienne in 1562. Versions of ancient scepticism were known to the Renaissance before this book appeared, via Cicero's *Academica* and, especially, Diogenes Laertius's *Life of Pyrrho*.[7] However, as the great historian of ancient philosophy, Jonathan Barnes, has claimed of Estienne's edition of Sextus:

> It made a sensation: widely read and vastly influential, it was cited in the disputes of the theologians and it was submitted to the scrutiny of philosophy. If ancient scepticism was not wholly unknown before the publication of Estienne's Sextus, it was little regarded and little respected: the Sextus put it in the limelight and made it the talk of the day.[8]

Supposedly based on the philosophical works of Pyrrho of Elis (c. 360–c. 270 BC), Sextus's handbook opened with an enumeration of the three philosophical schools at that time:

> When people are investigating any subject, the likely result is either a discovery, or a denial of discovery and a confession of inapprehensibility, or else a continuation of the investigation. This, no doubt, is why in the case of philosophical investigations, too, some have asserted that they have discovered the truth, some have asserted that it cannot be apprehended, and others are still investigating.
> Those who are called Dogmatists in the proper sense of the word think that they have discovered the truth – for example, the schools of Aristotle and Epicurus and the Stoics, and some others. The schools of Clitomachus and Carneades, and other Academics, have asserted that things cannot be apprehended. And the Sceptics are still investigating. (I. i. 1–3, p. 3)

Unlike the 'Dogmatists' who 'think that they have discovered the truth' and the 'Academics' who assert 'that things cannot be apprehended', sceptics 'are still investigating', searching, questing. As Barnes has it, 'The Greek word for "sceptic" means something like "inquisitive", "investigative"; and Sextus intends the word in its ordinary sense. If you undertake an inquiry, he says, one of three things will result: you will hit upon a solution to the problem, you will determine that it is impossible to hit upon a solution, or you will continue the search. . . . A sceptic, according to Sextus, is one who continues the search' (xx). In Sextus's own words, 'Scepticism is an ability to set out oppositions among things which appear and are thought of in any way at all, an ability by which, because of the equipollence in the opposed objects and accounts, we come first to suspension of judgement and afterwards to tranquility' (I. iv. 8, p. 4).[9]

This scepticism is Sextus's third kind of philosophy, grounded in 'equipollence', reaching for, if not always finding, tranquillity. It is the sceptical way of looking at the world that helped to shape the thought of Montaigne and then Shakespeare.[10] Montaigne clearly valued this Pyrrhonian approach, as he reveals especially in 'An Apologie of Raymond Sebond' (2.12). Rehearsing the opening of the *Outlines*, Montaigne claimed that

> Whosoever seeks for any thing, cometh at last to this conclusion and sayeth that either he hath found it, or that it cannot be found, or that he is still in pursuit after it. All Philosophy is divided into these three kinds. Her purpose is to seek out the truth, the knowledge, and the certainty.
>
> The Peripatetics, the Epicureans, the Stoics, and others have thought they had found it. . . .
>
> Clitomochus, Carneades, and the Academics have despaired the finding of it and judged that truth could not be conceived by our means. . . .
>
> Pyrrho and other Sceptics, or Epechists . . . say that they are still seeking after truth. (150–1; 290)

Montaigne sympathises with the Pyrrhonian view and its 'profession . . . ever to waver, to doubt, and to inquire. . . . Their effect is a pure, entire, and absolute surceasing and suspense of judgement. They use their reason to inquire and to debate, and not to stay and choose. Whosoever shall imagine a perpetual confession of ignorance and a judgement upright and without straggering to what occasion soever may chance – that man conceives the true Pyrrhonism' (151, 154; 291, 292).[11]

Will Hamlin has rightly pointed out that Montaigne was – despite his claims to the contrary – *not* a strict Pyrrhonian; his leaps to faith too often distanced him from the suspension of mind that was crucial to followers of Sextus: 'Had Montaigne been an adherent of "true Phyrrhonisme", he would have conformed to Roman Catholicism without affirming that it represented truth. Had he been a true Pyrrhonist, he could never have been a fideist, using the imbecility of reason to justify a leap of faith.'[12] Ann Hartle, too, has distinguished between Pyrrhonian scepticism and that of Montaigne. Whereas the former uses suspension of judgement ultimately to lead to 'imperturbability' or *ataraxia*, for Montaigne, 'the skeptical act with regard to human testimony is the initial suspension of the judgment that what I am hearing is impossible because it is incredible, and incredible because unfamiliar. It is an act of openness to the possible, to the unfamiliar. In this sense Montaigne's credulity *is* his skepticism.'[13]

All of this is to say that Shakespeare and Montaigne shared in their epistemology what Hamlin has called 'sceptical values': Shakespeare's essaying Montaigne definitely includes the 'placing in question [of] all authorities' and a 'diffidence and intellectual humility' in 'recognition of the limitations of human reason and perception'.[14]

But Montaigne almost certainly was not Shakespeare's only source for these 'sceptical values'. Thomas Nashe, in his 1591 Preface to Sir Philip Sidney's *Astrophil and Stella*, alluded to an English edition of Sextus: 'so that our opinion (as Sextus Empiricus affirmeth) gives the name of good or ill to everything. Out of whose works (lately translated into English for the benefit of unlearned writers) a man might collect a whole book of argument . . .'[15] Hamlin has made the convincing claim that the fragment known as *The Sceptick*, usually attributed to Sir Walter Ralegh and based on Book One, chapter 14 of Sextus's *Outlines*, is actually the translation alluded to by Nashe:

> the 'lost translation' is probably not lost at all. Four manuscript copies of *The Sceptick* survive, and collation of these four, combined with examination of relevant verbal evidence from Nashe, Rowlands, the 1560s Latin edition of Sextus's *Outlines*, the 1651 *Sceptick*, and Thomas Stanley's 1659 translation of Sextus, yields strong reasons for believing *The Sceptick* is itself the 'lost' translation rather than a distinct and derivative work.[16]

Hamlin's superb research has also documented the presence of copies of Sextus in British libraries from 1562 to 1625.[17] As Hamlin notes, '*The Sceptick* appeared in English not only because Sextus was seen as important, not only because he was talked about on the Continent, not only because he was championed by Montaigne, but also because the English, too, had their doubts.'[18] And Shakespeare was one of the English who had doubts.[19]

The section of Sextus from which *The Sceptick* derives (I. xiv. 35–177) contains the 'Ten Modes' of scepticism, and one of these is crucial for the Montaigne–Shakespeare nexus: the fifth mode,

> the one depending on positions and intervals and places – for depending on each of these the same objects appear different. For example, the same colonnade appears foreshortened when seen from one end, but completely

symmetrical when seen from the middle. The same boat appears from a distance small and stationary, but from close at hand large and in motion. The same tower appears from a distance round, but from close at hand square. These depend on intervals. . . . Since, then, all apparent things are observed in some place and from some interval and in some position, and each of these produces a great deal of variation in appearances, as we have suggested, we shall be forced to arrive at suspension of judgement by these modes too. For anyone wishing to give preference to some of these appearances over others will be attempting the impossible (I. xiv. 118–19; 121, pp. 31–2)

Arriving at a certain truth, or even a 'preference to some of these appearances over others', when so many 'positions and intervals and places' are involved, is 'impossible'. And although *The Sceptick* does not quote from the fifth mode directly, it does contain the following:

If we will hearken to men's opinions concerning one and the same matter, thinking thereby to come to the true knowledge of it, we shall find this to be impossible, for either we must believe what all men say of it, or what some men only say of it. To believe what all men say of one and the same thing is not possible, for then we shall believe contrarieties: for some men say that that very thing is pleasant which others say is displeasant. . . . This argument seemeth to be further confirmed if the differences of the senses of hearing, seeing, smelling, touching and tasting be considered, for that the senses differ it seemeth plain. Painted tables, in which the art of slanting is used, appear to the eye as if the parts of them were some higher and some lower than the other, but to the touch they seem not to be so. Honey seemeth to the tongue sweet, but unpleasant to the eye; so ointment doth recreate the smell, but it offendeth the taste; rain water is profitable to the eyes, but it hurteth the lungs. We may then tell how these things seem to our senses. But what they are in their own nature, we cannot; for why should not a man credit any one of his senses as well as the other.[20]

The allusion to the 'art of slanting' contains similarities with the fifth mode and is almost certainly a reference to anamorphic painting, in which – depending on the viewer's perspective – one thing can possess two discrete realities. This type of painting clearly intrigued Shakespeare: he alludes to it in *Twelfth Night* when Duke Orsino says, upon encountering the twins Viola/Cesario and Sebastian, 'One face, one voice, one habit, and two persons, / A natural perspective that is and is not!'[21]

Perspectivism, often linked to the philosophy of Friedrich Nietzsche – who in the nineteenth century linked Montaigne and Shakespeare – was available to Shakespeare and Montaigne through Sextus.[22] As we have seen, it is Montaigne who claimed, in 'Of the Institution and Education of Children' (1.26; 1.25 in Florio), that

> This great vniverse (which some multiply as Species vnder one Genus) is the true looking-glasse wherein we must looke, if we wil know whether we be of a good stamp, or in the right byase. To conclude, I would have this worldes-frame to be my Schollers choise-booke: So many strange humours, sundry sects, varying judgements, diverse opinions, different lawes, and fantastical customs teach vs to judge rightly of ours, and instruct our judgement to acknowledge his [ie, its] imperfections and naturall weakenesse, which is no easy an apprentiship. ('Of the Institution and Education of Children [1.25], 75)

As we have explored in the Introduction, 'apprentiship' was deeply connected to essaying, and this sifting through 'diverse opinions' is crucial to Montaigne's epistemology. Montaigne makes a similar point in the much later 'Of Experience' (3.13):

> We open the matter and spill it in distempering it. Of one subject we make a thousand, and, in multiplying and subdividing, we fall again into the infinity of Epicurus his atoms. It was never seen that two men judged alike of one same thing. And it is impossible to see two opinions exactly semblable, not only in diverse men but in any one same man at several hours. I commonly find something to doubt of where the commentary happily never deigned to touch as deeming it so plain. . . .
> Who would not say that glosses increase doubts and ignorance, since no book is to be seen, whether divine or profane, commonly read of all men, whose interpretation dims or tarnishes not the difficulty? (320; 635)

This emphasis on the 'diverse' nature of the world; the problem of 'byase'; and the impossibility 'to see two opinions exactly semblable, not only in diverse men, but in any one same man at several hours' are all concerns of Shakespeare's sceptical approach to knowledge. We see it in Hamlet's 'There are more things in Heaven and Earth, Horatio, / Than are dreamt of in our philosophy' (1.5.168–9);[23] his 'for there is nothing either good or bad but thinking makes it so' (2.2.244–5); and *All's Well That Ends Well*'s Lafew's 'They say miracles are past, and we have our philosophical persons, to make modern and familiar, things supernatural and causeless. Hence is it that we make trifles of terrors, ensconcing ourselves into seeming knowledge, when we should submit ourselves to an unknown fear' (2.3.1–5).[24] Shakespeare, like Montaigne, uses his scepticism to reveal, as Lars Engle has argued, 'the dangers of dogmatic arrogance and the failures of overly assertive norm-bearers. . . . Shakespeare is with Montaigne an early modern exemplar of a norm of scepticism about aggressive normativity.'[25]

Not all readers of Montaigne and Shakespeare see a critique of normativity, status quo, and the doxa in their scepticism, however. Max

Horkheimer, the brilliant philosopher of the Frankfurt School, wrote in 1938 that Montaigne's brand of 'unprincipled . . . scepticism' was politically weak, non-committal, and evasive:[26]

> Skepticism is a pathological form of intellectual independence; it is immune to truth as well as untruth. . . . Like dead religiosity, the churches, and hierarchy, a moribund skepticism – the closing off of human beings toward one another, their retreat into their own empty individuality – belongs to an intellectual disposition in contradiction with the current level of development of human powers. . . . There is no humanism without a clear position toward the historical problems of the epoch; it cannot exist as a mere profession of faith to itself. . . . Like the ancients, Montaigne concluded from the uncertainty of knowledge based on the senses or the understanding, as well as from the multiplicity of moral, metaphysical, and religious perspectives, that one simply cannot know anything. In contrast, the dialectic, in its negative application to ideas that consider themselves firm and absolute, sees the essence of the power of thought as that of the 'negative'.[27]

Scepticism is 'moribund' and retreats 'into its own empty individuality'. Marxist dialectic and what Horkheimer calls 'critical theory', on the other hand, refuse to close 'off human beings toward one another' and are able to challenge 'ideas that consider themselves firm and absolute'. For Horkheimer, 'Critical theory, in contrast to skepticism, does not make an antitheoretical absolutism of the insight into the inadequacy of things as they are and the transitoriness of cognition. Instead, even in the face of pessimistic assessments, critical theory is guided by the unswerving interest in a better future.'[28] In Horkheimer's vision, scepticism lacks the force to reconfigure fixed ideas and is stuck in the status quo instead of imagining alternate possibilities.[29]

Shakespeare has come under fire for being similarly non-committal and politically 'quietistic'. Alluding to observations made by Jacob Feis, J. M. Robertson claimed – without much if any disapprobation – that 'Montaigne was a Quietist, preaching and practicing withdrawal from public broils. But Shakespeare's own practice was on all fours with this.'[30] Much more recently, Gary Taylor has argued that 'to choose is to commit ourselves, and thereby to expose ourselves, and therefore – we do not want to choose. . . . Again and again, Shakespeare tells us stories in which we do not have to choose.'[31] For these critics, the Pyrrhonian 'equipollence' and suspension of commitment evinced by Montaigne and Shakespeare is a weakness rather than a strength and reaffirms rather than challenges the status quo.

What follows will, I hope, reveal the limitations of this position. Montaigne and Shakespeare, like their Pyrrhonian forebears, resist dogmatism but do not evade difficult philosophical and political positions.

Indeed, like Horkheimer's practiser of negative dialectic and critical theory, Montaigne and Shakespeare, I would argue, are 'guided by . . . [an] interest in a better future'.

Montaigne, Shakespeare, and the Discontinuous Self

Just as Montaigne and Shakespeare shared a view of the inevitability of multiple perspectives in any attempt to know the world, they shared a sense of the self's being potentially multiple and discontinuous: 'My selfe now, and my selfe anon, are indeede two; but when better; in good sooth I cannot tell,' Montaigne said in 'Of Vanitie' (3.9, 577). Or, as Montaigne put it in his 'Of the Inconstancie of Our Actions' (2.1),

> If I speak diversely of myself, it is because I look diversely upon myself. All contrarieties are found . . . according to some turn or removing, and in some fashion or other. Shamefaced, bashful, insolent, chaste, luxurious, peevish, prattling, silent, fond, doting, laborious, nice, delicate, ingenious, slow, dull, froward, humorous, debonair, wise, ignorant, false in words, true-speaking, both liberal, covetous, and prodigal. All these I perceive in some measure or other to be in me, according as I stir or turn myself. And whosoever shall heedfully survey and consider himself, shall find this volubility and discordance to be in himself, yea, and in his very judgement. I have nothing to say entirely, simply, and with the solidity of myself, without confusion, disorder, blending, mingling; and in one word, *Distinguo* is the most universal part of my logic. . . . We are all framed of flaps and patches, and of so shapeless and diverse a contexture, that every piece and every moment playeth his part. And there is as much difference found between us and ourselves as there is between ourselves and others. *Magnam rem puta, unum hominem agere. Esteem it a great matter, to play but one man.* (95, 98; 195, 196–7)

Just as Montaigne stressed the 'varying judgements' and 'diverse opinions' that made certainty so difficult to achieve, so here and throughout the *Essays* he 'speak[s] diversely' of himself because he 'look[s] diversely' upon himself.[32] Far from unified, the Montaignian self is filled with 'contrarieties': 'wise, ignorant, false in words, true-speaking, both liberal, covetous, and prodigal. All these I perceive in some measure or other to be in me.'[33] This paradoxical self is anything but stable: 'I have nothing to say entirely, simply, and with the solidity of myself'; instead, there is 'confusion, disorder, blending, mingling'. Shockingly, 'there is as much difference found between us and ourselves as there is between ourselves and others'. The self is, ultimately, theatrical: 'every piece and every moment playeth his part', and one should 'esteem it a great matter to play but one man'.

Similarly, Shakespeare's meditations on being are – perhaps unsurprisingly – often grounded in metaphors from acting and the theatre: 'I am not what I am' (Iago, *Othello*, 1.1.65); 'I am not that I play' (Viola, *Twelfth Night*, 1.5.164); 'I am not what I am' (Viola, *Twelfth Night*, 3.1.132); 'This is and is not Cressid' (Troilus, *Troilus and Cressida*, 5.2.146); 'I hold the world but as the world, Gratiano, / A stage, where everyone must play a part, / And mine a sad one' (Antonio, *Merchant of Venice*, 1.1.77–9); and 'Thus play I in one person many people / And none contented' (Richard, *Richard II*, 5.5.31–2).[34] Hamlet tries to distinguish himself from this multiple or discontinuous theatrical self when he tells his mother that – presumably *unlike* her – he has a unified self and is not an actor:

> Seems, madam? nay it is. I know not 'seems'.
> 'Tis not alone my inky cloak, good mother,
> Nor customary suits of solemn black,
> Nor windy suspiration of forced breath,
> No, nor the fruitful river in the eye,
> Nor the dejected haviour of the visage,
> Together with all forms, moods, shows of grief
> That can denote me truly. These indeed 'seem',
> For they are actions that a man might play;
> But I have that within which passeth show –
> These be but the trappings and suits of woe. (1.2.76–86)

Hamlet esteems it a great matter 'to play but one man' and catalogues the 'suits' and 'actions' and 'shows' that only seem, that are mere 'trappings' of the self within. These may – but often do not, he implies here – correspond to a single self. Whether inadequate or false, the outside self does not match the inside self. Like Montaigne's description of the discontinuous self in 'Of the Inconstancie', Hamlet's conception of being – at least in this moment – is both highly theatrical and doubtful that it is possible to be a unified self.

Shakespeare's Antony values singleness, too, but, for much of *Antony and Cleopatra*, he and the Romans lament his lapse into Egyptian doubleness. Perhaps his lowest point comes late in Act 4 when he tells Eros that he has lost all solidity and has become so multiple and amorphous that he does not know who he is. Asking Eros, 'thou yet behold'st me?' and receiving an affirmative answer, Antony describes the forms that clouds can take:

> Sometime we see a cloud that's dragonish,
> A vapour sometime like a bear or lion,
> A towered citadel, a pendent rock,

> A forkèd mountain, or blue promontory
> With trees upon't that nod unto the world
> And mock our eyes with air. Thou hast seen these signs;
> They are black vesper's pageants. (4.15.2–8)

Antony's cloud images are paradoxical: wispy and formless by nature, they also take the shape of strong, solid, even masculine beasts and things: dragons, bears, lions, citadels, rocks, mountains, trees. But 'That which is now a horse even with a thought / The rack distains, and makes it indistinct / As water is in water' (4.15.9–11). These dissolving clouds are Antony: 'My good knave Eros, now thy captain is / Even such a body. Here I am Antony, / Yet cannot hold this visible shape, my knave' (4.15.12–14).[35]

Shakespeare's sense of the discontinuous self is not always this complete or this bleak. Prospero will return to the idea of life as an 'insubstantial pageant faded' that 'leave[s] not a rack behind' (4.1.155, 156) in Act 4 of *The Tempest*, but he finds at least some recognition of the worth of his project in Act 5. Montaigne, too, did not always see the 'watery' nature of the self as an unequivocally negative quality. But the end of 'An Apologie' (2.12) – drawing almost verbatim on Jacques Amyot's French translation of Plutarch's moral essay 'On the Meaning of *Ei*' – reveals the humbling nature of human mutability:

> Thus can nothing be certainly established, nor of the one nor of the other, both the judging and the judged being in continual alteration and motion.
>
> We have no communication with being, for every human nature is ever in the middle between being born and dying, giving nothing of itself but an obscure appearance and shadow, and an uncertain and weak opinion. And if perhaps you fix your thought to take its being, it would be even as if one should go about to [grasp] the water: for how much the more he shall close and press that which by its own nature is ever gliding, so much the more he shall lose what he would hold and fasten. Thus, seeing all things are subject to pass from one change to another, reason, which therein seeketh a real subsistence, finds herself deceived as unable to apprehend anything subsistent and permanent; forsomuch as each thing either commeth to a being and is not yet altogether, or beginneth to die before it be born. (185–6; 350)

In this essay, indeed, Montaigne gives up on the possibility of singleness, of playing just one man. All is flux:

> *only God is, not according to any measure of time, but according to an immovable and unmoving eternity, not measured by time nor subject to any declination; before whom nothing is, nor nothing shall be after, nor more*

> *new or more recent; but a real being, which by one only* Now *or* Present, *filleth the* Ever, *and there is nothing that truly is but he alone.* Without saying he hath been or he shall be – without beginning and sans ending. (188; 351)

In the vision of 'An Apologie', the only being beyond diversity, mutability, and theatre is God. Shakespeare's most despairing versions of the watery self do not even have the comfort of a stabilising deity.

Montaigne, Shakespeare, and (Post-)Modernity

The uncertainty surrounding both knowledge and the self shared by many of Montaigne's essays and Shakespeare's plays has been of significant interest to critics of the twentieth and twenty-first centuries. Hugh Grady frames the recent debate in this way: as 'harbingers of modernity', Montaigne and Shakespeare can be seen as writers sharing 'a version of skepticism that champions intellectual freedom and puts into question all those ideas and traditions which underlie their eras' arrangement of wealth and power' or as promulgating 'wishful thinking of contemporary liberal and radical interpreters unmindful of Montaigne's and/or Shakespeare's conservatism'.[36] Grady is clearly more sympathetic to the former position, arguing in an earlier book that Montaigne

> was, of course, a political pragmatist who made sure his own works never provoked the ire of Church and State in France. Underneath that, however, is a potentially subversive skepticism and, interestingly in the modern context, an account of subjectivity which emphasizes its potential for resistance to power and ideology as these terms have come to be defined in the late twentieth century.[37]

Here we see a link between 'scepticism' and 'subjectivity' that has captivated critics looking at the two writers in this century and last. Jean Starobinski highlighted this connection in his extremely important *Montaigne in Motion*:

> Montaigne recognizes a desire for stability that runs counter to his natural disposition and is therefore destined to know full well the power of the current that it opposes. Is this an insuperable contradiction? No, it will be resolved, ultimately, by the acceptance of paradox, the coexistence of opposites, and the reconciliation of identity and otherness. . . . Montaigne reconciles himself to the fact that the world is inevitably a world of appearances, and that aesthetic form, and hence artifice and disguise, cannot be avoided in the pursuit of personal identity.[38]

Paradoxes, artifice, and disguise frustrate both the 'desire for stability' and 'the pursuit of personal identity'. This connection between a quest for knowledge and quest for self can, in very similar terms, be applied to the Shakespearean project. Haunted by masks and appearances, both authors accept and reconcile themselves to paradoxes in the epistemological and ontological realms.

In a justifiably famous essay linking the two writers, Robert Ellrodt argued for Montaigne and Shakespeare as pioneers of 'a form of self-consciousness which implies a simultaneous awareness of experience and the experiencing self: it arises whenever a thought or emotion is perceived as *my* thought, *my* emotion in the very moment of experience'.[39] This consciousness about selfhood did not necessarily mean that the self, or indeed the world, was any clearer or easier to discern. Virginia Woolf famously praised Shakespeare's 'mind as the type of the androgynous, of the man-womanly mind',[40] and said of Montaigne that

> It is impossible to extract a plain answer from that subtle, half smiling, half melancholy man, with the heavy-lidded eyes and the dreamy, quizzical expression. . . . Let us simmer over our incalculable cauldron, our enthralling confusion, our hotch-potch of impulses, our perpetual miracle – for the soul throws up wonders every second. Movement and change are the essence of our being; rigidity is death; conformity is death: let us say what comes into our heads, repeat ourselves, contradict ourselves, fling out the wildest nonsense, and follow the most fantastic fancies without caring what the world does or thinks or says. For nothing matters except life; and, of course, order. . . . 'Perhaps' is one of his favourite expressions; 'perhaps' and 'I think' and all the words which qualify the rash assumptions of human ignorance. Such words help one to muffle up opinions which it would be highly impolitic to speak outright.[41]

'Androgynous', 'half', 'incalculable', 'hotch-potch', 'perhaps' – these are all words that accurately describe the approach to knowledge and self of Montaigne and Shakespeare.

All is flux, but all is not meaningless in this world. Peter Holbrook has nicely linked the two writers' shared approach to the self-in-flux:

> For this is the other way in which Montaigne and Shakespeare seem to be soulmates: in their preoccupation, in a way that anticipates again the thought of such later life-philosophers as Emerson and Nietzsche, with the problems involved in becoming a person or, to use Nietzsche's terminology, in becoming oneself.[42]

Ellrodt has taken great pains to make a related point in his recent work. Reaching towards the kind of reconciliation discussed by Starobinski, he argues that 'The contradictions noted by Montaigne are not in harmony with the Stoic ideal of "playing but one man", but they are reconcilable with a self-consistency understood as truth to the permanent impulses of one's own nature, however diverse they may be. Mere consistency belongs with the characters of classical comedy or Jonsonian humors.' Similarly, Shakespeare 'could hardly doubt the unalterableness of fundamental dispositions acknowledged by the psychology of his age. He steered clear from a rigid application of it and probably believed like Montaigne that "Our being cannot subsist without this commixture" of contrary things.'[43] As we shall see in Chapter 3, contrariety and 'commixture' are essential parts of knowing and being for both Montaigne and Shakespeare. But Ellrodt has argued most recently that 'Thus, to acknowledge that "man, totally and throughout, is but patches and multi-coloured elements" . . . is an admission of complexity, not a negation of the existence of a self. That this unique self should happen to be "various and wavering" ("divers et ondoyant") . . . does not necessitate the attribution of "several" selves to each individual.' For Ellrodt, then, post-structuralists have gone too far: in Montaigne, 'the acknowledgment of the instability of the self is counterbalanced by the recognition of its permanence'.[44]

Writers with post-structuralist leanings have indeed emphasised a darker vision.[45] For the psychoanalyst, psychiatrist, and critic Jacques Lacan, 'Montaigne is truly the one who has centered himself, not around scepticism but around the living moment of the *aphanasis* ["fading"] of the subject. And it is in this that he is fruitful, that he is an eternal guide, who goes beyond whatever may be represented of the moment to be defined as a historical turning point.'[46] In another paper, Lacan argued that the subject is 'not only not free from contradiction, as we have known since Montaigne, but much more, since the Freudian experience designates it as the place of negation'.[47] For Lacan, Montaigne was seemingly less important for his scepticism than for the idea of a discontinuous, fading, contradictory self.

Philosophers have been drawn to Montaigne's link between the contradictory subject and an epistemology that recognises contradiction and uncertainty.[48] Writing before he could be a post-structuralist, Hugo Friedrich took a similar position and provocatively suggested Montaigne's counter-Enlightenment, counter-Cartesian tendencies – the humility that 'runs counter to the totalizing pretensions' of Descartes and his followers: 'His desire is to bring this naked humanity to light, for the tedious monotony of being significant flees before it. I am such a nothing – therefore I am: this is the amazing conclusion of Montaigne's self-knowledge.'[49] *Sum nihil ergo sum.*

In a similar fashion, philosophers Charles Taylor (1989) – who refers overtly to Friedrich – and Stephen Toulmin (1990) have argued for the existence of rival approaches to the self put forward by Montaigne and Descartes.[50] Both see Montaigne's version as a 'road not taken'. For Taylor,

> Its [Montaigne's modern individualism's] aim is to identify the individual in his or her unrepeatable difference, where Cartesianism gives us a science of the subject in its general essence. . . . 'There is no man (if he listen to himselfe) that doth not discover in himselfe a peculiar forme, that wrestleth against the institution, and against the tempests of passions which are contrary unto him' [3.2]. . . . The Cartesian quest is for an order of science, of clear and distinct knowledge in universal terms, which where possible will be the basis of instrumental control. The Montaignean aspiration is always to loosen the hold of such general categories of 'normal' operation and gradually prise our self-understanding free of the monumental weight of the universal interpretations, so that the shape of our originality can come to view. Its aim is not to find an intellectual order by which things in general can be surveyed, but rather to find the modes of expression which will allow the particular not to be overlooked.[51]

Toulmin argues that in a move from a humanist/Montaignian vision to a rationalist/Cartesian vision of the self and the world, there are losses as well as gains: 'Whether the 17th-century enthronement of "rationality" was a victory or a defeat for humanity depends on how we conceive of "rationality" itself: instead of the successes of the intellect having been unmixed blessings, they must be weighed against the losses that came from abandoning the 16th-century commitment to intellectual modesty, uncertainty, and toleration' (174).[52] For Toulmin, the goal of philosophy is to 'regain the humane wisdom of the Renaissance, without in turn losing the advantages we won during the three hundred years in which intellectual life was dominated by Cartesian philosophy'.[53]

To Taylor's emphasis on the clash between Montaignian particularity and Cartesian generality and Toulmin's focus on the tension between sixteenth-century uncertainty and seventeenth-century certainty, I would add the related importance of Montaignian – and Shakespearean – perspectivism: the ability to look at human problems and experience from multiple perspectives. Indeed, in a later book – *Return to Reason* (2001) – Toulmin linked Montaigne and Shakespeare as writers who 'gave you the full kaleidoscope of life. As such, they conveyed a sense of personal individuality. No one could mistake Hamlet for Sancho Panza, or Pantagruel for Othello: what counted were the differences among people, not the generalities they shared.'[54]

In calling attention to the particularity, uncertainty, and perspectivism of Montaigne and Shakespeare, however, I would argue that Foucault rather than Lacan should be our guide. Foucault often claimed that to read historically was to read not for inevitability but for contingency:

> To follow the complex course of descent is to maintain passing events in their proper dispersion; it is to identify the accidents, the minute deviations – or, conversely, the complete reversals – the errors, the false appraisals, and the faulty calculations that gave birth to those things that continue to exist and have value for us; it is to discover that truth or being does not lie at the root of what we know and what we are, but the exteriority of accidents.[55]

Something happened, was made, was constructed, but something else could take its place; history wanders onto a path – it errs – and it could wander onto a different path later.

> Recourse to history... is meaningful to the extent that history serves to show how that which is has not always been; that is, the things which seem most evident to us are always formed in the confluence of encounters and chances, during the course of a precarious and fragile history. What reason perceives as its necessity or, rather, what different forms of rationality offers [sic] as their necessary being, can perfectly well be shown to have a history; and the network of contingencies from which it emerges can be traced. Which is not to say, however, that these forms of rationality were irrational; it means that they reside on a base of human practice and human history – and that since these things have been made, they can be unmade, as long as we know how it was that they were made.[56]

This theory – born out of a reading of Nietzsche, who made a hero of Montaigne, whose best reader was Shakespeare – should remind us that the triumph of Descartes's modernity – the rage for certainty, for a stable self, for the *cogito* – need not be permanent. What Hamlin has called the 'Shakespeare–Montaigne–Sextus Nexus' reveals not only how to read the past but possibly how to *re-read* the past and alter the future.[57] That both knowledge and the self are partial and in flux *and* that both can be reshaped, for better and worse, are two of the many important lessons Shakespeare learned from Montaigne – lessons that we, in turn, can learn from our readings of these essays of the *Essays*.

Notes

1. Montaigne, 'An Apologie of Raymond Sebond' (2.12), *The Essayes or Morall, Politike and Millitarie Discourses* (1603), 294.

2. Ramachandran, *The Worldmakers*, 70.
3. Shakespeare, like Montaigne, can be seen to have taken in what Eric Auerbach called 'a stimulant, some kind of drug, a drink of death or of life depending on what one decides. It is the poison of freedom, of the abandonment of any fixed position, and of human autonomy'. See his 'Montaigne the Writer', in *Time, History, and Literature*, 211. In his *Mimesis*, Auerbach also sees the writers sharing 'perspective consciousness': 'The sphere of life represented in a particular instance is no longer the only one possible or a part of that only and clearly circumscribed one. Very often there is a switch from one sphere to another, and even in cases when this does not occur, we are able to discern as the basis of the representation a freer consciousness embracing an unlimited world. We have commented upon this in connection with Boccaccio and especially in connection with Rabelais; we could also have done so in connection with Montaigne' (321–2).
4. Montaigne, 'Of the Inconstancy of Our Actions' (2.1), in *Shakespeare's Montaigne*, ed. Greenblatt and Platt. Where available, quotations from Florio's Montaigne will come from this edition; citations will be included in the text and will list, first, this edition's page number and, second, the page number of the 1603 *Essayes* (98; 197). See Peter Holbrook's similar formulation: 'This Protean aspect to Montaigne's thought, writing, and selfhood is one of the ways he is most like Shakespeare, in whom we also find a bewildering multiplicity of perspectives. . . . [I]n both Shakespeare and Montaigne what makes for success in life involves in part at least the cultivating of a self which is unrepeatable and free' ('Introduction', *The Shakespearean International Yearbook* 6, pp. 8; 9).
5. I largely share the view of William M. Hamlin, in his 'The Shakespeare–Montaigne–Sextus Nexus': 'in the absence of incontestable demonstration of such a habit of reading, it might seem advisable to retreat to a less confident model of Montaigne-absorption, one based less on the premise of aggressive and eclectic proto-Althusserianism and more on a general sense of responsiveness to the wide range of opinions, attitudes, argumentative tactics and self-acknowledged contradictions embedded in the Frenchman's vast book. I have elsewhere characterised this range as a "Montaignean constellation", a cluster of ideas and discursive strategies loosely classifiable as "sceptical" despite simultaneously involving cognitive moves which constitute significant abandonments of Pyrrhonian and Academic assumptions' (22). Another compelling formula, which also draws on Renaissance scepticism, comes from Jourdan, *The Sparrow and the Flea*: 'Faith in the ineluctable mystery of things and the sovereign grandeur of being, coupled occasionally with rashness to force or confuse the turn of events and to make one's mark, but without frenzy as to failure or success, is the foundation of Montaigne's and Shakespeare's thought, and an essential ingredient in any worthwhile study of their work' (22). Similarly and more recently, Peter Mack has claimed that 'Shakespeare and Montaigne teach their audiences how to think ethically by exploring the implications of

opposed positions on issues more than by expounding a particular moral teaching.' See his 'Madness, Proverbial Wisdom and Philosophy in *King Lear*', in *Shakespeare and Renaissance Ethics*, ed. Gray and Cox, 285. Holbrook, in his 'Shakespeare, Montaigne and Classical Reason' from the same volume, goes even further, arguing for a shared scepticism towards reason and ethical choice in human affairs: 'One thing they have in common is a distrust of what I have called classical reason – hence of a large part of the ethical tradition generally, that which understands humanity as in principle capable of rational choice' (282).

6. Popkin, *The History of Scepticism*, xvii.
7. See Schmitt, 'The Rediscovery of Ancient Skepticism', in *The Skeptical Tradition*, ed. Burnyeat, 225–51.
8. Barnes, Introduction to Sextus Empiricus, *Outlines of Scepticism*, ed. Annas and Barnes, xi. All future references to the texts of Sextus will be to this edition unless otherwise noted and will follow the citation in parentheses.
9. See Cave, 'Imagining Scepticism in the Sixteenth Century', who calls this kind of Pyrrhonian scepticism 'an anti-systematic way of doing philosophy, an always unfinished enquiry in which unforeseen shifts and reversals are programmatically allowed for' (195).
10. This is a scepticism very different from that linked to Shakespeare by Stanley Cavell in his *Disowning Knowledge in Six Plays of Shakespeare*. I share Hamlin's view, in his *Tragedy and Scepticism in Shakespeare's England*, that Cavell's version is grounded less in Pyrrhonian scepticism than in Cartesian scepticism (something ultimately very different, as I will explore below): 'Descartes is ultimately less remarkable for his doubt than for the edifice of certainty his doubt enables him to build' (145). See also Grady, *Shakespeare, Machiavelli, and Montaigne*, 52n58.
11. Richard Popkin has argued for the additional importance of Pyrrhonian scepticism to Catholics like Montaigne: 'Not only had these ancient Pyrrhonists found the summit of human wisdom but also, as Montaigne and his disciples were to claim for the next century, they had supplied the best defense against the Reformation. Since the complete sceptic had no positive views, he could not have the wrong views. And since the Pyrrhonist accepted the laws and customs of his community, he would accept Catholicism. Finally, the complete sceptic was in the ideal state for receiving Revelation, if God so willed. The marriage of the Cross of Christ and the doubts of Pyrrho was the perfect combination to provide the ideology of the French Counter-Reformation' (51).
12. Hamlin, *Tragedy and Scepticism*, 65.
13. Hartle, *Michel de Montaigne*, 15, 23.
14. Hamlin, *Tragedy and Scepticism*, 142, 143. See also his 'What Did Montaigne's Skepticism Mean to Shakespeare and His Contemporaries?' where Hamlin discusses the '"synthesis" of Academic and Pyrrhonian skepticism' as 'a skeptical paradigm' that attracted Montaigne – and, through him, Shakespeare and his contemporaries – because of its 'common utility in

combating intolerance, fanaticism, closed-mindedness, and dogmatic pronouncement' (208; 209).
15. Nashe, *Works*, ed. McKerrow, 3: 332–3.
16. Hamlin, 'A Lost Translation Found?' 35–6. Hamlin's research on *The Sceptick* has convinced the authority on the history of scepticism, Richard Popkin. See his *History of Scepticism*, 18–19.
17. Hamlin, *Tragedy and Scepticism*, 32–4.
18. Hamlin, *Tragedy and Scepticism*, 53.
19. For Shakespeare and Sextus's ten modes, see Pierce, 'Shakespeare and the Ten Modes of Scepticism'.
20. Hamlin, 'A Lost Translation Found?' 49–50. See *Outlines*, I. xiv. 91–4, pp. 25–6.
21. Shakespeare, *Twelfth Night*, 5.1.208–9, in *The Norton Shakespeare*, second edition. Unless otherwise noted, all further citations from the plays of Shakespeare are to this edition and are annotated within the text. See also *Richard II*, 2.2.14–27, and *Antony and Cleopatra*, 2.5.117–18. Portia's 'Nothing is good, I see, without respect; / Methinks it sounds much sweeter than by day' (*Merchant*, 5.1.98–9) may also be an allusion to anamorphic or perspective painting.
22. For Nietzsche on Montaigne and Shakespeare, see 'Richard Wagner in Bayreuth', 207. For Nietzsche and perspectivism, see Hales and Welshon, 'Truth, Paradox, and Nietzschean Perspectivism'.
23. I adopt the First Folio's 'our' because it includes Hamlet as one of those whose 'philosophy' needs reconfiguration.
24. See Sherman, 'The Aesthetic Strategies of Skepticism': 'A structural homology links skepticism – with its system for producing either-or exigencies between which it refuses to adjudicate – and these parallel theoretical developments with their syntax of alternative interpretation' (112).
25. Engle, 'Shakespearean Normativity in *All's Well That Ends Well*', 267.
26. Horkheimer, 'Montaigne and the Function of Skepticism', 290.
27. Horkheimer, 'Montaigne and the Function of Skepticism', 307; 308–9.
28. Horkheimer, 'Montaigne and the Function of Skepticism', 311.
29. Horkheimer – who is well aware of Nietzsche's reading of Montaigne and the claim that Shakespeare was Montaigne's 'best reader' – is disappointed in Nietzsche's fondness for Montaigne's thought. He calls Nietzsche's praise in 'Richard Wagner in Bayreuth' 'ambiguous' (303). Later works, Horkheimer admits, show a Nietzsche who 'glorifies the personality' of Montaigne and 'makes of him a hero, which he certainly was not' (303, 304).
30. Robertson, *Montaigne and Shakespeare*, 188.
31. Gary Taylor, 'Judgment', in *New Ways of Looking at Old Texts II*, 93–4.
32. For a nice link between knowledge and self in Montaigne, see Todorov, *Imperfect Garden*: 'Montaigne does not justify love of the self, here, but knowledge of the self. In the present case, that leads him to a progressive identification of his being with his project of knowledge.... It is no longer the man who produces the book, it is the book that makes the man' (149).

33. For the importance of the word 'contrarieties' and its variants to some 'intriguing places' in sceptical texts, see Hamlin, 'A Lost Translation Found?', 49n48. Florio uses the word again – in another passage discussing human diversity – in 'An Apologie' (2.12): 'What differences of sense and reason, what contrarietie of immaginations, doth the diversitie of our passions present vnto vs?' (330).
34. The 'seven ages of man' speech of *As You Like It*'s Jaques, which famously begins 'All the world's a stage, / And all the men and women merely players', arguably does not suggest the discontinuous self in the same way. Nonetheless, it imagines seven distinct roles played throughout one's life (2.7.138–65). For Jaques, playing just one man is inconceivable.
35. See also my *Shakespeare and the Culture of Paradox*, 182–8.
36. Grady, 'Afterword', 174.
37. Grady, *Shakespeare, Machiavelli, and Montaigne*, 5. See also 109–25. Despite all of his important work bringing back the writers of the 'Frankfurt School (especially Adorno, Benjamin, and Horkheimer)' to discussions of Renaissance literary history (16), Grady does not account for the disjunction between his Frankfurt School-inspired take on Montaigne's 'potentially subversive skepticism' and Horkheimer's sense of Montaigne's scepticism as the antithesis of subversive.
38. Starobinski, *Montaigne in Motion*, 26, 86.
39. Ellrodt, 'Self-Consciousness in Montaigne and Shakespeare',42.
40. Woolf, *A Room of One's Own*, 171.
41. Woolf, 'Montaigne', in *The Common Reader*, 91 and 94.
42. Holbrook, 'Introduction', 8.
43. Ellrodt, 'Self-Consistency in Montaigne and Shakespeare', 140, 143. For the Montaigne quotation, see 'Of Experience' (3.13), 649.
44. Ellrodt, *Montaigne and Shakespeare*, 16–17; 8. In this late work, Ellrodt also distances Montaigne and Shakespeare from the 'cultural and moral relativism supposed to be constant in the *Essays*. Montaigne does insist on the diversity of customs (notably in I, xxiii; II, xii; and III, xiii), but to notice a diversity does not mean you countenance it' (150). See also Todorov, *Imperfect Garden*: 'The individual, Montaigne declares, has no essence that would resist the vagaries of existence. But this does not mean, on another level, that this individual has no stability or that one can never generalize from one individual to another' (142).
45. See most recently Kritzman, *The Fabulous Imagination*. Although by no means unremittingly pessimistic, Kritzman brings a poststructuralist sensibility to Montaigne's views on selfhood and knowledge: 'The narrative self depicted in the *Essays*, endlessly reconfigured by the imagination, produces a monstrous form that is forever in a state of crisis because of its inability to assume the shape of a single image. . . . [T]he essays are expositions of ambivalence and the unresolved tension of living in the world' (15, 23).
46. Lacan, *The Four Fundamental Concepts of Psycho-analysis*, 223–4.
47. Lacan, 'Presentation on Psychical Causality', in *Écrits*, 146.

48. See Belsey, 'Psychoanalysis and Early Modern Culture': 'My own best guess is that Lacan finds in Montaigne's apparent inconsequentiality, in the appearance of free association that characterizes the essays, a contrast with the rigorously thetic, law-abiding self-discipline of an Enlightenment philosophy confident that nothing in principle exceeds its totalizing grasp. . . . The essay genre itself, Montaigne's invention, is precisely tentative, provisional, allusive, and anecdotal. Its form runs counter to the totalizing pretensions that would go on to characterize the philosophy of Descartes and his successors. Enlightenment prose sets out to follow a rational sequence and eschews digression' (268, 269). Jean-François Lyotard, in his *The Postmodern Condition*, has noted the affiliations between Montaigne and the essay on the one hand and post-structuralism on the other: 'A postmodern artist or writer is in the position of a philosopher: the text he writes, the work he produces are not in principle governed by preestablished rules, and they cannot be judged according to a determining judgment, by applying familiar categories to the text or work. Those rules and categories are what the work of art itself is looking for. The artist and the writer, then, are working without rules in order to formulate the rules of what *will have been done*. . . . It seems to me that the essay (Montaigne) is postmodern' (81). See most recently Zalloua, 'Essaying Trouble': '. . . Montaigne's essaying of the subject emerges against the backdrop of a dominant humanism, whose pull in the late Renaissance he disputes', which Zalloua connects to Judith Butler's 'decentering of the subject' and 'anti-humanism' (162).
49. Friedrich, *Montaigne*, 18.
50. See also Burrow, 'Frisks, Skips and Jumps', for his playful but useful distinction between Descartes's retiring to the 'stove' to derive the *cogito* and Montaigne's retiring to his tower to write the *Essays*. For Burrow, 'stove people think that you can strip everything away and rebuild reality from precepts; tower people reckon that writing about and exploring or refining beliefs is the best you can do. For tower people, the process of writing and arguing is what thinking is; it is not concluding. . . . Thinking is done not by starting from the beginning, but by thinking onwards and backwards and hoping some clarification will emerge' (22). Noting that philosophers like Ludwig Wittgenstein, Michael Oakeshott, Richard Rorty, Bernard Williams, and Martha Nussbaum 'breathe the air of the tower far more easily than they do that of the stove', Burrow speculates that Montaigne may 'one day come to seem as significant a figure in the history of philosophy as Descartes' (22).
51. Charles Taylor, *Sources of the Self*, 182.
52. In her *The Cunning of Uncertainty*, Helen Nowotny, though not highlighting Montaigne, argues that an embrace of uncertainty is crucial to contemporary scientific research: 'The cunning of uncertainty is a subversive force, ready to serve us if we are ready to go along with it. It may break up the routines adopted over time and reorder priorities by opening a fresh view of the future. It can be a humbling experience but also a wholesome one if it produces clarity where dense mental fog was before. It encourages us

not to skirt ambiguity and ambivalence, but to realize that they enrich the scope of meaning and, ultimately, of experience. At times it reminds us that there are not only truths and lies, but a zone in the middle which can shift, or be shifted, either way. Embracing uncertainty and entering into collusion with its cunning remains an open-ended process' (172).
53. Toulmin, *Cosmopolis*, 174.
54. Toulmin, *Return to Reason*, 30. For Montaigne's connection to the perspectivalism and anti-foundationalism of American pragmatism, see Ferrari, 'Continental Skepticism and American Pragmatism'.
55. Foucault, 'Nietzsche, Genealogy, History', in *The Foucault Reader*, 81.
56. Foucault, 'Structuralism and Post-Structuralism', in *Aesthetics, Method, and Epistemology*, 450. More recently, see Kritzman: 'The exemplarity of the Montaignian imagination teaches us that we can transcend the dominant positivism of our current age by seeing things otherwise' (26). See also Nowotny, who argues for the power of uncertainty – in arts and science research – to reveal that 'it could be otherwise' (xiv). Grady sees a shared forward-looking scepticism in both Montaigne and Shakespeare: 'Shakespeare and Montaigne, I argue, give a common answer to the Machiavellian reduction which had robbed the world of value and enchantment. Yet they cannot return the certainties, the vanished floor under the mythopoeic rug which modernity had so unceremoniously removed. Yes, there are values, there is beauty, there are ethics. But they cannot be grounded within the general nature of things or the will of a mysterious and absent God. Instead, Montaigne and Shakespeare can only display them and contrast them with the world that obtains without them – and perhaps posit a utopian hope for an intersubjectively constructed world more receptive to them' (*Shakespeare, Machiavelli, and Montaigne*, 125). For a different interpretation, see Spencer, *Shakespeare and the Nature of Man*, who links rather than separates the two Renaissance thinkers and their effect on Shakespeare: Montaigne and Machiavelli were authors who similarly shook 'to its foundations' 'the old orderly scheme' and who presented Shakespeare with an 'intellectual and emotional' conflict that he had to negotiate in his plays (49, 50).
57. Ann Hartle, in her *Montaigne and the Origins of Modern Philosophy*, links philosophical possibility in Montaigne to what she calls 'astonished familiarity', in which 'the ordinary is miraculous. The new is just the most familiar, what was there all along, but hidden'. 'Essaying', then, is in this way part of 'the production of the marvelous' (91, 94, 108–9).

Chapter 2

'A little thing doth divert and turn us': Fictions, Mourning, and Playing in 'Of Diverting or Diversion' and *Hamlet*

Hamlet sits paradoxically at the centre and on the edge of the Montaignian Shakespeare. When linking Hamlet to Montaigne, critics have typically turned to 'An Apologie of Raymond Sebond', with its cataloguing of and arguments for scepticism.[1] But I want to claim that 'Of Diverting or Diversion' speaks to *Hamlet* just as strongly, even though its seeming lack of verbal sources causes it rarely to be discussed with the play. While there are in fact verbal connections between 'Of Diverting' and *Hamlet*, the main connection between essay and play is the anatomy of diversion that Hamlet and *Hamlet* share with Montaigne. In essay and play, diversion as an essentially human way of managing grief, passion, and despair coexists in the same work with diversion as the epitome of human delusion and escapist fantasy. Linking theatre to diversion, both authors show us an ambivalence towards playing that Shakespeare foregrounds in Hamlet's ambivalence towards action, whether vengeful or dramatic. Diversion provides possibilities in both texts, but essay and play are ultimately equivocal about whether these possibilities are fruitful or destructive.

These connections between essay and play help make the case for *Hamlet*'s centrality to this book, and I will turn to them shortly. But because of the dating of the various versions of *Hamlet*, some critics have contested the idea that the play could have been shaped by the *Essays*. The first part of this chapter, then, will show the ways in which Shakespeare could have essayed Montaigne before writing some of the texts of *Hamlet*.

George Coffin Taylor clearly thought *Hamlet* was a Montaignian play and produced the data to prove it. He asserted in 1925 that not only the verbal echoes – *Hamlet* shares the lead in most 'Montaigne words to the page' and has far more Montaigne words in total than any other Shakespeare play – but also 'the date, the philosophical nature of the play and the general consensus of substantiated and unsubstantiated opinion of those who have heretofore interested themselves in the subject of Montaigne and Shakspere [sic] at all' make 'a strong case ... for *Hamlet* as the play of all plays marked by the Montaigne influence. However strong this influence upon *Lear* may be, all considerations point to *Hamlet* as the play in which it is strongest and most pervasive.'[2]

It is possible, of course, that Shakespeare encountered Montaigne even before the 1603 translation. He could have read the essays in the original, since he had French connections and had enough French to give us the language lesson in *Henry V*. William Carew Hazlitt suggested a particular avenue for Shakespeare's receiving access to the French text:

> These Quineys [from Stratford], who were mercers and vintners, and had relations with London, if not with the wine-growing provinces of France, notably Bordeaux itself, were persons of exceptional culture, and Thomas, who subsequently espoused Judith Shakespeare, was a most likely man to invest in one of the earlier Bordeaux editions of the *Essays* on their first appearance.[3]

And, perhaps less fancifully, Shakespeare's landlords in London's Silver Street, just about the time that Montaigne's *Essays* were first published in English, were French Huguenots. Shakespeare befriended them enough that he would help convince one of their employees to marry their daughter in 1604 and, when the relationship between father and son-in-law went sour, Shakespeare would testify on the family's behalf in 1612.[4]

Another way Shakespeare could have received pre-1603 access to Montaigne is, like Sir William Cornwallis – who almost certainly alludes to Florio's translation in his own *Essayes* of 1600 – to have seen the *Essays* in manuscript.[5] And Florio's translation was licensed on 4 June 1600.[6] So we need not fear linking *Hamlet* to Montaigne, as John Sterling did in 1838, purely because of the date of publication: 'the external facts appear to contradict any notion of a French ancestry for the Dane, as the play is said to have been produced in 1600, and the translation of the "Essays" not for three years later'.[7]

Indeed, for Hugh Grady, leaning on the exact dates of Shakespeare's encounter with Montaigne misses the point:

> I will take it for granted that when the plays put recognizable Machiavellian and Montaignean concepts in the mouths of their characters, or create chains of cause and effect which parallel those in contemporary political texts like Machiavelli's *The Prince* or *The Discourses*, it is reasonable to assume that discursive dynamics are at work even if we cannot be certain

of what microcircuitry was responsible for each specific transmission. In the end, it matters little whether Shakespeare directly read either Machiavelli or Montaigne. What matters is that we can observe the discursive parallels among them, parallels which help us to read the plays in new (and sometimes old) ways and which help us to see the extent to which Shakespeare participated in the creation of intellectual modernity as he entertained and challenged his audiences . . .

Here again I am following Foucault's notions that discourses circulate in societies in fluid ways not necessarily dependent on direct author-to-author contact; or, as an older critical idiom had it, sometimes ideas are 'in the air'. I believe that Shakespeare and Montaigne are linked at least through such an indirect connection, and I want to draw attention to the fundamental ways in which both of these quintessential early modern writers employ shifting viewpoints, critical rationality, and suspicion of final conclusions and system-building.[8]

Grady and I come to similar conclusions about the Montaigne–Shakespeare connection, and we both argue for *Hamlet* as a text in which 'a Montaignean moment emerges'.[9]

Still, given the scepticism surrounding Shakespeare's debt to Montaigne, I think it is wise to use 1603 as a point of departure, to depend a little more on the '"source-and-influence" dynamics of traditional positivist historicism' than Grady would like to.[10] In this case, I concur with J. M. Robertson, who argued that 'It is necessary to produce proofs, and to look narrowly to dates. . . . We must therefore keep closely in view the divergences between this text [Q1] and that of the Second Quarto, printed in 1604, in which the transmuting touch of Shakespeare is broadly evident. . . . [And] as it is from Florio that he is seen to have copied in the passages where his copying is beyond dispute, it is on Florio's translation that we must proceed.'[11]

Textual Histories

There are several versions of *Hamlet* in its earliest printed form, and there is a dispute over their dates. So the crucial question is whether Shakespeare could have essayed Montaigne in English before writing *Hamlet*.

The key terms of the debate concerning the composition of the 1603 First Quarto (Q1) – which are arguably still those in play today – were set by Charles Knight and John Payne Collier in the mid-nineteenth century.[12] For Knight, Q1 was evidence of 'the author working on his first sketch', while for Collier Q1 consists of a misquoting of the original

Shakespearean text, a 'memorial reconstruction', as it would come to be called.[13] This tension was distilled nicely by Tycho Mommsen in 1857: the distinction was between 'first sketches' and 'mere representations of the genuine text'.[14] But as Zachary Lesser shrewdly points out, both views 'imagined Shakespeare's authorship along Romantic lines': Shakespeare as the sole creator of *Hamlet* with Q1 as his early sketch (Knight) and Shakespeare as the master author of the Second Quarto (Q2) and Folio (F), whose genuine work has been corrupted in memorial reconstruction (Collier/Mommsen).[15]

A turning point came in the Clarendon Shakespeare, edited by William George Clark and William Aldis Wright in 1872, which introduced the idea that Q1 was a messier text than had been previously argued. Shakespeare was working with an inferior version of the play, and they claimed 'with some diffidence'

> That there was an old play on the story of Hamlet, some portions of which are still preserved in the quarto of 1603; that about the year 1602 Shakespeare took this and began to remodel it for the stage, as he had done with other plays; that the quarto of 1603 represents the play after it had been retouched by him to a certain extent, but before his alterations were complete: and that in the quarto of 1604 we have for the first time the Hamlet of Shakespeare.... A close examination of the quarto of 1603 will convince anyone that it contains some of Shakespeare's undoubted work, mixed with a great deal that is not his, and will confirm our theory that the text, imperfect as it is, represents an older play in a transition state, while it was undergoing a remodeling but had not received more than the first touches of the master's hand.[16]

For Lesser, 'in this passage we can see the true birth of the *Ur-Hamlet* ["an old play on the story of Hamlet"]. What is crucially new about Clark and Wright's theory is its integration of the pre-Shakespearean *Hamlet* into Shakespeare's own texts.'[17]

With the birth of the *Ur-Hamlet* came the birth of what Lesser calls 'disintegrationism'.[18] Fearing this metamorphosis, F. J. Furnivall lamented in 1880 that

> in 1872 the Cambridge editors of the Clarendon Press *Hamlet* ... propounded a new theory of the First Quarto of the play (1603); and this theory, when carefully examined and worked out, just robs Shakspere [sic] of about four-fifths of the conception of the characters of Hamlet, Claudius, Gertrude, Ophelia, and Laertes: 'Flat burglary as ever was committed!'[19]

As Lesser notes, Furnivall's fears were confirmed by the disintegrationists, among them F. G. Fleay, E. E. Stoll, L. L. Schücking, and

J. M. Robertson: 'the disintegrationists would go well beyond Clark and Wright, finding other hands even in the Q2/F text of the play. . . . *Hamlet* would become a layered text resulting from a multistep process of revision, with Shakespeare altering and incorporating the work of several other playwrights.'[20]

The Collier–Knight debate has been revived in recent works on Q1 by Kathleen Irace, Tiffany Stern, James Marino, Steven Urkowitz, and Terri Bourus.[21] Irace and Stern play the role of Collier (and Mommsen), arguing for, with new research, the notion of Q1 being a 'memorial reconstruction and the first of many theatrical reworkings of *Hamlet*, not Shakespeare's first thoughts or the vestiges of the *Ur-Hamlet*' (Irace) and a 'noted play' (Stern).[22] Building on earlier work by Urkowitz, Bourus – with some of the invective characteristic of the original skirmish – takes the Knight position, claiming that Q1 is Shakespeare's roughest draft. Marino is somewhere in between, seeing, according to Lesser, 'more continuity than disjuncture between the pre-Shakespearean *Hamlet*, Q1, Q2, and F'.[23]

The idea that Q1 is the first draft of the play is obviously important for the notion that Shakespeare essayed Montaigne in English as he was revising *Hamlet*.[24] In his important 1986 article, '"Well-sayd olde Mole": Burying Three *Hamlet*s in Modern Editions', Urkowitz argued for Shakespeare's hand in all three versions. Fresh from his research on the two versions of *King Lear*,[25] Urkowitz focused on several 'theatrical instances of triple-variants. These include alternative readings which would produce different events or patterns of events in stage productions of the alternative texts.'[26] As Bourus would do later, he also discusses the proximity of Q1 to the sources of the Hamlet story, and the subsequent departure from these sources in the later texts, focusing specifically on the changing portrayal of Gertrude:

> If, as the conventional explanation has it, theatrical pirates indeed produced the First Quarto text, they worked most peculiarly, accidentally reinventing details of a play Shakespeare had abandoned from his sources. . . . Alternatively, of course, if the First Quarto derives from an early Shakespearean version, then the line of alteration simply fits what we observe repeatedly in the work of other writers, that is, successive rewrites move further away from original source material.[27]

For Urkowitz, the idea that there is an 'essential *Hamlet*' is an 'idealized shadow'; it is time, instead, to examine 'the extant legacy of theatrical treasure in the multiple texts left us by a playwright made like us of flesh and blood'.[28]

Bourus makes a more wide-ranging argument for Shakespeare's involvement in *Hamlet* Q1, seeing it not just as Shakespeare's early rough draft but as the *Ur-Hamlet* itself.[29] Bourus dismantles arguments for the authorial roles of piratical publishers, actors, and reporters. For her, the play that, for example, Gabriel Harvey and Thomas Lodge saw was Q1, 'the first play that young Shakespeare wrote without a collaborator . . . performed in London in 1589 at the Theatre, that first single-purpose English arena, erected only 13 years before'.[30] Then there were two revisions: 'The first, most radical revision took place in 1602, 13 years after the original version had been staged; it is best represented by the 1623 Folio text. The second revision took place, apparently, in 1604, and unlike the first revision it may have been purely literary; it is best represented by the 1604 Quarto text.'[31] Bourus is not concerned with Montaigne's presence in Q2 – she is more concerned with the death of fathers and sons and with the revision of the 1.2 'seems' speech – but her arguments and dating work nicely to shore up the argument for a Montaignian *Hamlet*.[32]

Whether we accept Irace's revised notion of memorial reconstruction,[33] Stern's noted text, Marino's 'continuing incremental revisions', or Bourus's very early Q1 and 1604 Q2, all of these scholars pave the way for a *Hamlet* shaped by a reading of Florio's Montaigne. Despite their varying positions, all would agree that *Hamlet* was not a finished product in 1600–1, even though Harvey wrote approvingly of it around that time.[34] It is impossible to know the ultimate answers to these questions of *Hamlet*'s origins. But not knowing should not prohibit us from interrogating the extent to which essaying Florio's Montaigne helped Shakespeare make *Hamlet* into *Hamlet*, into 'the Hamlet of Shakespeare'.[35]

Two early literary-historical treatments of a Montaignian *Hamlet* worried much less about these important arguments. Although with wildly different conclusions, Jacob Feis and J. M. Robertson saw the differences between the 1603 First Quarto and the 1604–5 Second Quarto of *Hamlet* as utterly crucial in tracking the influence of Montaigne on Shakespeare. For Feis,

> In closely examining the innovations by which the augmented second quarto edition (1604) distinguishes itself from the first quarto, published the year before (1603), we find that almost every one of these innovations is directed against the principles of the new philosophical work – *The Essayes of Michel Montaigne* – which had appeared at that time in England, and which was brought out under the high auspices of the foremost noblemen and protectors of literature in this country. . . . [M]ost of the freshly added philosophical thoughts, and many characteristic peculiarities, have clear reference to the philosophy of a certain book and the character of its author – namely, to Michel Montaigne and his 'Essais'.[36]

The second quarto, Feis argued, 'distinguished itself' from the first by the presence of the 'freshly added philosophical thoughts' of Montaigne. Agreeing with Sterling that 'the Prince of Denmark is very nearly a Montaigne',[37] Feis saw Montaigne's presence in the post-1603 *Hamlet* as part of a Shakespearean critique of the French essayist's newly translated ideas. By channelling Montaigne's ideas into the sceptical and ineffectual Hamlet, Feis argued, Shakespeare was distancing himself from rather than allying himself with the Frenchman.[38]

Robertson was equally adamant about the influence of Montaigne on the Second Quarto of *Hamlet* but far less critical of Montaigne:

> And when finally it is found that, with only one exception, all the passages in question have been added to the play in the Second Quarto, after the publication of Florio's translation, it seems hardly possible to doubt the translation influenced the dramatist in his work. . . . the influence is from the very start of that high sort in which he that takes becomes co-thinker with him that gives, Shakespeare's absorption of Montaigne being as vital as Montaigne's own assimilation of the thought of the classics.[39]

For Robertson, there is no doubt that *Hamlet* – in its Second Quarto form – marks the beginning of the Montaignian Shakespeare: 'on the one hand . . . there is no sign worth considering of a Montaigne influence on Shakespeare before HAMLET; and, on the other hand . . . the influence to some extent continues beyond that play'.[40]

T. S. Eliot, beginning with a review of Robertson's *The Problem of 'Hamlet'*, saw no difficulty linking Shakespeare's *Hamlet* to Montaigne:

> Why he attempted it [a revision of *Hamlet*] at all is an insoluble puzzle; under compulsion of what experience he attempted to express the inexpressibly horrible, we cannot ever know. We need a great many facts in his biography; and we should like to know whether, and when, and after or at the same time as what personal experience, he read Montaigne, II., xii.: 'Apologie de Raimond Sebond'. We should have, finally, to know something which is by hypothesis unknowable, for we assume it to be an experience which, in the manner indicated, exceeded the facts. We should have to understand things which Shakespeare did not understand himself.[41]

In reviewing Taylor's book in 1925, Eliot combined this sense of ultimate 'unknowability' as to Shakespeare's thinking with the sense that Montaigne – and especially Florio's Englished version of the *Essays* – had a role to play in Shakespearean composition:

> And in bringing more clearly to light this *verbal* influence Mr. Taylor supplies a corrective to the invariable human impulse to look for mystery and

excitement. For certainly it was not the influence of one philosopher on another. As Mr. Taylor reminds us, no two critics can agree on what Shakespeare's 'philosophy' was – if he had one. . . . Montaigne is just the sort of writer to provide a stimulant to a poet; for what the poet looks for in his reading is not a philosophy – not a body of doctrine or even a consistent point of view which he endeavors to *understand* – but a point of departure. The attitude of a *craftsman* like Shakespeare – whose business was to write plays, not to think – is very different from that of the philosopher or even the literary critic.

Not that Montaigne did not influence Shakespeare in ways which we can never know. Mr. Taylor does not deny the existence of some deeper influence than an influence of vocabulary. But he refrains – and for this abstention must be given all praise – from attempting to plumb these depths. There was almost certainly some emotional influence. . . . But what and how much we shall never know. It is not only the external history of Shakespeare's life that is deficient. It is that internal history, which may have much or may have little relation to the external facts, that internal crisis over which our imagination is tempted to brood too long – it is this that we shall never know.[42]

Eliot does not doubt that Shakespeare used Montaigne as a 'departure'; the verbal echoes unearthed by Taylor confirm this 'influence of vocabulary' and help Eliot build on the ideas in his Robertson review. Eliot's scepticism is reserved for the attempt to determine what Shakespeare was feeling and thinking – 'that internal history' – as he essayed Montaigne.[43]

The key moments that Eliot leans on surround Taylor's discussion of *Hamlet*, and it is interesting that Taylor, *pace* Eliot, sees *Hamlet* as the place where intellectual and verbal influences may coincide. Noting, as many have before and since, that 'about the time when Florio's version of the *Essays* was published (1603), a change seems to come over the spirit of Shakespeare's plays', Taylor speculates on the reasons: 'It may be that something in the life of Shakspere would (if known) explain it – some personal tragedy, or bad health, or a burning of the candle at both ends, or a woman, or, perhaps a combination of all of these, and, in addition, his reading of Montaigne at this particular time. As a guess among guesses, the Montaigne guess is as good as any.'[44] Taylor – who, it should be noted, is not at all concerned about the date of *Hamlet* posing an influence problem – starts by positing *Hamlet* as a particularly Montaignian play, and then claiming that the verbal 'facts' bear out 'this natural surmise':

Underlying all the more extensive treatments of the Montaigne–Shakespeare controversy is discernible a sort of feeling that *Hamlet* is the play in which Montaigne's influence is strongest. . . . If the influence of Montaigne the thinker was to be found at all in Shakespeare, one would be most likely to find it in that play, which, whatever else it may be, is preeminently the drama of thought. ... He stands 'environ'd with a wilderness' of doubts, and he alone among Shakespeare's characters gives the impression of one eternally attempting to pass beyond the flaming ramparts of the world. It is small wonder that the general vein of skepticism and questioning running through *Hamlet* should have set students looking here first for the influence of Montaigne. This natural surmise is borne out by the facts. The average of Montaigne words to the page makes for this conclusion; the large proportion of parallels in Montaigne and Hamlet points almost undeniably to it.[45]

Although Taylor allows that 'a strong case is made out for *Hamlet* as the play of all plays marked by the Montaignian influence', he is still most comfortable with 'the phrasal influence of Montaigne as the most important single point developed by this discussion', providing as it does both an escape from 'that portion of the field where the quicksands lie' and the ability 'to plant one's feet again on ground more or less solid'.[46]

Taylor's brilliant work revolves around the verbal echoes that impressed Eliot so much, and we need to keep eyes and ears open for these parallels. Admitting with Eliot that 'we shall never know', I nonetheless want to 'plumb these depths' a little more than would have made Eliot comfortable. I hope, then, to find in Montaigne some of the sources of 'departure' that Eliot did think were valid to consider.

'Of Diverting or Diversion'

With that idea in mind, I would like to begin with a close reading of Montaigne's 'Of Diverting or Diversion' (3.4) and examine its explorations of the way that diversions – thoughts of love, imaginings, theatrical performances, dreams – help us manage loss, despair, and mourning. I will argue that Montaigne's ambivalence towards diversions – at times he sees them as essential, even beautiful, and at other times highly misleading, illusory, and escapist – aligns nicely with similar ambivalences in Hamlet's thinking, especially in his meditations on mourning and theatricality in the first two acts.

Montaigne begins his essay with a focus on the managing of the specifically feminine mourning of his friend. Most women, he says, are 'artificial and ceremonious' in 'their discourses [of mourning]', but this friend is 'a truly afflicted lady', and Montaigne tells us of his strategy for caring for her, which introduces the concept of diversion:

> After I had for awhile applied myself to her torment, I attempted not to cure it by strong and lively reasons, either because I want them or because I supposed I might otherwise effect my purpose the better. Nor did I cull out the several fashions of comfort prescribed by philosophy: that the thing

lamented is not ill, as *Cleanthes* [says]; or but a little ill, as the Peripatetics; that to lament is neither just nor commendable, as *Chrisippus*; nor this of *Epicurus*, most agreeing with my manner, to translate the conceit of irksome into delightsome things; nor to make a load of all this mass, dispensing the same as one hath occasion, as *Cicero*. But fair and softly declining our discourses, and by degrees bending them unto subjects more near, then a little more remote, even as she more or less inclined to me. I unperceivably removed those doleful humours from her so that, as long as I was with her, so long I kept her in cheerful countenance and untroubled fashion, wherein I used diversion.[47]

Avoiding 'strong and lively' methods, Montaigne 'fair and softly declin[ed] our discourses . . . bending them' until he was able to remove 'those doleful humours from her' and keep 'her in cheerful countenance' by means of this use of 'diversion'. He also admits that he had not finished the job and perhaps had not been forceful enough, since later visitors did not find her changed: 'Those which in the same service succeeded me found her no whit amended: the reason was, I had not yet driven my wedge to the root' (227; 500).

Montaigne next explores 'some kinds of public diversions' from the recent and the classical past. First, he mentions the case of the Lord of Himbercourt, who negotiated not once but twice with the angry townspeople of Liege, upset about yielding the town to the Duke of Burgundy. 'Diverting their head-long fury and dissipating the same with vain and frivolous consultations,' he 'lulled them into so secure a sleep that he gained the day, which was his chiefest drift and only aimed scope' (228; 500). Drawing on a tale from Ovid's *Metamorphoses*, Montaigne also mentions how Hippomenes defeated Atalanta in a foot race, won her hand in marriage, and avoided his own death by diverting her attention in the race using the careful placement of 'alluring' golden apples given to him by Venus. Eventually, 'by this digressing and diverting, the goal and the advantage of the course was judged his' (228, 229; 500). Finally, Montaigne makes the general point that doctors often use diversion to effect cures when more direct approaches will not work:

> When physicians cannot purge the rheum, they divert and remove the same unto some less dangerous part. I also perceive it to be the most ordinary receite [remedy] for the mind's diseases. . . . One makes it seldom to shock mischiefs with direct resistance. One makes it neither bear nor break, but shun or divert the blow. (229; 500)

So who can succeed without relying on diversions? Only those 'of the first rank', like Socrates, can stay upon the thing itself, to examine, and judge it. It belongeth to one only *Socrates* to accost and entertain death with an undaunted ordinary visage, to become familiar and play with it. He seeketh for no comfort out of the thing itself. To die seemeth unto him a natural and indifferent accident. Thereon he wishly fixeth his sight and thereon he resolveth without looking elsewhere. (229; 500–1)

We get the sense here of what Montaigne will say more forcefully later in the essay: that, while relying on diversion is necessary and definitely human, there is a moral superiority to those who can avoid it and 'stay upon the thing itself'. This question of whether to divert or not to divert is central to Hamlet – and *Hamlet* – as well.

Most people, unlike Socrates, 'divert their consideration from death' (230; 501) in a variety of ways, especially with prayer and 'heavens-raised devotion': 'One may well commend their religion, but not properly their constancy' (229, 230; 501). And human beings do not just swerve from a focus on death; they rarely grapple directly with life itself: 'We ever think on somewhat else: either the hope of a better life doth settle and support us, or the confidence of our children's worth, or the future glory of our name, or the avoiding of these lives' mischiefs, or the revenge hanging over their heads that have caused and procured our death' (231; 501).

When he moves onto examples, though, Montaigne cannot help returning to death: his exempla reveal ways in which famous men have diverted their thoughts from the horrors of mortality. First, we are told of how Xenophon initially succumbed to despair and removed his crown when he first heard of his son Gryllus's death. But, 'finding upon better relation how valiantly he died, he took it up and put it on his head again' (231; 501). Next, we read that Epicurus 'at his death comforted himself in the eternity and worth of his writings. . . . All glorious and honourable labours are made tolerable' (231; 502). Xenophon, Montaigne tells us, claims that 'the same wound and the same toil . . . toucheth not a general of an army as it doth a private soldier', presumably because the former will glean plaudits and glory and the latter will not (231; 502). Epaminondas, too, diverted himself and 'took his death much the more cheerfully, being informed that the victory remained on his side. . . . And such other like circumstances amuse, divert, and remove us from the consideration of the thing itself' (231; 502).

Ultimately, for Montaigne, diversion in such matters is supremely human (Socrates, of course, being the exception). For 'even the arguments of philosophy at each clap wrest and turn the matter aside and scarcely wipe away the scab whereof' (231–2; 502). The great Zeno, 'the first man of the first philosophical school and superintendent of the rest . . . against death cried out: *No evil is honourable; death is; therefore is death no evil*' (232; 502). The great minds of the past still needed to think on death by means of diversion: 'I love to see that these principal wits cannot rid themselves of our company. As perfect and absolute as they would be, they are still but gross and simple' (232; 502).

What is important for readers of *Hamlet* is that Montaigne goes on to build his case for the compassionate humanity of diversion by contrasting it with revenge. Acknowledging that '*Revenge is a sweet-pleasing passion, of a great natural impression,*' he tells the story of his counsel of a 'young prince' (almost certainly Henri de Navarre, eventually King Henry IV of France) *against* using revenge:

> To divert of late a prince from it, I told him not he was to offer the one side of his cheek to him who had struck him on the other in regard of charity; nor displayed I unto him the tragical events poesy bestoweth upon that passion. There I left him and strove to make him taste the beauty of a contrary image: the honour, the favour, and the good will he should acquire by gentleness and goodness. I diverted him to ambition. (232; 502)

Significantly, Montaigne counselled a third way – neither passive turning the other cheek, nor reading about and meditating on the tragedies of employing vengeance found in 'poesy'. Instead, Montaigne 'diverted him to ambition', by focusing on the benefits to the prince's reputation – 'the honour, the favour, and the good will' he would acquire by practising 'gentleness and goodness'. The implications of choosing to divert oneself from vengeance and focusing on both ambition and honour are issues to which we will return when we look to link this essay to *Hamlet*.

Montaigne's praise of diversion shifts to a meditation on managing an 'affection in love' that is 'over-powerful'. The answer? '*Disperse or dissipate the same* . . . weaken it with dividing, and protract it with diverting the same' (232; 502). While it is acceptable to have one 'regent or chief master desire', managing it by division and dissipation will not allow it to 'misuse and tyrannize you' (232; 502). What is especially interesting in what follows is that Montaigne tells us he used love as a diversion to help him overcome 'heavy displeasure', almost certainly the grief caused by mourning the loss of Etienne de La Boétie. Given what preceded this discussion, we might assume that the 'regent or chief master desire' was that for his friend, the death of whom required him to seek diversion to avoid the tyranny of that feeling:

> I had peradventure lost myself in it had I only relied upon my own strength. Needing a vehement diversion to withdraw me from it, I did by art and study

make myself a lover, whereto my age assisted me. Love discharged and diverted me from the inconvenience, which good will and amity had caused me.

So it is in all things else. A sharp conceit possesseth and a violent imagination holdeth me; I find it a shorter course to alter and divert than to tame and vanquish the same. If I cannot substitute a contrary unto it, at least I present another unto it. *Change ever easeth, variety dissolveth, and shifting dissipateth.* (233; 502)

Time, as well as mutability, has a role to play in the easing of pain. And though the memory of an old friend never goes away – 'a wise man seeth little less his friend dying at the end of five and twenty years than at the beginning of the first year' – diversions mitigate that feeling and allow one to carry on: 'so many other cogitations cross this that it languisheth and in the end groweth weary' (233; 502).

At the core of this essay, then, is how diversion dissipates strong, often devastating emotion. And it is important to note that here Montaigne links diversion to change, variety, and shifting – and soon will connect it to a related idea: theatricality. For in the next section Montaigne discusses how women use diversion both to keep gossip from spreading and to cover up their real emotions:

I have also seen some women, who to divert the opinions and conjectures of the babbling people and to divert the fond tattling of some, did by counterfeit and dissembled affections overshadow and cloak true affections. (233; 502)

But the problem with this acting is something that Quintilian taught the Renaissance and that haunted Ben Jonson (and probably Shakespeare, too): the role can replace the reality. 'I have noted some who, in dissembling and counterfeiting, have suffered themselves to be entrapped wittingly and in good earnest, quitting their true and original humor for the feigned' (233–4; 503).[48]

And it is here that Montaigne's attitude towards diversion starts to change. It is as if, in remembering the effect of diversion on his feelings for his friend, as well as the linking of diversion to feminine feigning and theatricality, Montaigne shifts his focus to the negative side of our need to divert, shift, and change. Whereas earlier Montaigne concentrated on the human – even humanising – elements of diversion, he begins to focus on the negative elements, starting with its superficiality: '*A little thing doth divert and turn us, for a small thing holds us.* We do not respect subjects in gross and lone; they are circumstances or small and superficial images that move and touch us, and vain rinds which rebound from subjects' (234; 503). Elsewhere in the *Essays* – and even in this essay – Montaigne counsels human beings to think small, not to overreach, to remember that we are not God. But the emphasis here is on our misguided love of surface, 'superficial images', and 'vain rinds'.

Montaigne's confession that small things move and disturb him is beautiful and makes him seem one of us, but he clearly sees this trait as a weakness here:

> The remembrance of a farewell, or of an action, of a particular grace, or of a last commendation afflict us. . . . The word and the tune wound me – even as a preacher's exclamations do often move their auditory more than their reasons, and as the pitiful groan of a beast yearneth us, though it be killed for our own use – without poising or entering therewhilst into the true and massy essence of my subject. . . . They are the foundations of my mourning. (234; 503)

Montaigne seems disappointed in us and himself for valuing particulars over universals and preacher's 'exclamations' over their 'reasons', as well as for having 'the foundations of my mourning' being other than 'the true and massy essence of my subject'. Montaigne continues chastising himself for focusing on the wrong things, using his kidney stone as an example: 'I considered how slight causes and frivolous objects imagination nourished in me the grief to lose my life; with what atoms the consequence and difficulty of my dislodging was contrived in my mind; to what idle conceits and frivolous cogitations we give place in so weighty a case or important affair' (234; 503).

Then, in a move very much like Hamlet's in 2.2 to which we must return, Montaigne links the focus on the trivialities of bodily pain to the power of the seemingly weak forces of language and art to move us:

> So do the plaints and fables of trouble vex our minds, and the wailing laments of *Dido* and *Ariadne* passionate even those that believe them not in *Virgil* nor in *Catullus*. It is an argument of an obstinate nature and indurate heart not to be moved therewith. . . . And no wisdom goeth so far as by due judgement to conceive aright the evident cause of a sorrow and grief too lively and wholly. That it suffer or admit no accession [except] by presence, when eyes and ears have their share therein, parts that cannot be agitated but by vain accidents. (235; 503)

Montaigne asserts that we can get close to an understanding of pain and mourning only through the diversion of 'fables': what we experience through our 'eyes and ears', such as the 'wailing laments of *Dido* and *Ariadne*'.[49] And rhetors and actors underscore this plight in being moved by their own performances:

> Is it reason that even arts should serve their purposes, and make their profit of our imbecility and natural blockishness? An orator, (sayeth Rhetoric), in

the play of his pleading, shall be moved at the sound of his own voice and by his feigned agitations, and suffer himself to be cozened by the passion he representeth. Imprinting a lively and essential sorrow by the juggling he acteth, to transfer it into the judges, whom of the two it concerneth less. As the persons hired at our funerals who, to aid the ceremony of mourning, make sale of their tears by measure and of their sorrow by weight. For although they strive to act it in a borrowed form, yet by habituating and ordering their countenance, it is certain they are often wholly transported into it and entertain the impression of a true and unfeigned melancholy. (235–6; 503–4)

For Montaigne, in this section of the essay, mourning and grief are part of a theatre of sorrow: the actors move the audience but also take their own representations for the things themselves: representing and acting, though initially presented 'in borrowed form', become 'true and unfeigned melancholy'.

Not just women, then, but everyone is capable of becoming what they play – or everyone is capable of playing the woman's part. For Quintilian returns in this section of Montaigne's essay as a warning against the dangers of diversion. Montaigne makes an analogy between the professional mourners mentioned above ('the persons hired at our funerals who . . . aid the ceremony of mourning') and actors ('comedians') who get lost in their performances:

> *Quintilian* reporteth to have seen comedians so far engaged in a sorrowful part that they wept after being come to their lodgings; and of himself, that having undertaken to move a certain passion in another, he had found himself surprised, not only with shedding of tears but with a paleness of countenance and behaviour of a man truly dejected with grief. (236; 504)[50]

And this feigning, this being 'engaged in a sorrowful part', ultimately proves distasteful to Montaigne because it gets us too far away from the thing – or the person:

> when we lose a late acquaintance, [we] strive to load him with new and forged praises and to make him far other now that we are deprived of his sight than he seemed to be when we enjoyed and beheld him. As if mourning were an instructing party, or tears cleared our understanding by washing the same. (236; 504)

As a result of this falsification in mourning, Montaigne wants nothing to do with any similar sorts of eulogies when he is gone: 'I renounce from this time forward all the favourable testimonies any man shall afford me, not because I shall deserve them but because I shall be dead' (236–7; 504).

Montaigne finishes the essay by further denouncing diversion, linking it to falsehood, dreams, and escapism. Thinking and imagining that become reality are now not sources of solace and comfort but ones of delusion:

> Let me think of building castles in *Spain*, my imagination will forge me commodities and afford me means and delights wherewith my mind is really tickled and essentially gladded. How often do we pester our spirits with anger or sadness by such shadows and entangle ourselves into fantastical passions which alter both our mind and body? What astonished, flearing, and confused mumps and mows doth this dotage stir up in our visages! What skippings and agitations of members and voice! Seems it not by this man, alone, that he hath false visions of a multitude of other men with whom he doth negotiate, or some inward goblin that torments him?
>
> Inquire of yourself, where is the object of this alteration? Is there anything but us in nature, except subsisting nullity, over whom it hath any power? (237; 504)

And this obsession with imaginings, 'fantastical passions', and 'inward goblins' can be a matter of life and death – not just in valuing falsehoods in the act of mourning but in making decisions that can lead to death: Montaigne's final examples are of Cambyses – who killed his brother, though he loved him dearly, because he dreamed this brother would be King of Persia; Aristodemus, who 'killed himself upon a conceit he took of some ill presage'; and King Midas, who did the same, 'being troubled and vexed by a certain unpleasing dream of his own' (237; 504). Montaigne cynically concludes, 'It is the right way to prize one's life at the right worth of it, to forgo it for a dream' (237; 504), adding that the soul and mind blame the body for all of human weakness.[51] Finishing with a celebration of the mind over the body in Propertius – 'The mind's way first should rightly be assign'd' – Montaigne, who has in the last half of this essay taken the mind to task for its fantasies and dreams, sardonically closes by saying, 'It hath surely much reason to speak of it' (238; 504–5). And yet to him, what is this 'subsisting nullity', this quintessence of dust?

A Montaignian *Hamlet*

Hamlet's meditation on acting and seeming begins very early in the play in all of its versions and has obvious affinities with 'Of Diverting'. Furthermore, the speech gains both anger with regard to mourning and a focus on metatheatricality when Q1 becomes Q2. In the First Quarto,

Hamlet addresses the King and focuses primarily on an inner/outer contrast, 'in conventional terms:'[52]

> My lord, t'is not the sable sute I weare:
> No nor the teares that still stand in my eyes,
> Nor the distracted hauiour in the visage,
> Nor all together mixt with outward semblance,
> Is equall to the sorrow of my heart,
> Him haue I lost I must of force forgoe,
> These but the ornaments and sutes of woe. (2.33–9)[53]

The tension between 'outward semblance' and the inner 'sorrow of my heart' is clear, but Hamlet's anger and metadramatic focus become pronounced in the revision, which is addressed to his mother as he pounces on her word 'seems':

> Seems, madam? Nay, it *is*. I know not 'seems'.
> 'Tis not alone my inky cloak, good-mother,
> Nor customary suits of solemn black,
> Nor windy suspiration of forced breath,
> No, nor the fruitful river in the eye,
> Nor the dejected haviour of the visage,
> Together with all forms, moods, shows [shapes – Q2] of grief
> That can denote me truly. These indeed 'seem',
> For they are actions that a man might play;
> But I have that within which passeth show –
> These but the trappings and suits of woe.[54]

As Roland Mushat Frye has taught us, the 'inky cloak' reminds us that Hamlet is still in the mourning garment wholly appropriate to his historical moment and station:

> that 'inky cloak' . . . would have enveloped him completely, leaving only his face and hands exposed. This is not the short cape to which we are usually treated in period costuming of Hamlet, but the voluminous outer mourning garment worn in the stately funerals of this period. . . . Hamlet has continued to wear that cloak, covering him from head to foot, as though by it he could alone counterbalance the scandalous unseemliness and even irreverence displayed in the dress of all of those about him.[55]

The change from Q1 to Q2, then, adds a focus on Hamlet's mourning attire, from merely the 'sable sute', which has its analogue in the Q2/F 'suits of solemn black', to the 'inky cloak'. Hamlet's costume calls attention to his ongoing state of mourning, despite the fact that others have moved on to celebrate the recent marriage long before the conventional mourning period was over.[56] For Bourus, this revision is significant because the change suggests a Shakespeare recently living with the death of his father, John Shakespeare: 'Beginning in September 1601, he would have personally inhabited the "inky cloak" of an adult son grieving for his father.'[57] Although it is far from certain that Shakespeare himself, not being of noble or royal station, would have worn the kind of cloak that Frye describes, the changed text does highlight the act of mourning. But, as Bourus also notes, the same cloak is part of an increased cluster of words that bring playing into the speech and heighten its metadramatic quality.[58]

I find these arguments very compelling, but I would like to think of the alterations in the passage in terms of Shakespeare's essaying 'Of Diversion', which is interested in the extent to which both mourning and playacting can be diversions that, for better and worse, take us away from the truth. Shakespeare makes a microscopic verbal change that may suggest the influence of the essay. In a rare line from the texts that is virtually identical, a key difference exists. In listing the components of his outward sorrow, Hamlet in Q1 mentions 'the distracted hauiour in the visage', whereas in Q2 he refers to 'the deiected hauior of the visage'.[59] In the spirit of Taylor, I point out that there is a significant verbal echo of Montaigne, in a passage we have examined earlier:

> *Quintilian* reporteth to have seen comedians so far engaged in a sorrowful part that they wept after being come to their lodgings; and of himself, that having undertaken to move a certain passion in another, he had found himself surprised, not only with shedding of tears but **with a paleness of countenance and behaviour of a man truly dejected with grief.** (236; 504, emphasis mine)

The 'distracted hauiour' of Q1 becomes a 'deiected hauior' in Q2, nicely echoing Florio's original 'behauiour of a man truly deiected with griefe'. But even more important is the context of the echo: it comes in a passage that focuses on how playing a strong emotion can yield real versions of that emotion. Indeed, one of the themes of Montaigne's essay concerns the boundary between feigning and true emotion. Earlier in the essay, Montaigne focuses on the female penchant for such behaviour – 'who to divert the opinions and conjectures of the babbling people and to divert the fond tattling of some, did by counterfeit and dissembled affections overshadow and cloak true affections' – alluding to the ideas of Quintilian that he will overtly mention later in the essay.

This negotiation between playing and actually feeling an emotion is part of Hamlet's scathing critique of his mother, one that, as we have suggested, becomes more scathing – and, significantly, more metadramatic in focus – in the move from Q1 to Q2. The First Quarto does contain 'sute', 'visage', 'outward semblance', and 'ornaments and sutes of woe' – and all of these words have some connection to playing. But, just as Montaigne makes actors central to his essay, so Q2 makes the theatrical metaphor explicit, as Hamlet contrasts real emotion with feigned feeling. He 'know[s] not seems', and the Q2 Hamlet expands on the catalogue of ways of seeming: 'suits of solemn black', 'windy suspiration of forced breath', 'river in the eye', 'dejected haviour of the visage'. None of these 'forms, moods, shapes' can 'denote [him] truly' but instead are connected to 'show' and 'trappings and . . . suits of woe' – 'actions that a man might play' in the theatre.

The metadramatic patterns established here are only amplified in Act 2, when the players come to Elsinore, and Hamlet requests, first, that a player recite 'One speech in it I truly loved, 'twas Aeneas' tale to Dido, and there about of it especially when he speaks of Priam's slaughter. If it live in your memory begin at this line . . .' (2.2.426–9). The Pyrrhus episode is more developed in the revised versions – more space is given to a speech from a play within a play – but more significant is Hamlet's meditation on the tension between played and feigned emotion – which, I argue, shows Shakespeare essaying 'Of Diversion'. The Hamlet of Q1 mentions the players and contrasts them with himself, beginning with a discussion of Hecuba:

> Why these Players here draw water from eyes:
> For Hecuba, why what is Hecuba to him, or he to Hecuba?
> What would he do and if he had my losse?
> His father murdred, and a Crowne bereft him,
> He would turne all his teares to droppes of blood,
> Amaze the standers by with his laments,
> Strike more then wonder in the iudiciall eares,
> Confound the ignorant, and make mute the wise,
> Indeede his passion would be generall. (7.356–65)

Without a doubt, Q1 Hamlet focuses on the performance: he remarks on how the players evoke tears from their audience by invoking Hecuba, and imagines how powerful the effects would be on the 'standers by' if they played in the theatre of *his* world – filled with 'losse', a 'father murdred, and a Crowne bereft him'. 'Teares' would be turned to 'droppes of blood' in the 'eyes', and the 'wonder' of his tale would 'Amaze the standers by with his laments', striking 'iudiciall eares', confounding 'the ignorant' and making 'mute the wise'. Indeed, all witnesses would be affected by the player's 'passion'.

But the revised speech further heightens the metadramatic language and deepens the sense of the tension between the fictive and the real. Indeed, the revised Hamlet thinks this tension is 'monstrous'. Focusing on the single player, Hamlet cannot believe that the actor, 'But in a fiction, in a dream of passion', can have such an effect – fictions and dreams overtly get connected to theatrical performance. And, as in Hamlet's revised 'seems' speech, his revised 'Hecuba' speech expands into a catalogue of dramatic effects, detailing the player's method in a way the Q1 version did not:

> this player here . . .
> Could force his soul so to his whole [Q2: owne] conceit
> That from her working all his visage wanned [Q2: wand; F: warm'd]
> Tears in his eyes, distraction in's [Q2: in his] aspect,
> A broken voice, and his whole function suiting
> With forms to his conceit? And all for nothing.
> For Hecuba! (2.2.528; 530–5)

This anatomy of the affective elements of performance deepens the metadramatic quality of the speech but also brings Hamlet's language closer to Montaigne's comments on the actor in Quintilian who 'found himself surprised' not only with the 'shedding of tears' but also with the 'paleness of countenance and behavior of a man truly dejected with grief' (236; 504). Hamlet shares a fascination with the ability of a fiction to affect both the performer and his audience, collapsing the boundaries between playing and being along the way.

The mention of Hecuba is important for other than metadramatic reasons, of course. One of Hamlet's motivations for summoning this speech from a remembered play is to hear about a properly grieving mother and wife, and for the Renaissance, Hecuba was, according to Harry Levin, 'the *ne plus ultra* of misfortune'.[60] As we have seen, although Montaigne does not mention Hecuba in 'Of Diverting', he does mention 'the wailing laments of *Dido* and *Ariadne* passionate', and they are linked to the power of 'plaints and fables of trouble' to 'vex our minds' – even those of readers who do not accept them as fact, 'those that believe them not in *Virgil* nor in *Catullus*' (235; 503). To resist these 'passionate' fictions is to be 'of an obstinate nature and indurate heart' (235; 503). Diversions in Montaigne, and in *Hamlet*, are double-edged: they have the power to soothe pain and to change reality, but they also lead one to a realm of illusion, dreams, and (sometimes fatal) delusion. For Montaigne, diversion ultimately takes one too far from the thing itself, and Hamlet's distaste for theatre – he hates it even though, perhaps because, he needs it – grows as the play unfolds. This was, Hamlet might say, sometime a paradox but now the time gives it proof.

One 'thing itself' is death, and, as we have seen, Montaigne holds up Socrates as one of the few examples of a human being who would 'stay upon the thing itself, to examine, and judge it' (229; 500) – even if the 'thing' is death. While we might not want to say with John Sterling that 'the Prince of Denmark is very nearly a Montaigne',[61] it is tempting to see the Hamlet of the Graveyard Scene as very nearly Montaigne's Socrates. For Hamlet – who arguably was once like Montaigne's typical human beings who are not 'of the first rank' and who focus 'on somewhat else: either the hope of a better life' or 'the future glory of our name' (231; 501) – has in 5.1 become someone who 'seeketh for no comfort out of the thing itself. To die seemeth unto him a natural and indifferent accident. Thereon he wishly fixeth his sight and thereon he resolveth without looking elsewhere' (229; 500–1).

Across all three versions of *Hamlet*, this new approach to death is present. But in the most famous moment of the Graveyard Scene, a Q2/F revision accentuates the problems of diversionary imagination that we find in Montaigne's essay. Looking at his former jester Yorick's skull in Q1, Hamlet tells Horatio: 'I knew him, Horatio, a fellow of infinite mirth. He hath caried me twenty times vpon his backe. Here hung those lippes that I have kissed a hundred times, and to see, now they abhorre me' (16.84–6). But in Q2, Hamlet focuses on the ability of the imagination – rather than of the lips – to abhor him: 'hee hath bore [borne F] me on his backe a thousand times, and now how abhorred in my imagination it is' (5.1.172–3). In the Folio text, the abhorrent quality of the imagination is even clearer, as Hamlet says, 'And how abhorred my Imagination is.' The 'it' of Q2, perhaps a reference to the general memory that his imagination is summoning, has dropped out; in F, he finds the 'Imagination' abhorrent, just as he earlier found 'a fiction . . . a dream of passion' to be 'monstrous' (2.2, 529, 528). The point is clear in both revised texts: he is trying to get back to the thing itself, but imagination gets in the way, even when looking at a bare skull.

One other revision is even more telling with regard to death and things themselves. In meditating upon the levelling power of death, Hamlet talks to Horatio about lawyers, mocking their obsessions with minutiae – that which would take them away from the thing itself that is death. In Q1 Hamlet says,

> Looke you, there's another *Horatio*.
> Why mai't not be the scull of some Lawyer?
> Me thinkes he should indite that fellow

> Of an action of Batterie, for knocking
> Him about the pate with's shouel: now where is your
> Quirkes and quillets now... (13.35–8)⁶²

In Q2 and F, the passage reads, 'where be his quiddities [Q2; F: Quiddits] now, his quillets, his cases, his tenures, and his tricks?' (5.1.91–3). In some sense, this is just an amplification of the legal language, but the addition of 'quiddities'/'quiddits' is important. For though 'quiddities' and 'quillets' were virtually synonymous as meaning 'verbal quibbles or niceties', it is the 'quiddities' and 'quiddits' of the revised texts that echo the Latin *quidditas*, which means 'the essential nature of a thing'.[63] Therefore, lawyers – unlike Montaigne's Socrates and the perspective that the new Hamlet aspires to – get bogged down in the illusion of grasping for *quidditas* but in the end do not 'stay upon the thing itself' because '*A little thing doth divert and turn us, for a small thing holds us*' (234; 503). And Montaigne is ultimately, at least in this essay, pessimistic about the power of the 'little ... small thing', 'superficial images', and 'vain rinds' (234; 503). The focus on the true *quidditas* is lost; the trivial quiddity takes its place. Yet Hamlet's – and *Hamlet*'s – take on such diversions seems slightly more open-ended than Montaigne's. Hamlet ironically comments on the difficulty of achieving *quidditas* by mocking those who imagine they have it. Indeed, he suggests that he understands that a quiddity may be more than a quibble: he knows a quiddity from a *quidditas*, just as he knows a hawk from a handsaw.

One final diversion raised by Montaigne's essay is crucial to *Hamlet* and the play's evolution. Whether the first version of *Hamlet* was the *Ur-Hamlet*, or whether the *Ur-Hamlet* was in fact Q1, what is clear is that revenge has been associated with the play for at least as long as Thomas Lodge's remarks in 1596: the Ghost 'cried so miserally at the Theater like an oyster wife, *Hamlet, revenge*'.[64] This exploration of revenge could be seen as an inspiration for revision: the *Hamlet* of Q1 – a revenge play – shifts to the *Hamlets* of Q2 and F, which become plays about revenge.[65] Or as David Kastan puts it, imagining Shakespeare's negotiation with the *Ur-Hamlet*: 'In shaping a play that interrogates rather than merely enacts the rhythms of revenge, Shakespeare creates something that is more than a revenge play ...'[66]

Montaigne, as we have examined, meditates on revenge in 'Of Diverting' and reports on his attempting 'to divert a late prince from it'. Revenge is best avoided, Montaigne says, not by ignoring your wronger or by reading about the poetical history of tragic acts of revenge but by diverting one's thoughts from revenge to those of ambition – for one's honour and reputation above all else: 'the honour, the favour, and the good will he should acquire by gentleness and goodness' (232; 502). Hamlet's deferral of revenge may co-exist with his ambition if we take this Montaignian angle.[67] And Montaigne's English translator, John Florio, would have understood this version of ambition: in his Italian–English dictionary, *A Worlde of* Wordes (1598), Florio defined *Ambitioso* as 'ambitious, very desirous of honor'.[68]

For like Montaigne's prince, Hamlet cannot – especially with his father's plea to 'Revenge his most foul and unnatural murder' (1.5.25) – 'offer the one side of his cheek to him who had struck him on the other' (232; 502). Nor can he bury himself in 'the tragical events poesy bestoweth upon that passion' (232; 502), though one can see him essaying this approach in having the Player rehearse the story of avenging Pyrrhus, rooted in Virgil's *Aeneid*. Instead, Hamlet can be seen to be following ambition – but not Claudius's version, which is nakedly political: 'I am still possessed / Of those effects for why I did the murder – / My crown, mine own ambition, and my queen' (3.3.53–5).

Hamlet's alternative version of ambition is linked to Montaignian ideas from inside and outside 'Of Diverting'. In a section not in Q1 (and not in Q2, either), Rosencrantz and Guildenstern discuss with Hamlet the reasons Hamlet thinks Denmark is a prison. When Rosencrantz says, 'We think not so, my lord,' Hamlet replies, 'Why, then 'tis none to you, for there is nothing either good or bad but thinking makes it so' (2.2.243–5). Harold Jenkins links this 'common reflection' to Montaigne's 'That the Taste of Goods or Evilles Doth Greatly Depend on the Opinion We Have of Them' (1.40).[69] The Montaignian source could also be 'That to Philosophize Is to Learn How to Die' (1.20, 1.19): 'Life in itself is neither good nor evil; it is the place of good or evil according as you prepare it for them' (29; 37).

Montaigne does seem to be echoed, and he hovers around not only the discussion of the subjective nature of certain judgements but also the discussion of ambition among Hamlet and his friends:

Ros.	Why, then your ambition makes it one; 'tis too narrow for your mind.
Ham.	O God, I could be bounded in a nutshell and count myself a king of infinite space, were it not that I have bad dreams.
Gui.	Which dreams indeed are ambition; for the very substance of the ambitious is merely the shadow of a dream.
Ham.	A dream itself is but a shadow.
Ros.	Truly, and I hold ambition of so airy and light a quality that it is but a shadow's shadow.
Ham.	Then are our beggars bodies, and our monarchs and outstretched heroes the beggars' shadows. (2.2.246–57)[70]

The scholars debate the nature of ambition, and Hamlet quickly sidesteps the idea that his ambition is the political version to which Claudius will allude.[71] Indeed, ambition gets linked by all three characters to dreams, illusions, and shadows; ambition is a fiction that, ultimately, connects kings and beggars. In fact, because they are presumably without the illusion of ambition, beggars are arguably more substantial ('bodies') than ambitious kings and heroes ('beggars' shadows'). Hamlet makes a similar levelling point later in the play: 'We fat all creatures else to fat us, and we fat ourselves for maggots. Your fat king and your lean beggar is but variable service – two dishes, but to one table. That's the end' (4.3.22–5). In this earlier exchange, though, it is the shadow of ambition rather than death that is the levelling agent. All powerful people chase the shadow of ambition, just as all must die.

From this point forward, Hamlet will attempt to essay a Montaignian path: away from vengeance via the diversions of fictions and theatre. He will try both to pursue an ambition – based not on power or on 'the future glory of our name' but on ethics and honour – and, simultaneously, to avoid the pitfall of prizing 'one's life at the right worth of it, to forgo it for a dream'. To divert or not divert – that remains the question.

Notes

1. See, among many others, Eliot, 'Hamlet and His Problems', 941; George Coffin Taylor, *Shakspere's Debt to Montaigne*, 40–1; Elldrodt, 'Self-Consciousness in Montaigne and Shakespeare', esp. 41; King, *Hamlet's Search for Meaning*, esp. 58–60; and Hamlin, 'Montaigne and Shakespeare', esp. 336n38.
2. Taylor, *Shakspere's Debt*, 40–1. Taylor consistently spells 'Shakespeare' as 'Shakspere'. Taylor's charts have *Hamlet* tied (with *Lear* and *The Tempest*) for first with 3.4 'Montaigne words' per page and the clear winner with 125 words in the play (32). The table charting 'the number of passages in each play' has *Hamlet* the decisive winner with 51; the next closest is *Lear* with 23 (28–9).
3. William Carew Hazlitt, *Shakespear[e]*, 156.
4. See E. K. Chambers, *William Shakespeare*, 2: 90–5; Honan, *Shakespeare*, 325–9; and Nicholl, *The Lodger Shakespeare*.
5. For a clear statement of this position, see the Danish scholar George Brandes, in his *William Shakespeare*, who made the link between *Hamlet* and Montaigne in 1898 and was not troubled when Montaignian echoes appeared in *Hamlet* as early as Q1: 'When such passages occur in the First Quarto (1603), we must assume either that Shakespeare knew the French original, or that – as is likely enough – he may have had an opportunity

of reading Florio's translation before it was published. It happened not infrequently in those days that a book was handed round in manuscript among the author's private friends five or six years before it was given to the public. Florio's close connection with the household of Southampton renders it almost certain that Shakespeare must have been acquainted with him' (352). More recently, see Anzai, *Shakespeare and Montaigne Reconsidered*: 'The publication of Florio's Montaigne was in 1603, whereas the date of composition of Hamlet is usually conjectured to be 1600–1601; the composition of *Hamlet* is prior to the publication of *The Essayes*. However, it is quite possible that Shakespeare read his friend's translation in manuscript, as his own sonnets were read widely among his friends in manuscript before publication in 1609' (90n1). Most recently, this possibility has been challenged by the editors of the *New Oxford Shakespeare*, who ignore the Cornwallis allusion: 'scribal copies of such a large book would have been expensive, and we possess no other evidence that it circulated in advance of publication'. See Taylor and Egan (eds), *The New Oxford Shakespeare: Authorship Companion*, 543.

6. See Cornwallis [the Younger], 'Of Censuring' (Essay 12), *Essayes*, H4r–v; Cornwallis, *Essayes*, ed. Allen, ix–xxiii, 42; and Yates, 213. See also Knowles, '*Hamlet* and Counter-Humanism': 'We know that a manuscript of Florio's translation was in circulation before its publication in 1603. Florio's patron Southampton was also Shakespeare's, but it seems that a manuscript was in circulation outside Southampton's household, since in his own essays written before 1600 Sir William Cornwallis praises the translation of his model' (1053). For a different perspective, see Hamlin, *Montaigne's English Journey*, for the claim that the Cornwallis reference suggests 'that Cornwallis had access to one of the other efforts at English translation of the *Essais* to which Florio alludes. . . . I find it difficult not to suspect that at least one other (possibly partial) English version of Montaigne was circulating in the late 1590s, and that Shakespeare might well have been exposed to it before he later encountered Florio's published *Essayes*' (242–3n18).
7. [Sterling], 'Art. IV', A review of 'Observations on an Autograph . . .', 321–2. See, too, Harold Jenkins, in William Shakespeare, *Hamlet*, The Arden Shakespeare, ed. Jenkins, esp. 108–12: 'Perhaps no single word or group of words is sufficiently remarkable for its use to be conclusive in itself; but they have cumulative weight. . . . I incline therefore to think that of the ideas which Shakespeare so lavishly bestowed on Hamlet a few at least were prompted by his recent reading in Florio's Montaigne' (110).
8. Grady, *Shakespeare, Machiavelli, and Montaigne*, 29–30; 52. To be fair, Grady does list the possibilities for Shakespeare's encountering Montaigne before 1603. See 49–52.
9. Grady, *Shakespeare, Machiavelli, and Montaigne*, 264.
10. Grady, *Shakespeare, Machiavelli, and Montaigne*, 5.
11. Robertson, *Montaigne and Shakespeare*, 39; 40.

12. See Lesser, *Hamlet after Q1*.
13. For Collier, the problem was an in-house stenographer; for Tycho Mommsen, it was a combination of 'an actor, who put down, from memory, a sketch of the original play, as it was acted, and who wrote very illegibly; the other [was] that of a bad poet, most probably "a bookseller's hack", who, without any personal intercourse with the writer of the notes, availed himself of them to make up this early copy of "Hamlet". Numerous mistakes of the ear fall to the share of the former contributor, whereas much more numerous misconceptions of the eye, and wrong outpiecings, are to be attributed to the latter. The compositor may have added to these blunderings.' See Mommsen, '"Hamlet", 1603; and "Romeo and Juliet", 1597', 182. For a recent survey of the stenographic idea, see Stern, 'Sermons, Plays, and Note-Takers', 1–23.
14. Mommsen, '"Hamlet", 1603; and "Romeo and Juliet", 1597', 182.
15. Lesser, *Hamlet after Q1*, 53. Although he doesn't mention Montaigne, Charles Knight – the first major proponent of the revision theory – argues for a growing sophistication and intellectual development between the two quartos that certainly could include Shakespeare's having read Montaigne: there was a 'growth ... of the great poet's command over language ... [and] the higher qualities of his intellect ... his profound philosophy, his wonderful penetration into what is most hidden and obscure in men's characters and motives .... It is the contemplative part of his nature which is elaborated in the perfect copy' (quoted in William Shakespeare, *Hamlet*, ed. Furness, *A New Variorum Edition of Shakespeare*, 4: 15–16. See also the anonymous author of an article in the *Edinburgh Review* LXXXI (April 1845): 'Q1 gives us ... a form exhibiting such dissimilarities from the later one, as indicate not obscurely the process of the poet's mind, from the unripe fervor of early manhood to the calmer and more philosophic inspiration of perfect maturity .... In other words, the older Play evolves but partially either of the Prince's contemplative character, – the philosophic and the poetic, – those deep and fine touches of a moody and cheerless yet noble philosophy' (378, 380; quoted in *Hamlet*, ed. Furness, 4: 18–19). This view is scoffed at by Richard Grant White in 1883, who noted 'Q1 was hastily printed to meet an urgent popular demand and ... the philosophical part of the play would be at once the most difficult to obtain by surreptitious means, and the least valued by the persons to supply whose cravings that edition was published .... To minds undisciplined in thought, abstract truth is difficult of apprehension and of recollection; whereas, a mere child can remember a story' (quoted in *Hamlet*, ed. Furness, 4: 27).
16. Clark and Wright, eds. *Hamlet, Prince of Denmark*, The Clarendon Shakespeare, x–xii. See Lesser, *Hamlet after Q1*, 55.
17. Lesser, *Hamlet after Q1*, 55–6.
18. As Lesser notes, the term was coined by the detractors of the disintegrationists, most famously in E. K. Chambers's critique in his British Academy

Lecture of 1924, 'The Disintegration of Shakespeare'. As Cary DiPietro says in his 'The Shakespeare Edition in Industrial Capitalism', Chambers's 'title neatly summarized a range of textual activities associated with the reattributing of Shakespeare's plays to non-Shakespearian sources' (147).
19. Furnivall, 'Is the Character of Hamlet Shakspere's Creation or Not?', 101. See Lesser, *Hamlet after Q1*, 173.
20. Lesser, *Hamlet after Q1*, 173.
21. Irace, 'Origins and Agents of Q1 *Hamlet*', in Clayton (ed.), *The* Hamlet *First Published (Q1), 1603,* and Irace, ed. *The First Quarto of Hamlet*, 1–27, esp. 20; Stern, 'Sermons, Plays, and Note-Takers'; Marino, *Owning William Shakespeare*, esp. 75–106; Urkowitz, '"Well-sayd olde Mole"', in Ziegler, ed, *Shakespeare Study Today*, and Urkowitz, 'Back to Basics', in Clayton, ed; and Bourus, *Young Shakespeare's Young Hamlet*.
22. Irace, 'Origins and Agents', 118, and Stern, 'Sermons, Plays, and Note-Takers', 1.
23. Lesser, *Hamlet after Q1*, 258n34.
24. For the most recent articulation of this position, see Frampton, '"To Be, or Not to Be"'.
25. Urkowitz, *Shakespeare's Revision of* King Lear.
26. Urkowitz, '"Well-sayd olde Mole"', 55.
27. Urkowitz, '"Well-sayd olde Mole"', 48, 49. On Belleforest as a source especially for Q1, see Bourus, *Young Shakespeare's Young Hamlet*, 99–100, and Margrethe Jolly, '*Hamlet* and the French Connection'. Jolly's conclusion – which is cited favourably by Bourus – contains the interesting fact that, although 'Q1 is 55 per cent of Q2's length, Q1's borrowings [from Belleforest] are not a mere 55 per cent of Q2's borrowings. Proportionally, the borrowings occur at almost twice the density in Q1 than in Q2 . . . . Altogether Q1 has more borrowings despite being the shorter play. . . . The development of characters, the increase in delay between plans to entrap Hamlet and the actual attempts to do so, and some of the more subtle touches in Q2 could all be due to that revision process, and are consistent with the concept of a developing dramatist' (103, 104).
28. Urkowitz, '"Well-sayd olde Mole"', 68, 69.
29. This is the tentative conclusion of the *New Oxford Shakespeare* editors, a group that includes Bourus. For some very helpful discussion of the dating possibilities of *Hamlet* – and how the publication of Florio's translation of Montaigne may help with the dating – see *New Oxford Shakespeare: Authorship Companion*, ed. Taylor and Egan, 542–8, esp. 542–3.
30. Bourus, *Young Shakespeare's Young Hamlet*, 212.
31. Bourus, *Young Shakespeare's Young Hamlet*, 210.
32. Not in Q1 but present in 1.2 of Q2 and F is an intriguing passage not mentioned by Bourus that may have come from *Florio's* Montaigne rather than Montaigne himself. In his 'Epistle Dedicatorie', defending the dedication of the *Essayes* to 'two so severallie all-worthy Ladies', Florio asserts, 'But to any in the right, it would be judged wrong, to disjoyne them in ought

who were neerer in kinde, then ever in kindnesse (*Essayes*, trans. Florio, Sig A2). Hamlet famously responds to Claudius, who has just called him 'my Cosin *Hamlet*, and my sonne', 'A little more then kin, and lesse then kind' (See *The Three-Text-Hamlet: Parallel Texts of the First and Second Quartos and First Folio*, ed. Bernice W. Kliman and Paul Bertram, second edition [New York: AMS Press, Inc., 2003], 18–19). Thanks to Saul Frampton for this reference.

33. In her 'Origins and Agents of Q1 *Hamlet*' – though arguing for an initial memorial reconstruction – Irace sees Shakespeare and/or his company tinkering with it from this early drafting up to and beyond the publication of Q1 in 1603 (118–20). Different still is the position of Paul Menzer, *The Hamlets*, who sees 'memorial reconstruction' as akin to writing rather than piracy. For Menzer, 'Q1 is a separate *Hamlet* project – an independent act of creation by a person or persons unknown, and . . . it involves their memory of earlier versions of the *Hamlet* tale as well as, obviously, Shakespeare's *Hamlet*. . . . [M]any of Q1's paradoxes evaporate if we consider that the text records the memory of a performance with access – as audience, as actor, as a reader in part – to a *Hamlet* at various times, at various places, and at and on various stages' (20; 39).
34. See Bourus, *Young Shakespeare's Young Hamlet*, 138–9.
35. In this regard, Alan C. Dessen's agnostic take in his 'Weighing the Options in Q1', in Clayton (ed.), 65–78, is refreshing: 'The best way to confront the anomalies and confusions of Q1 is therefore to rely upon what I think of as a two-track system: to look at representative features with at least two options in mind so as to ask whether such elements are consistent with abridgement-memorial reconstruction or with Q1 as an earlier yet-to-be-fully-developed version. If, for example, a passage is not to be found in Q1, does that mean it has been forgotten or screened by the reporter-abridger, or that it has not yet been conceived or written?' (68). The later Urkowitz ('Back to Basics') also is more agnostic – and at peace with his unknowing: 'What harm would come if readers could see how the three early texts transform *Hamlet* into different fluid shapes, even though we cannot be sure about the provenance of each word or even each scene? . . . Editors fiercely insist that they produce 'authoritative' *Hamlets*, which they defend against all other authoritative *Hamlets*. But theatrical art fiercely resists such authority by the very nature of its ephemeral performances' (289).
36. Feis, *Shakspere and Montaigne*, 5; 36.
37. [Sterling], 'Art. IV', A review of 'Observations on an Autograph . . .', 321.
38. Patrick Gray, in his '"HIDE THY SELFE": Montaigne, Hamlet and Epicurean Ethics', in *Shakespeare and Renaissance Ethics*, ed. Gray and Cox, argues for a neo-Feisian gap between Shakespeare on the one hand and Hamlet and Montaigne on the other: 'Shakespeare in *Hamlet* presents not only a critique of Epicurean ethics but also a critique or "assay" of Montaigne himself, insofar as Montaigne can be said to be

an Epicurean . . . . Hamlet is modeled on Montaigne himself. If so, the reasons for his delay are fairly straightforward. Hamlet is rendered ineffective politically, or at least severely hindered, by precisely the same set of character flaws that Montaigne attributes to himself repeatedly in his *Essays*: temperamental indifference; a tendency to escape into solipsistic daydreams; irresolution; a reluctance to assume responsibility; and a corresponding, fatalistic tendency simply to drift with the ebb and flow of fortune' (219–20, 228). Gray wisely adds, though, that 'Montaigne acknowledges that Epicurean withdrawal from public life, although attractive to him personally, may not be a panacea, and in fact may be entirely worthy of moral opprobrium that in his own time, as well as antiquity, it tended to incur. Like Shakespeare, he registers the dark side of Epicurean *otium*, its potentially tragic consequences' (233). Although not critical of Montaigne's ideas, Rhodri Lewis, in his *Hamlet and the Vision of Darkness*, has also recently argued that Shakespeare's use of Montaigne in *Hamlet* is one of contrast rather than similarity: 'Hamlet's soliloquies are designed to look like they have some share in the Montaignian moment. The essayist is another persona that Hamlet attempts to put on, and that does not fit him. Where Montaigne bears with himself tolerantly and amusedly, secure in his belief that he makes sense (however obscurely) through his *Essais* and before his God, Hamlet is rash, angry, impatient, and reluctant to ask himself even the most elementary questions. If Polonius marks the destructive blindness of Ciceronian moral philosophy, then Hamlet's example suggests that Montaigne's optimistically circuitous individualism offers no viable alternative' (36).

39. Robertson, *Montaigne and Shakespeare*, 65.
40. Robertson, *Montaigne and Shakespeare*, 66.
41. Eliot, 'Hamlet and His Problems', 941. The essay appears, in slightly altered forms, in Eliot's *The Sacred Wood*, 95–103, and his *Selected Essays: 1917–1932*, 141–6.
42. Eliot, 'Shakespeare and Montaigne', 895.
43. William Empson, '*Hamlet* When New', when talking about the fact that 'Everybody [in *Hamlet*] is "acting a part" except Horatio', takes it for granted that Shakespeare had read Montaigne and that this reading had some bearing on the key ideas of *Hamlet*: 'The Elizabethans, though both more formal and more boisterous than most people nowadays, were well able to see the need for sincerity; and it is agreed that Shakespeare had been reading Montaigne about how quickly one's moods can change, so that to appear consistent requires "acting", a line of thought which is still current' (26; 27). A few years later, Harry Levin, in his excellent *The Question of Hamlet*, also assumes Montaigne's influence on Shakespeare: 'His [Hamlet's] position is a point of vantage from which we may look out with Shakespeare – and with the author whose reflective mood he is dramatising, Montaigne – upon 'this miserable human condition'. Hamlet is both the

doubter and the doubt. . . . Shakespeare was also one of the first and most devoted readers of Montaigne in Florio's translation, as is evidenced by numerous turns of speech and by a certain essayistic movement of thought. . . . But, in retrospection, his mentor is Montaigne; the soliloquies are like the *Essays* in balancing arguments with counter-arguments, in pursuing wayward ideas and unmasking stubborn illusions' (7, 11, 72).

44. Taylor, *Shakspere's Debt*, 39, 40.
45. Taylor, *Shakspere's Debt*, 40–1. See 13–16 and 53–4 for his charts providing the data on verbal echoes.
46. Taylor, *Shakspere's Debt*, 41.
47. Montaigne, 'Of Diverting or Diversion' (3.4), in *Shakespeare's Montaigne*, ed. Greenblatt and Platt. Where available, quotations from Florio's Montaigne will come from this edition; citations will be included in the text and will list, first, this edition's page number and, second, the page number of *The Essayes, or Morall, Politike and Millitarie Discourses* (1603), 226–7; 499–500.
48. See Quintilian, *Institutio oratoria*, I.xi, and Jonson, *Timber: or, Discoveries*, in *Ben Jonson*, ed. Herford, Simpson, and Simpson, 8: 597.
49. See *Hamlet*, 2.2.529, 535–6, where the focus is on 'a fiction, a dream of passion' and 'Hecuba'. For the importance of Hecuba – to *Hamlet* and early-modern English drama – see the important essay by Tanya Pollard, 'What's Hecuba to Shakespeare?' and, more recently, her *Greek Tragic Women on Shakespearean Stages*, esp. 117–42.
50. This entire section is influenced by Quintilian, VI.ii, especially sections 32–6. Warren Boutcher recently noted this connection in his *The School of Montaigne in Early Modern Europe: Volume II, The Reader–Writer*, 212n74. Montaigne has already alluded to the phenomenon earlier when discussing women who become what they play. See also Hamlet's advice to the Players, *Hamlet*, 3.2.1–40, and his speech on seeming.
51. Screech's translation better captures the irony: 'Abandoning your life for a dream is to value it for exactly what it is worth' (Montaigne, *Complete Essays*, trans. Screech, 945). See also the original French: 'C'est priser sa vie justement ce qu'elle est, de l'abandonner pour un songe' (Montaigne, *Les Essais*, ed. Balsamo, Magnien, and Magnien-Simonin, 881).
52. See Bourus, *Young Shakespeare's Young Hamlet*, 200.
53. For Q1 citations, I use, unless otherwise noted, the scene and line numbers of Irace (ed.), *The First Quarto of Hamlet*. I have not, however, modernised the spelling.
54. Shakespeare, *Hamlet*, 1.2.76–86, in *The Norton Shakespeare*, second edition. Unless otherwise noted, all further citations from the plays of Shakespeare are to this edition and are annotated within the text.
55. Frye, *The Renaissance Hamlet*, 92–4. But see Kastan, *A Will to Believe*, who suggests that there may be a doctrinal gap between the Protestant and Catholic takes on Hamlet's inky cloak (124–5).

56. See Frye, 82–102, esp. 84–5 and 99–100.
57. Bourus, *Young Shakespeare's Young Hamlet*, 200–1.
58. This intersection might also be biographical: 'But that grieving son was also a professional player, an actor who may well have worn such "suits of woe" on stage, from time to time, performing "shapes of grief" that were merely played' (Bourus, *Young Shakespeare's Young Hamlet*, 201).
59. It is 'the deiected hauiour of the Visage' in the Folio.
60. See Levin, *The Question of Hamlet*, 141–64, esp. 162.
61. [Sterling], 'Art. IV', A review of 'Observations on an Autograph . . .', 321.
62. Modernised and set as prose in Irace (ed.), 86.
63. This is actually the first definition in the *OED*, 1a: 'Chiefly *Philos*. The inherent nature or essence of a person or thing; what makes a thing what it is'. Definition 2a is 'A subtlety or nicety in argument; a quibble.' See also Jenkins, 383n97.
64. Lodge, *VVits Miserie*, sig. h4v. Modernised in Bourus, *Young Shakespeare's Young Hamlet*, 144–5.
65. See also Shapiro, *A Year in the Life of Shakespeare*: 'You can feel in these lines [about Pyrrhus] the hold that this kind of revenge drama once had on Shakespeare as well as his appreciation of a moral clarity that was no longer credible. It's one of the keys to understanding what makes *Hamlet* so distinctive: even as he paints over an earlier work of art, Shakespeare allows traces of what's been whitewashed to remain visible' (291).
66. Kastan, '"His semblable is his mirror"', 122.
67. See Kastan, '"His semblable is his mirror"': 'Shakespeare's prince can never fully credit the impulse to revenge' (112).
68. Florio, *A Worlde of Wordes*, n.p.
69. Shakespeare, *Hamlet*, The Arden Shakespeare, ed. Jenkins, 250n249–50; 467–8.
70. This same section includes Hamlet's bitter speech about the 'quintessence of dust', which arguably has its source in 2.12:

> **Ham.** . . .this goodly frame the earth seems to me a sterile promontory, this most excellent canopy the air, look you, this brave o'erhanging firmament, this majestical roof fretted with golden fire, why, it appeareth nothing to me but a foul and pestilent congregation of vapours. What piece of work is a man, how noble in reason, how infinite in faculties, in form and moving how express and admirable, in action how like an angel, in apprehension how like a god: the beauty of the world, the paragon of animals – and yet, to me, what is this quintessence of dust? (2.2.289–98).

Compare Montaigne, trans. Florio: 'Who hath perswaded him, that this admirable mooving of heavens-vaults; that the eternal light of these lampes so fiercely rowling over his head; that the horror-moving and continuall motion of the infinite vaste Ocean, were established, and continue so manie ages for his commoditie and service? Is it possible to imagine any thing so rediculous, as this miserable and wretched creature, which is not so much as maister of himselfe, exposed and subject to offences of all things, and yet dareth call himselfe Maister and Emperour of this Vniverse?' (*Essayes*, II.12, 258).

71. See Jenkins: 'It would be convenient to be able to say (with John Dover Wilson) that they are employed to test a theory of the King's that Hamlet's 'distemper' is due to frustrated ambition (for the throne). . . . But that goes beyond the text' (250n252).

Chapter 3

Mingled Yarns and Hybrid Worlds: 'We Taste Nothing Purely', *Measure for Measure*, and *All's Well That Ends Well*

Wee are double in our selves, which is the cause, that what wee beleeve, we beleeve it not, and cannot rid our selves of that . . . which we condemne.

(Montaigne, 'Of Glorie' [2.16])[1]

Our life is composed, as is the harmonie of the World, of contrary things; so of divers tunes, some pleasant, some harsh, some sharpe, some flat, some low, and some high: What would that Musition say, that should love but some one of them? He ought to know how to vse them severally and how to entermingle them. So should we both of goods and evils, which are consubstantiall to our life. Our being cannot subsist without this commixture, whereto one side is no lesse necessarie than the other.

(Montaigne, 'Of Experience' [3.13])[2]

The web of our life is of a mingled yarn, good and ill together. Our virtues would be proud if our faults whipped them not, and our crimes would despair if they were not cherished by our virtues.

(Shakespeare, *All's Well That Ends Well*)[3]

In the last chapter, Shakespeare essayed Montaigne and found ambiguity and ambivalence: for Hamlet, as for Montaigne, diversions bring joy but also escapism and even death. The plays and the essay examined in this chapter go further, foregrounding – and arguably taking as their subject matter – the ambiguity and paradox of human experience.

This doubleness is characteristic of the so-called problem plays – for our purposes, *All's Well That Ends Well* and *Measure for Measure* – which explore 'mingled yarns' of 'good and ill together', while blending comedy and potential tragedy. They seem especially shaped by Montaigne's 'We Taste Nothing Purely' (2.20), verbally and formally, as well as intellectually.[4] Indeed, they can be seen as dramatic essays – *tastings* – of the opening sentences of Montaigne's essay: 'The weakness of our condition causeth that things in their natural simplicity and purity cannot fall into our use. The elements we enjoy are altered, metals likewise, yea gold must be empared with some other stuff to make it fit for our service.'[5]

These strangely hybrid, 'impure' plays have been linked since the late nineteenth century. In *Shakspere* [sic] *and His Predecessors* (1896), F. S. Boas grouped three plays together as problem plays or unpleasant, dark comedies – *Measure for Measure*, *All's Well That Ends Well*, and *Troilus and Cressida*.[6] The label was affixed to these plays because all seemed to strain their genres; in *Measure* and *All's Well*, the strain comes in the use of conventional qualities of comedy – and particularly the happy, festive energies in their endings – to rein in some very troubling plots and themes.

Boas claimed that there is no 'settlement of difficulties . . . [T]hroughout these plays we move along dim, untrodden paths, and at the close our feeling is neither of simple joy nor pain; we are excited, fascinated, perplexed, for the issues raised preclude a completely satisfactory outcome.'[7] George Hunter suggested that these plays have a unity that is different from either comedy or tragedy and 'whose aim is to discuss or expose the problems [they raise] rather than to lead them to a conclusion. The injustice that appears in Shakespeare's "problem plays" is . . . the injustice of life which prevents inner ideals from being realized, the same injustice that appears in all his serious plays.'[8] A. P. Rossiter has argued that these plays *both* undercut tragedy by focusing on human shortcomings and depravity instead of tragic dignity *and* undercut comedy with their pessimism and even cynicism, revealing a serious side to traditionally funny subjects: 'I mean, rather, a kind of drama in which the contemplation of man is on the one hand held back from the "admiration" and "commiseration" (as Sidney put it) of tragedy; and on the other, denied the wholehearted (or heart-whole) enjoyments of human irrationality and human sentiment of comedy.'[9] Alexander Leggatt claimed that 'the neat patterns of the story [in the problem plays] . . . are imposed on the awkward, intractable material of an unromantic world, where people simply will not behave'.[10] Finally, Lars Engle has argued that what links the plays is 'an acknowledgment of the impure negotiation of purposes that renders any final judgment on anything questionable, and an apparent disposition to take some comfort from that acknowledgment'.[11] Shakespeare seems to be searching for a new form, a new genre, a different poetic key, which he will find – after an intense exploration of tragedy – in the last plays or romances.[12]

It is not a stretch, then, to imagine Montaigne's 'We Taste Nothing Purely' shaping plays that, in their form and central ideas, both are impure and are about impurity. Indeed, the problem plays seem to engage with Montaigne's central thesis, laid out in the opening paragraphs of the essay: '*Of the pleasures and goods we have, there is none exempted from some mixture of evil and incommodity*' (190; 389). 'Goods' are mixed with 'evil', and 'pleasures' with 'incommodity', inconvenience, difficulty. Not surprisingly, Montaigne moves early on to a meditation on the way this blending of 'pleasures' and 'evil' is connected to sex:

> Our exceeding voluptuousness hath some air of groaning and wailing. Would you not say it dyeth with anguish? Yea, when we forge its image in her excellency, we deck it with epithets of sickish and dolorous qualities: languor, effeminacy, weakness, fainting, and *Morbidezza*, a great testimony of their consanguinity and consubstantiality. (190; 389)

The sexual act is filled with both 'voluptuousness' and pleasure on the one hand and 'groaning', 'wailing', and 'anguish' on the other. Its representations, too, are characterised by 'consanguinity and consubstantiality': the image of desire at its peak ('excellency') is nevertheless decked with 'sickish and dolorous qualities', as well as '*Morbidezza*' (which Florio glosses in his dictionary as 'wantonnesse, ranknesse, softnes').[13]

The sexual act and its representations turn out to be synecdoches for the general 'consanguinity and consubstantiality' of human experience. All moods are blended, 'excessive joy hath more severity than jollity; extreme and full content, more settledness than cheerfulness. . . . Ease consumeth us' (190; 389). Montaigne then quotes 'an old Greek verse' that claims, '"The gods sell us all the goods they give us." That is to say, they give us not one pure and perfect, and that which we buy not with the price of some evil' (190–1; 389).[14] Nothing is pure – and nothing is without some cost.

Montaigne next discusses the inextricability of pleasure and pain, or at least pleasure and difficulty. 'Travell [travail] and pleasure', seeming opposites and 'most unlike in nature, are notwithstanding followed together by a kind I wot not what natural conjunction. *Socrates* sayeth that some god attempted to huddle up together and confound sorrow and voluptuousness, but being unable to effect it, he bethought himself to couple them together, at least by the tail' (191; 389). Similarly, Montaigne invokes Metrodorus' claim that 'in sadness there is some alloy of pleasure', and more specifically – alluding to

Attalus in Seneca – asserts that 'the remembrance of our last [lost] friends is as pleasing to us as bitterness in wine that is over old . . . and as of sweetly-sour apples' (191; 389). Joy and sorrow, then, are blended emotions: 'the extremity of laughing intermingles itself with tears' (191–2; 389). Painters, Montaigne says, confirm this intermingling, being 'of opinion that *the motions and wrinkles in the face which serve to weep serve also to laugh*. Verily, before one or other be determined to express which, behold the picture['s] success; you are in doubt toward which one inclineth' (191; 389). As before with poetic descriptions of sexual acts, pictorial representations – like the thing represented – reveal the doubleness of the world.

At this point, Montaigne returns to sex, asserting that no man could bear pure, unmitigated desire: 'Let us suppose all his several members were for ever possessed with a pleasure like unto that of generation, even in the highest point that may be – I find him unable to bear so pure, so constant, and so universal a sensuality' (192; 389). Even if he could taste desire purely, Montaigne continues, he would not want to: 'Truly, he flies when he is even upon the nick and naturally hasteneth to escape it, as from a step whereon he cannot stay or contain himself, and feareth to sinketh into it' (192; 389).

This meditation on sexuality is followed by a broader yet more personal exploration of his own ethical blendedness: 'When I religiously confess myself unto myself, I find the best good I have hath some vicious taint' (192; 389). Montaigne suspects that even Plato, as he listened for the music of the spheres, would have 'heard some harsh tune of human mixture, but an obscure tune, and only sensible unto himself' (192; 389). He concludes this section by claiming that *'Man all in all is but a botching and parti-coloured work'* (192; 389). Shakespeare's Feste, the 'parti-coloured', motley Fool in *Twelfth Night*, though a pre-1603 character, shares Montaigne's view (and Florio's metaphor): 'bid the dishonest man mend himself: if he mend, he is no longer dishonest; if he cannot, let the botcher mend him. Any thing that's mended is but patched. Virtue that transgresses is but patched with sin, and sin that amends is but patched with virtue' (1.5.38–43).

This patched and multi-coloured quality of human beings makes the legal world a fraught one, and Montaigne tackles this problem here (as he does in many of his essays):

> *The very laws of justice cannot subsist without some commixture of injustice. And Plato sayeth, They undertake to cut off Hydra's heads that pretend to remove all incommodities and inconveniences from the laws. . . . Every great example hath some touch of injustice, which is requited by the common good against particulars*, sayeth Tacitus. (192; 389–90)

There can be no justice without a 'commixture' of injustice. Trying to get things absolutely right, in the legal sphere, is impossible: to attempt to erase 'incommodities and inconveniences' from the legal system is to cut off Hydra's heads; eradicating one of them inevitably breeds others. Further, the universal element of laws – the 'great example' – leads to 'some touch of injustice', and 'particulars' have to be sacrificed to 'the common good'. Montaigne's source seems to be Jean Bodin's *Methodus*, which quotes both the Plato passage and the Tacitus passage on the same page.[15] This is the realm of equity, which Bodin wrote about in another book, *The Six Bookes of a Commonweale*, book 6, chapter 6: 'the law without equitie, is as a bodie without a soule, for that it concerning but thinges in generall, leaueth the particular circumstances, which are infinit, to be by equalitie [i.e., equity] sought out according to the exigence of the places, times, and persons'.[16] As we will see, too, these ideas are central to the problems of *Measure for Measure*.

Montaigne concludes the essay by returning to a more general meditation on the problems raised by the mixed quality of human experience. As a result of these difficulties, Montaigne recommends that 'human enterprises should be managed more grossly and superficially and have a good and great part of them left for the rights of fortune' (193; 390). Recognising the limitations of human control, we should try not to analyze things 'so nicely and so profoundly. A man loseth himself about the considerations of so many contrary lusters and diverse forms' (193; 390). Quoting Livy, Montaigne notes, '*Their minds were astonished while they revolved things so different*' (193; 390). As an example of such astonishment, Montaigne mentions the story of Cicero's Simonides's pondering King Hieron's question, 'What is the being and nature of God?' Faced with 'sundry subtle and sharp considerations unto him' and, 'doubting which might be the likeliest, he altogether despaireth of the truth' (193; 390).

This is a model for all of us: 'Whosoever searcheth all the circumstances and embraceth all the consequences thereof, hindereth his election' (193; 390). In order not to be paralysed by possibility, we should not only submit to 'the rights of fortune' but also think with a more narrow scope: '*A mean engine doth equally conduct and sufficeth for the executions of great and little weights*. It is commonly seen that the best husbands [i.e., managers] and the thriftiest are those who cannot tell how they are so, and that these cunning arithmeticians do seldom thrive by it' (193; 390). The essay concludes, then, on a note of resignation: nothing is pure, and the ability to negotiate this impurity is compromised by our very impurity. Those who reason less intricately get closer to the answers. The rest, with Simonides, most likely 'despaireth of the truth'.

Measure for Measure

Coming from Montaigne's essay to *Measure for Measure* – as Shakespeare might have done – one is struck by the absence of purity everywhere: in ethics, religion, rational certainty, even – and at times especially – language. The world of Vienna is morally, religiously, intellectually, and linguistically an extremely messy place. I have argued elsewhere that the play is a site of paradox, and nearly every scene contains paradoxical ideas, language, or both.[17] But it is also a site of Montaignian impurity, where 'The weakness of our condition causeth that things in their natural simplicity and purity cannot fall into our use. The elements we enjoy are altered, metals likewise, yea gold must be empared with some other stuff to make it fit for our service,' especially in the legal world, in which '*The very laws of justice cannot subsist without some commixture of injustice.*'[18]

The play opens with governmental disorder in Vienna. Duke Vincentio, we learn in 1.3, has allowed the laws to go unenforced to such an extent that he feels it would now be unjust to enact them himself:

> Sith 'twas my fault to give the people scope,
> 'Twould be my tyranny to strike and gall them
> For what I bid them do – for we bid this be done,
> When evil deeds have their permissive pass,
> And not the punishment. Therefore indeed, my father,
> I have on Angelo imposed the office,
> Who may in th'ambush of my name strike home,
> And yet my nature never in the fight
> T'allow in slander. (1.3.35–43)

This later explanation sheds some retrospective light on the Duke's choice in 1.1 of Angelo as his deputy, when Escalus – whose 'own science / Exceeds, in that, the lists of all advice / My strength can give you' (1.1.5–7) and who is 'first in question' (1.1.46) – would seem to be a better choice. But the Duke does not want the scales of Escalus merely to balance right and wrong; he wants wrong severely redressed. And Angelo is the man to do it:

> Lord Angelo is precise;
> Stands at a guard with envy, scarce confesses
> That his blood flows, or that his appetite
> Is more to bread than stone. (1.3.50–3)

The Duke, too, has a Montaignian sense that we taste nothing purely: 'Hence shall we see / If power change purpose, what our seemers be'

(1.3.53–4). Shakespeare further highlights the impurity at the heart of the play by having the first crime that Angelo seeks to enforce be an extremely ambiguous one. In 1.2 we see Claudio paraded through the streets in a display of power for the state, and he describes his crime in paradoxical terms. Answering Lucio's query, 'whence comes this restraint', Claudio answers, 'From too much liberty, Lucio, liberty' (1.2.104–5). But Claudio's crime is not unequivocal lechery or adultery; it is based in a 'true contract' (1.2.122) and seems to have been a spousal *de futuro*, one that was conditional but binding if the couple had, as Claudio and Juliet had, intercourse.[19] So they are and are not married, and Angelo's pure reading of the law seems misplaced in this murky, impure world.

Our sense of Vienna's murkiness is heightened when Claudio asks Lucio to get his sister – a would-be nun about to 'receive her approbation' (1.2.155) – to intercede on his behalf. Claudio thinks she might be successful with 'the strict deputy' (1.2.158) because

> in her youth
> There is a prone and speechless dialect,
> Such as move men: beside, she hath prosperous art
> When she will play with reason and discourse,
> And well she can persuade. (1.2.159–63)

The second talent – Isabella's 'prosperous art' – is clear; Claudio is alluding to the art of rhetoric, in which Isabella can 'persuade' by playing 'with reason and discourse'. Even here, the suggestions are more complicated than they appear at first. Rhetoric has – and had in this period – negative connotations of artifice, duplicity, and manipulation, and the verb 'play' suggests frivolity at best and sexual dalliance at worst. But the other attribute that Claudio claims for Isabella is that much more unclear. Whereas it obviously contrasts with (at least) verbal rhetoric – it is 'speechless dialect' – what 'prone' means here is famously vexed. Possibly a textual corruption, it could also suggest an eagerness that, when combined with rhetoric, 'move[s] men' as well as persuades them.[20]

Lucio, unsurprisingly, removes the ambiguity from the description when he confronts Isabella in 1.4. For Lucio, Isabella is a woman, and women have special powers. Addressing her initially as 'virgin, if you be – as those cheek-roses / Proclaim you are no less' (1.4.16–17), Lucio later exhorts her to

> Go to Lord Angelo;
> And let him learn to know, when maidens sue,
> Men give like gods, but when they weep and kneel,
> All their petitions are as freely theirs
> As they themselves would owe them. (1.4.79–83)

More intensely than Claudio, Lucio suggests that there is a female power of moving and persuasion that is heightened when the woman is a 'maiden'. He will join Isabella as a coach and director in 2.2, helping her use all of her talents to argue for Claudio's life in front of Angelo.

Before this scene, though, Shakespeare gives an often comic take on the muddy world of Vienna. Escalus begins the scene quite seriously, trying to remind Angelo that no one is perfect and that rigid certainty in legal matters is problematic:

> **Ang.** We must not make a scarecrow of the law,
> Setting it up to fear the birds of prey,
> And let it keep one shape, till custom make it
> Their perch, and not their terror.
> **Esc.**   Ay, but yet
> Let us be keen and rather cut a little,
> Than fall and bruise to death . . .
> Let but your honour know –
> Whom I believe to be most strait in virtue –
> That in the working of your own affections,
> Had time cohered with place, or place with wishing,
> Or that the resolute acting of your blood
> Could have attained th'effect of your own purpose –
> Whether you had not sometime in your life
> Erred in this point which now you censure him,
> And pulled the law upon you. (2.1.1–6; 8–16)

Escalus, showing the sense of balance that his name denotes, tries to get Angelo to be less severe and reminds him that he, too, is human – that we taste nothing purely. Angelo's response is typically rigid:

> 'Tis one thing to be tempted, Escalus,
> Another thing to fall . . .
> You may not so extenuate his offence,
> For I have had such faults; but rather tell me,
> When I that censure him do so offend,
> Let mine own judgement pattern out my death,
> And nothing come in partial. (17–18; 27–31)

The last clause is crucial and marks Angelo as an anti-Montaignian character. Montaigne's world is one in which most if not everything is partial; for Angelo, the ideal is that 'nothing come in partial', that nothing is extenuated, that all things in his legal and intellectual world are pure.

The rest of the scene is starkly different, dominated by the comedy surrounding Constable Elbow's difficulty with the English language; what he says is often the opposite of what he means. That he is connected to the enforcement of the law deepens and darkens the point, however, since Angelo's focus on the letter of the law takes a beating here, at least indirectly. And the scene is an example of what Stephen Greenblatt has called 'anticipatory, or proleptic, parody', in which comic versions of important events and ideas occur *before* the serious ones, thereby diminishing lofty notions before they are presented as official and significant. The effect is a turning of a sceptical eye on the affairs of state and the political world.[21]

A case in point comes early in Elbow's attempt to explain to Escalus and Angelo the wrongdoings of Pompey the bawd and Master Froth, who seems to have propositioned Elbow's wife: 'If it please your honour, I am the poor Duke's constable, and my name is Elbow. I do lean upon justice, sir; and do bring in here before your good honour two notorious benefactors' (45–7). The upside-down diction of Elbow offends Angelo's sense of clarity: 'Benefactors! Well: what benefactors are they? Are they not malefactors?' (48–9).

But Elbow will not settle into predictable, standard speech: 'If it please your honour, I know not well what they are; but precise villains they are, that I am sure of, and void of all profanation in the world that good Christians ought to have' (50–2). Elbow does not know what they are, but he is certain they are villains; yet they are 'void of all profanation'. He goes on to confuse 'detest' with 'attest' (63–70) and 'honourable' with 'dishonourable' (78–80), prompting Escalus to ask Angelo, 'Do you hear how he misplaces?' (81). Pompey adds to the topsy-turvyness by twice saying, 'I hope here be truths' (116, 121). Truth, of course, is very difficult to find 'here', especially when linguistic turbulence is so evident. One of the many sites of impurity in Vienna, then, is language, and Angelo loses patience with the errors and misplacings:

> This will last out a night in Russia,
> When nights are longest there. I'll take my leave,
> And leave you to the hearing of the cause,
> Hoping you'll find good cause to whip them all. (122–5)

In contrast, Escalus patiently inquires into Elbow's job status, gently planning to replace him from among 'some six or seven, the most sufficient of your parish' (241–2). He also gives Pompey one last chance.

This kindness is clearly preferable to Angelo's surliness, but because Pompey will break the law again – as we see in Act 3 – the Duke's appointment of Angelo over Escalus to clean up Vienna makes a kind of sense. And the case of Pompey is connected to the case of Claudio at scene's end. As soon as Elbow leaves, Escalus and a Justice discuss Claudio's fate:

> **Esc.** It grieves me for the death of Claudio –
> But there's no remedy.
> **Justice.** Lord Angelo is severe.
> **Esc.**   It is but needful.
> Mercy is not itself that oft looks so.
> Pardon is till the nurse of second woe
> But yet, poor Claudio! There is no remedy. (249–55)

In a few lines, Escalus reveals how torn he is. Claudio's imminent death 'grieves' him, but he will not agree to the Justice's claim that Angelo is 'severe'. Instead, Escalus attempts to take the official position that 'Pardon is the nurse of second woe' – something we might suspect will be true with Pompey's pardon – only to return once more to his pity for Claudio, finishing in despair: 'There is no remedy.' Thus, even the lighthearted quality of parts of 2.1 suggest darker themes: not to pardon is to be severe and inhuman, but pardon is presumably what got Vienna into its morally messy present state. Angelo's rigid certainty about justice is proleptically challenged, but Shakespeare suggests that too much forgiveness and legal laxity are problematic, too.

Enter Isabella, then, who will sue for pardon of her brother in 2.2 and 2.4. Although she is very clear about her own moral world, her argument with Angelo is about how limited and ambivalent human power is, especially when compared with that of God:

> Why, all the souls that were forfeit once,
> And He that might the vantage best have took
> Found out the remedy. How would you be,
> If He which is the top of judgement should
> But judge you, as you are? O, think on that,
> And mercy then will breathe within your lips,
> Like man new made.

* * *

>   Could great men thunder
> As Jove himself does, Jove would never be quiet,
> For every pelting petty officer
> Would use his heaven for thunder, nothing but thunder.
> Merciful heaven,
> Thou rather with thy sharp and sulphurous bolt
> Split'st the unwedgeable and gnarlèd oak

> Than the soft myrtle. But man, proud man,
> Dressed in a little brief authority,
> Most ignorant of what he's most assured.
>
> * * *
>
> We cannot weigh our brother with ourself.
> Great men may jest with saints; 'tis wit in them,
> But in the less, foul profanation.
>
> * * *
>
> That in the captain's but a choleric word,
> Which in the soldier is flat blasphemy.
>
> * * *
>
> Because authority, though it err like others,
> Hath yet a kind of medicine in itself
> That skins the vice o'th'top. Go to your bosom;
> Knock there, and ask your heart what it doth know
> That's like my brother's fault. If it confess
> A natural guiltiness such as is his,
> Let it not sound a thought upon your tongue
> Against my brother's life. (2.2.75–81; 113–22; 129–31; 33–4; 137–44)

In this remarkable set of speeches, Isabella attempts to interject a perspectivalism into Angelo's life. Most of her examples seek to remind him of the differences between human and divine perspectives, especially in the realm of politics and power: 'Jove' and 'Merciful heaven' are contrasted with the 'tyrannous . . . giant' (109–10), with 'proud man, / Dressed in a little brief authority.' But, even in the strictly human realm, when it comes to justice, we taste nothing purely: 'great men' can jest with saints, but the 'lesser' cannot; the captain is allowed to do what the soldier is not; and those in 'authority' can cover their vices and flaws in a way that 'others' are not able to.

Although Isabella may not convince Angelo of the flaws in any specific position, both her 'persuasion' and her 'speechless dialect' move him to such an extent that he entertains that some things might indeed 'come in partial'. After he has agreed to see her again the next day, Angelo reveals in soliloquy that his sense of the pure order of things has been disturbed:

> What's this? What's this? Is this her fault or mine?
> The tempter or the tempted, who sins most, ha?
>
> * * *

> What dost thou; or what art thou, Angelo?
> Dost thou desire her foully for those things
> That make her good?
>
> * * *
>
> O cunning enemy, that, to catch a saint,
> With saints dost bait thy hook. Most dangerous
> Is that temptation that doth goad us on
> To sin in loving virtue. Never could the strumpet,
> With all her double vigour – art and nature –
> Once stir my temper; but this virtuous maid
> Subdues me quite. Ever till now,
> When men were fond, I smiled, and wondered how.
> (167–8; 177–9; 184–9)

Sinning 'in loving virtue' and erotically subdued by 'this virtuous maid', Angelo has discovered the blended sense of the world. He no longer knows what he does or is.

But this confusion of categories leads Angelo not to a higher, more flexible intellectual or moral viewpoint but instead into self-loathing and depravity. Again in soliloquy, he announces to us at the opening of 2.4 that, since his world is upside down, he will turn moral uncertainty into a new certainty and become evil:

> When I would pray and think, I think and pray
> To several subjects: heaven hath my empty words,
> Whilst my invention, hearing not my tongue,
> Anchors on Isabel; God in my mouth,
> As if I did but only chew his name,
> And in my heart the strong and swelling evil
> Of my conception. The state whereon I studied
> Is like a good thing, being often read,
> Grown seared and tedious. Yea, my gravity,
> Wherein – let no man hear me – I take pride,
> Could I with boot change for an idle plume
> Which the air beats in vain. O place, O form,
> How often dost thou with thy case, thy habit,
> Wrench awe from fools, and tie the wiser souls
> To thy false seeming! Blood, thou art blood.
> Let's write 'good angel' on the devil's horn –
> 'Tis [not] the devil's crest. (2.4.1–17)

Through Angelo, Shakespeare explores the problem of tasting nothing purely: the mixed nature of the world can allow for the manipulation of appearances and the exploitation of ambiguity. Using the 'place' and 'form' of his authority, Angelo becomes the corrupt leader that Isabella posited in 2.2. By writing '"good angel" on the devil's horn', he makes sure that the crest will no longer be seen as the devil's because writing and seeming will trump reality and truth. As he tells Isabella after she rejects his sex-for-Claudio's-freedom proposal, 'by the affection that now guides me most, / I'll prove a tyrant to him. As for you, / Say what you can, my false o'erweighs your true' (168–70).

Shakespeare has seemed to set up a fairly clear binary: on the one hand is the corrupt underworld of Vienna, joined by the corrupt deputy who should clean up the city's ills, and on the other the kind-hearted, all-knowing Duke and the morally pure Isabella. But Shakespeare won't let us have literary moral purity, either, and the second half of the play brings both the Duke and Isabella into *Measure*'s murkiness. From the outset, the Duke's going undercover may seem shady, but his posing as a Friar to hear Claudio's confession and the various machinations of his plot to foil Angelo bring him further into ethical ambiguity.

When the Duke comes to speak with Claudio, he tells Claudio to 'Be absolute for death' because 'Either death or life / Shall thereby be the sweeter' (3.1.5–6). But there is nothing absolute about the Duke's thesis. In fact, his claims are based in paradox, arguing that anything Claudio might value in life on earth is actually worthless:

> Reason thus with life.
> If I do lose thee, I do lose a thing
> That none but fools would keep. A breath thou art,
> Servile to all the skyey influences
> That dost this habitation where thou keep'st
> Hourly afflict. (6–11)

In a series of 'Thou art not' clauses, the Duke tells Claudio that what he thinks he is, he is not:

> Thou art not thyself,
> For thou exist'st on many a thousand grains
> That issue out of dust. Happy thou art not,
> For what thou hast not, still thou striv'st to get,
> And what thou hast, forget'st. Thou art not certain,
> For thy complexion shifts to strange effects
> After the moon. If thou art rich, thou'rt poor,
> For like an ass whose back with ingots bows,
> Thou bear'st thy heavy riches but a journey.
> And death unloads thee. (19–28)

Nothing on earth is as it seems, then: he is 'not certain, for [his] complexion shifts to strange effects, / After the moon.' Being 'absolute for death' is as close to 'absolute' as Claudio will get. As he tells the Duke, 'I humbly thank you. / To sue to live, I find I seek to die, / And seeking death I find life. Let it come on' (41–3).

But we taste nothing purely. Isabella tells Claudio that 'There is a devilish mercy in the judge, / If you'll implore it, that will free your life, / But fetter you till death' (63–5). There is a hope of life, but it brings death, indeed 'perpetual durance' (65, 66). When Claudio finds out the terms offered by Angelo, his terror of death returns, and he tells Isabella 'death is a fearful thing' (116) and

> but to die, and go we know not where . . .
> The weariest and most loathéd worldly life
> That age, ache, penury, and imprisonment
> Can lay on nature is a paradise
> To what we fear of death. (116; 129–32)

Claudio turns the Friar/Duke's reasoning upside down: all of 'the heartache and the thousand natural shocks / That flesh is heir to' (*Hamlet*, 3.1.64–5) are preferable to the uncertainty of death. Isabella – whom we have heard say 'Then Isabel live chaste, and brother die / More than our brother is our chastity' (2.4.184–5) – sees Claudio's wanting her to accept the deal as evidence of his depravity:

> O, fie, fie, fie!
> Thy sin's not accidental, but a trade.
> Mercy to thee would prove itself a bawd.
> 'Tis best that thou diest quickly. (3.1.150–3)

At this moment of extreme familial discord, the Duke enters and – asserting that, as Claudio's confessor, he has been told that Angelo was testing Isabella and was happy to receive 'that gracious denial' – tells Claudio once more that 'Tomorrow you must die – go to your knees and make ready' (3.1.167; 170–1).

If the Duke's actions to this point have stretched the boundaries of ethical behaviour, things get only more morally suspect from this point on. Disguised as a Friar, he has spied on his people, has taken Claudio's confession, and has lied to Claudio about taking Angelo's. But the scheme he introduces here – a bed trick that Isabella has to pretend to take part in – is so questionable that he feels the need to defend it to Isabella herself: 'If you think well to carry this as you may, the doubleness of the benefit defends the deceit from reproof' (246–8). The ends (doubly) justify the means, and the ability to save Claudio's life, as well as to undo Mariana's sorrow and restore her reputation, convinces Isabella to pretend to be the sexual agent in the bed trick. That there may be other 'benefits' – somewhere in this part of the play the Duke falls in love with Isabella and will propose marriage to her at the end – makes the Duke's involvement of Isabella in a sexual plot more than a little troubling: 'Haste you speedily to Angelo – if for this night he entreat you to his bed, give him promise of satisfaction' (251–3).

The Duke's journeys around the city have taught him – or confirmed for him – the moral murkiness of life in Vienna. When Escalus asks the Duke – disguised as 'a brother / Of gracious order, late come from the See, / In special business from his Holiness' (3.1.444–6) – 'What news abroad i'th'world?' (447), the Duke responds with a paradox befitting the city:

> None, but that there is so great a fever on goodness that the dissolution of it must cure it. Novelty is only in request, and it is as dangerous to be aged in any kind of course as it is virtuous to be inconstant in any undertaking. There is scarce truth enough alive to make societies secure, but security enough to make fellowships accursed. Much upon this riddle runs the wisdom of the world. The news is old enough, yet it is every day's news. (448–55)

The news isn't new, it's old: goodness is so sick that it needs the 'dissolution' of death to cure it, novelty trumps age, and inconstancy is a virtue.[22] These are paradoxical times, and 'much upon this riddle runs the world'. And paradox slides into duplicity and deception, as the specific case of Angelo has revealed:

> O, what may man within him hide,
> Though angel on the outward side!
> How may likeness, made in crimes,
> Making practice on the times
> To draw with idle spiders' strings,
> Most ponderous and substantial things?
> Craft against vice I must apply.
> With Angelo tonight shall lie
> His old betrothèd, but despisèd:
> So disguise shall, by th' disguisèd,
> Pay with falsehood false exacting,
> And perform an old contracting. (491–502)

The 'outward side' hides that 'within', and the Duke himself must engage in 'craft', 'disguise' – which he already has done, in his Friar garb – and 'falsehood' in order to counter 'vice', 'disguise', and 'false exacting'. Later, when describing the plot to Mariana, the Duke strikes a similar chord, reminding her that

> He is your husband on a pre-contract:
> To bring you thus together 'tis no sin,
> Sith that the justice of your title to him
> Doth flourish the deceit. (4.1.68–71)

Although he denies that his plan is tainted with sin, the Duke cannot be, and does not pretend to be, above impurity.

Just as nothing is tasted purely in *Measure for Measure*, nothing runs smoothly in the Duke's plot. Despite Angelo's promise to free Claudio after Isabella has given herself to him sexually – achieved by the bed trick, with Mariana as substitute – Angelo fears Claudio's wrath and orders him executed anyway; he wants proof that Claudio has been killed and demands to see his head. Barnardine, whom the Duke proposes as a substitute, refuses to be executed; and it is the Provost who then suggests sending Angelo the head of Ragusine, 'a most notorious pirate, / A man of Claudio's years, his beard and head / Just of his colour' (4.3.63–5). In the impure world of Vienna, the Duke resorts to the use of tricks: the bed trick (Mariana is the substitute for Isabella) and head trick (Ragusine's head is the substitute for Claudio's). Most troubling of all is what Harry Berger has called the 'dead trick': the Duke's pretending to Isabella that Claudio has been executed, even though the Duke has, in Ragusine, just found the solution to keep Claudio alive: 'He hath released him, Isabel, from the world. / His head is off and sent to Angelo' (4.3.107–8).[23] The Duke-as-Friar tells her that the Duke is returning, 'And you shall have your bosom on this wretch, / Grace of the Duke, revenges to your heart, / And general honour' (126–8). Isabella's response – in a line syllabically shared with the Friar – reveals her complicity in and submission to the plot: 'I am directed by you' (128).

Using craft against vice was at least somewhat defensible. But why does the Duke feel it is acceptable to use craft against *virtue*? The Duke has let us in on his secret, though the answer adds more murkiness and less clarity: 'But I will keep her ignorant of her good, / To make her heavenly comforts of despair, / When it is least expected' (101–3). The Duke seems more interested in political – and, ultimately, romantic – comedy than he does in Isabella's wellbeing. The ironic reversal of expectation – turning the tragic into the comic – seems to override all else.[24] And the end of *Measure for Measure* brings dramatic form into the world of impurities.[25]

Part of the difficulty of seeing the Duke's play, as well as Shakespeare's play, as a romantic comedy is Isabella. As a nun-in-training, she seeks to avoid the sexual world typical of the romance plot – a world which is all the more raunchy, embedded as it is in licentious Vienna. But, as strange as it may seem, Isabella is the ideally 'impure' heroine that this hybrid play needs. This is not to say that there is anything sexually impure about Isabella. But her clarity that 'more than our brother is our chastity' seems – and probably seemed at the time of the play's origin – harsh and unyielding, almost Angelo-esque.[26] And some sort of merciful intervention is required at play's end because the Duke has sentenced Angelo to death, and Mariana – revealing her knowledge that we taste nothing purely – has begged Isabella to forgive her newly-wed husband:

> They say best men are moulded out of faults,
> And, for the most, become much more the better
> For being a little bad. So may my husband.
> O, Isabel will you not lend a knee? (5.1.431–4)

Isabella complies, but her speech on Angelo's behalf is not a clear-cut request for mercy:

> Let him not die. My brother had but justice,
> In that he did the thing for which he died.
> For Angelo,
> His act did not o'ertake his bad intent,
> And must be buried but as an intent
> That perished by the way. Thoughts are no subjects,
> Intents but merely thoughts. (5.1.440–6)

First, Isabella maintains that Claudio was correctly sentenced, while Angelo would be killed for an act he did not actually commit; she upholds the letter of the law in her brother's case. It is a speech that poses as merciful but is not.[27] And, although Mariana takes Isabella's speech as a plea for mercy, none is granted until the Duke unveils Claudio and thus Angelo's crime disappears. What follows is a series of pardons and proposed marriages, an 'orgy of clemency', in A. D. Nuttall's words.[28] Shakespeare seems to be essaying Montaigne and his source: '*Every great example hath some touch of injustice, which is requited by the common good against particulars*, sayeth *Tacitus*' (192; 389–90).

The ending of the play is thus filled with romantic impurities, and comic marriage is in the forefront here. The betrothal that led to the imprisonment of Juliet and nearly led to the death of Claudio is shown to be part of the healthiest relationship of all; the other marriages and proposed marriages are problematic. Angelo's marriage to Mariana seems like a punishment, and Lucio's imminent wedding to Kate Keepdown most certainly is one: 'Marrying a punk, my lord, is pressing to death, whipping, and hanging' (5.1.515–16). Further, the carefully constructed romantic drama 'directed' by Duke Vincentio is anything but pure comedy. He first proposes to Isabella at the moment that she and Claudio have been reunited and are almost certainly embracing. Although directors sometimes deal with this textual awkwardness by staging an icy silence between Claudio and Isabella, a loving embrace between brother and sister can take the place of words. Indeed, the Duke breaks off his first proposal abruptly because he sees that he has botched his discovery scene, that Isabella is preoccupied: 'Give me your hand, and say you will be mine. / He is my brother too. But fitter time for that' (5.1.486–7). Line 487 breaks in half, as the Duke retreats from his proposal and turns to Angelo and Lucio, dooming them both to married states. When he returns to Isabella to give his second proposal, he is much more careful, much more conditional, much more, one might say, Montaignian:

> Dear Isabel,
> I have a motion much imports your good,
> Whereto, if you'll a willing ear incline,
> What's mine is yours, and what is yours is mine.
> So bring us to our palace, where we'll show
> What's yet behind that's meet you all should know. (527–32)

The Duke, one more time, tries to harmonise the discord of his play and Shakespeare's, fusing 'yours' and 'mine' and finishing with a rhymed couplet.[29] But Isabella famously does not respond to this second proposal, leaving open the possibility that, at the very least, we have a deferred comedy and perhaps a broken one. Genre has combined with thematic ideas, then, and comic structure – in the dramas of both Duke Vincentio and Shakespeare – is added to the impurities of Vienna's politics and sexuality: 'The elements we enjoy are altered, metals likewise, yea gold must be empared with some other stuff to make it fit for our service.'

All's Well That Ends Well

The self-conscious title of *All's Well That Ends Well* both suggests and mocks the purity of comic form, continuing the anatomy of comedy in *Measure for Measure*.[30] Arthur Kirsch has claimed that '*All's Well That Ends Well* may indeed constitute the most detailed and comprehensive appropriation of Montaigne in the Shakespeare canon.'[31] He leans heavily on Montaigne's 'Upon Some Verses of Virgil' (3.5), but his argument could just as easily be applied to 'We Taste Nothing Purely':

> Montaigne's central theme . . . and one that suggests that the sharpest and deepest resemblance between the essay and *All's Well*, is that this 'purpose [sexual desire]', with all its paradoxes, incarnates the paradoxes of human nature itself. He stresses in the essay, as he does throughout his work, that in all respects our bodies and souls are intertwined, and with them, our pleasures and pains, our virtues and vices. 'Our life consisteth partly in folly, and partly in wisedome. Hee that writes of it but reverently and regularly, misses the better moitie of it. I excuse me not unto my selfe, and if I did, I would rather excuse my excuses, than any fault else of mine [Montaigne, *Essayes*, 3.5.532].'[32]

One of the significant ways that *All's Well* evinces its Montaignian impurity is in its paradoxes, which constantly challenge categories. The play opens with the Countess lamenting her 'delivering my son from me', which will result in her having to 'bury a second husband' (1.1.1–2). Later in the second scene Parolles tells Helena, 'Loss of virginity is rational increase, and there was never virgin got till virginity was first lost' (1.1.120–2), and, just after their discussion of virginity, Helena thinks about Bertram's future life in France: 'His humble ambition, proud humility, / His jarring concord and his discord dulcet, / His faith, his sweet disaster' (1.1.158–60). From the very first scene, then, the play world is one of mingled yarns.

The most significant of these first-scene paradoxes is one that is slightly less apparent today than it would have been in the early days of the play's existence: the gap between noble birth and noble action, which is suggested by the Countess in her early speech to her son, Bertram, and which is a prominent theme throughout the play:

> Be thou blessed, Bertram, and succeed thy father
> In manners as in shape. Thy blood and virtue
> Contend for empire in thee, and thy goodness
> Share with thy birthright. (1.1.54–7)

Bertram's mother does not assume that natural nobility in 'shape', 'blood', and 'birthright' will yield the acquired, nurtured qualities of 'manners', 'virtue', and 'goodness'.

The Countess furthers this thesis in 1.3 when she tells Helena that she is, in a sense, Helena's mother – in spite of the natural argument to the contrary:

> Why not a mother? When I said 'a mother',
> Methought you saw a serpent. What's in 'mother'
> That you start at it? I say I am your mother,
> And put you in the catalogue of those
> That were enwombèd mine. 'Tis often seen
> Adoption strives with nature, and choice breeds
> A native slip to us from foreign seeds. (1.3.124–30)

For the Countess, 'Adoption strives with nature', but this is not a catastrophic thing. The boundary between nature and what Montaigne would call custom is porous; with time, 'foreign seeds' become 'native slips', and adopted daughters end up in the 'catalogue of those / That were enwombèd mine.' Helena wants nothing to do with being the Countess's daughter, but not because of some strict idea of the purity of blood and birthright but because 'Can't no other / But, I your daughter, he must be my brother?' (1.3.149–50). Loving and desiring Bertram, Helena invokes the natural separation between her and the Countess (and thus Bertram) in order to sidestep any possibility of incest. But the play suggests that, in general, nature and nurture are a mingled yarn.

Nowhere is this more clear than in the King's speech to Bertram about blood in 2.3. Having been cured by Helena, the King makes good on his bargain to give to Helena 'with thy kingly hand / What husband in thy power I will command' (2.1.192–3). When Helena picks Bertram, the latter is horrified both because he has not chosen her himself – 'In such a business give me leave to use / The help of mine own eyes' (2.3.103–4) – and because he considers the class difference insurmountable: 'She had her breeding at my father's charge. / A poor physician's daughter, my wife? Disdain / Rather corrupt me ever' (2.3.110–12). The King's response shows that he – like the Countess – sees nature and custom to be blendable, mixable, interchangeable:

> 'Tis only the title thou disdain'st in her, the which
> I can build up. Strange is it that our bloods,
> Of colour, weight, and heat, poured all together,
> Would quite confound distinction, yet stands off
> In differences so mighty. If she be
> All that is virtuous, save what thou dislik'st –
> 'A poor physician's daughter' – thou dislik'st
> Of virtue for the name. But do not so.

From lowest place when virtuous things proceed,
The place is dignified by th'doer's deed.
Where great additions swell's, and virtue none,
It is a dropsied honour. Good alone
Is good without a name; vileness is so;
The property by what it is should go,
Not by the title. She is young, wise, fair.
In these to nature she's immediate heir,
And these breed honour. That is honour's scorn
Which challenges itself as honour's born
And is not like the sire; honours thrive,
When rather from our acts we them derive
Than our foregoers. The mere word's a slave,
Debauched on every tomb, on every grave
A lying trophy, and as oft is dumb
Where dust and damned oblivion is the tomb
Of honoured bones indeed. What should be said?
If thou canst like this creature as a maid,
I can create the rest. Virtue and she
Is her own dower; honour and wealth from me. (2.3.113–40)

This extraordinary speech continues the Montaignian theme of 2.20 in *All's Well*: we taste nothing purely, even – perhaps especially – social class. Yarns are not the only thing envisioned as mingled in this play: for the King, mingled blood is indistinguishable blood, and his deconstruction of nobility and 'honour' continues the point the Countess has been making. Noble 'blood' and birthright are not intrinsically connected to noble action. Convinced that Helena is 'All that is virtuous', the King promises Bertram that, by royal fiat, he can adjust the class distinction that is merely conventional and customary: he can easily 'build up' the title that Bertram is so disturbed by.

The King goes further, though, and pokes holes in the entire system – the system that, interestingly, holds up his claim to power. Titles, names, words are 'lying trophies' unless there is honour – and honourable deeds – behind them. Further, they are sources of disease rather than health: 'Where great additions swell's, and virtue none, / It is a dropsied honour.' But far from being a Montaignian hero, Bertram is utterly unmoved by the ideas of the French essayist delivered to him by the French monarch: 'I cannot love her, nor will strive to do't' (2.3.141). And the King is forced to reassert the system whose mutability and fragility he has just exposed: 'My honour's at the stake, which to defeat / I must produce my power' (2.3.145–6). Bertram's resistance to the royal proclamation has threatened the King's very traditional 'honour', and he must reassert his royal authority and 'produce' his 'power'. He forces Bertram to marry Helena, and Bertram pretends to agree: 'Pardon, my gracious lord, for I submit / My fancy to your eyes' (163–4). But Bertram will leave France in order to fight in the Italian wars before consummating his marriage – indeed, without giving Helena a kiss.

The scepticism towards political power runs throughout the play, in scenes both before and after this one, and royal authority is deeply connected to the play's focus on the world's categorical impurity. The levelling tendency of *All's Well*, put forth by the King himself in 2.3, begins with the King's health issues, especially if the fistula is located in the anus – which then as now it almost certainly would have been.[33] The King is one of us – suffering pain and indignity, as well as life-threatening disease. As Montaigne reminded us on the final page of the *Essays*, '*And sit we upon the highest throne of the world, yet sit we upon our own tail*' (3.13, 340; 664). *All's Well's* King, as the play opens, presumably cannot even 'sit . . . upon' his 'own tail'.[34] Although the King and Helena ultimately reach a harmonious arrangement in 2.1, the omnipotence of the King is nevertheless challenged in this scene. The King initially rejects Helena's help because

> our most learnèd doctors leave us, and
> The congregated College have concluded
> That laboring art can never ransom nature
> From her inaidable estate. (2.1.114–17)

Despite what he argues elsewhere, here the King asserts that nature trumps 'laboring art', culture, and convention. But Helena responds by chiding the King for eschewing potentially divine help:

> Inspirèd merit so by breath is barred.
> It is not so with him that all things knows
> As 'tis with us that square our guess by shows;
> But most it is presumption in us when
> The help of heaven we count the act of men. (2.1.147–51)

Just as Isabella chided Angelo for presuming to have God-like powers, Helena chides the King for his presuming to know all that God can do. The difference here is that, while Helena is separating God and King – challenging the idea of the King as being 'God's substitute' (*Richard II*, 1.2.37) that was crucial to James I's political ideology – Helena is also suggesting that she, and not the King, has the divinely 'inspirèd merit' that is being barred by the King's very human 'breath'. In highlighting the limitations and impurity at the heart of human power, Helena is at her most Montaignian, especially when she reminds the King of God's tendency to use weak agents to convey his power and message:

> He that of greatest works is finisher
> Oft does them by the weakest minister.
> So holy writ in babes hath judgement shown
> When judges have been babes; great floods have flow'n
> From simple sources, and great seas have dried.
> When miracles by th'greatest have been denied. (2.1.134–9)

Montaigne, in fact, said as much in another essay: 'The participation which we have of the knowledge of truth, whatsoever she is, it is not by our strength we have gotten it. God hath sufficiently taught it us, in that he hath made choice of the simple, common, and ignorant to teach us his wonderful secrets' (2.12, 147; 289).

But because in Shakespeare we taste nothing purely, Helena's implication both that she is the 'weakest minister' and that she and not the King has received the divine breath merely shifts the arrogance that Montaigne is constantly chiding us for: 'Is it possible to imagine anything so ridiculous as this miserable and wretched creature, which is not so much as master of himself, exposed and subject to offences of all things, and yet dareth to call himself master and emperour of this universe?' (2.12,142; 258).

The venerable courtier Lafeu's Montaignian response to Helena's 'miracle' continues the play's sceptical approach to human knowledge: 'They say that miracles are past, and we have our philosophical persons to make modern and familiar things supernatural and causeless. Hence it is that we make trifles of terrors, ensconcing ourselves into seeming knowledge when we should submit ourselves to an unknown fear' (2.3.1–5).[35] Lafeu also tells us that a ballad has been written about the King's healing that confirms Helena's earlier claim (though without the hint of arrogance); its title is 'A showing of a heavenly effect in an earthly actor' (2.3.22–3). In this impure, uncertain world, the ways of God are largely 'unknown' and 'causeless'; when they are partially revealed, they are evinced in unpredictable ways.[36]

As her promised reward for curing the King, Helena is given Bertram as a husband. But winning and then being rejected by Bertram restores Helena's Montaignian humility, and her meditations on desire after participating in the bed trick reveal her kinship with the French essayist:

> But O, strange men,
> That can such sweet use make of what they hate,
> When saucy trusting of the cozened thoughts

Defiles the pitchy night; so lust doth play
With what it loathes, for that which is away. (4.4.21–5)

Desire forces men to make 'sweet use . . . of what they hate' and lust to 'play / With what it loathes'. Although Arthur Kirsch sees 'Upon Some Verses of Virgil' (3.5) as the Montaignian key-text for *All's Well*, his remarks focus on the mixed quality of the play's take on sexuality and could easily have been linked to 2.20:

> Even more important than these specific analogues, moreover, is their common denominator, an unremitting focus upon erotic love and a consciousness of sexuality itself as an extreme instance of the mixed nature of our being. This was Montaigne's most important legacy to Shakespeare in *All's Well That Ends Well* and should, I think, be a necessary emphasis in any interpretation of the play, for the source of most critical dissatisfaction with the play is ultimately an unwillingness to accept its sexual preoccupations.[37]

Like Hirsch, I would argue that sexuality provides a synecdoche for 'the mixed nature of our being', and this is a link that Montaigne consistently makes in 'We Taste Nothing Purely'. The Brothers Dumaine, even more than Helena and Lafeu, are the Montaignists of *All's Well*. Their meditations on the 'mingled yarn' of human affairs come directly out of a discussion of Bertram's peccadillos. Discussing the report of Helena's death, the brothers have the following discussion leading up to the 'mingled yarn' quotation, which I include for context:

> **Second Lord Dumaine** I am heartily sorry that he'll be glad of this.
> **First Lord Dumaine** How mightily sometimes we make us comforts of our losses.
> **Second Lord Dumaine** And how mightily some other times we drown our gain in tears. The great dignity that his valour hath here acquired for him shall at home be encountered with a shame as ample.
> **First Lord Dumaine** The web of our life is of a mingled yarn, good and ill together. Our virtues would be proud if our faults whipped them not, and our crimes would despair if they were not cherished by our virtues. (4.3.61–72)

Comforts in loss, tears in gain, shame in dignity and valour – many mingled yarns populate this play.[38]

And as he does in *Measure for Measure*, so does Shakespeare here, connecting the impurity of the intellectual content of the play to its ending and thus its form and genre. The play tries to end well, and as Bard Cosman has noted, at least the King has a well end.[39] But the efforts to rehabilitate the superficial and lying Parolles by having him at least partly forgiven by his chief critic, Lafeu, are undermined by the seemingly unredeemable Bertram. Like Isabella with Angelo, Helena tries to forgive Bertram. But she has also beaten him at his game by solving his riddle: she has his ring and presumably is carrying his child. Learning her Montaignian lessons about the gaps in human experience – especially where love is concerned – she tells the King and Bertram that she is 'but the shadow of a wife you see, / The name and not the thing' (5.3.303–4). Before, of course, she was the thing itself – a Hamletian *quidditas* – that needed a mere name, a mere title; her reduction to a shadow and name hardly seems comically promising. Striving for comic happiness, Bertram responds, 'Both, both. O, pardon!' (305). But that gesture is compromised by an address – not to Helena but to the King – that focuses on the conditional: 'If she, my liege, can make me know this clearly, / I'll love her dearly, ever ever dearly' (312–13). Renaissance literature is filled with questions about proof of paternity, and Bertram seems to have a loophole if he wants one.

The King, too, does not give us the closure we might hope for – either in his final speech or in the Epilogue. Befitting this play in which we taste nothing purely, the King cannot be sure that this comedy will end well, despite his reaching for the rhymed couplet that should help achieve his goal: 'All yet seems well; and if it end so meet, / The bitter past, more welcome is the sweet' (329–30). The King's 'seems' is important because it registers doubt about whether all actually is well.[40] Further, his 'if' reminds us of Bertram's 'if', reminds us not only that all *may not* be well but that the problems *may not* have ended: to reformulate the phrase yet again, all *may* be well *if* it ends well. With this conclusion that points beyond the frame of the play, Shakespeare reveals a doubt that generic restrictions – particularly those of comedy – can contain an adequate version of human experience.[41]

And there's one more twist. The title is invoked a final time in the Epilogue:

> The King's a beggar now the play is done.
> All is well ended if this suit be won:
> That you express content, which we will pay
> With strife to please you, day exceeding day. (1–4)

The King has become a beggar – a beggar for applause. This move reminds us that kings on stage were not royalty, were relative beggars – indeed, actors were linked by statute in Shakespeare's day to 'rogues, vagabonds, and sturdy beggars'.[42] And, of course, this move can be connected to the King's astonishing views on class and nobility in Act 2;

no one's blood is distinguishable from anyone else's, and thus a King can easily become a beggar, as Hamlet has taught us.[43] Bringing back the conditional 'if', these lines also underscore that theatrical success was and is about audience satisfaction; comedies and happy endings typically provide the most pleasure. Thus, there is another potentially cynical angle on the end of this play: the drama ends well *if* people like it and come back to the Globe, paying to see it and other plays by Shakespeare and his company. So it is ironically fitting that, admitting it both seeks witnesses who will 'express content' and strives 'to please' them, *All's Well* has been deemed unpleasant, broken, and 'unsmiling', indeed 'one of Shakespeare's least performed and least loved comedies'.[44] As with so much else in this play – and the problem plays more generally – Montaigne seems to be hovering and haunting: 'Excessive joy hath more severity than jollity; extreme and full content, more settledness than cheerfulness' (2.20, 190; 389). The incompleteness that one finds in Montaigne and Shakespeare is often less than pleasant; open-endedness can suggest ongoing searches but also brokenness.[45] To essay – to taste – is to taste impurely. All can never end well, really.

Notes

1. Montaigne, 'Of Glorie' (2.16), *The Essayes, or Morall, Politike and Millitarie Discourses* (1603), 360.
2. Montaigne, 'Of Experience' (3.13), *The Essayes*, 648–9.
3. Shakespeare, *All's Well That Ends Well*, 4.3.69–72, in *The Norton Shakespeare*, second edition. Unless otherwise noted, all further citations from the plays of Shakespeare are to this edition and are annotated within the text.
4. Linking the problem plays to Montaigne – though not specifically this essay – A. P. Rossiter has called attention to the plays' 'shiftingness': 'But Doubt – the true Montaignian doubt (*Que sçay-je?*) – has its own 'unknown fear' when the scepticism is about the maskedness of man. . . . I throw out the term *shiftingness*. All the firm points of view or *points d'appui* fail one, or are felt to be fallible: in Ulysses, Isabella, Helena; even in Order, as represented by the Duke. Hence the "problem"-quality, and the ease with which any critic who takes a firm line is cancelled out by another. To pursue this shiftingness I should have to explore at length the world of the 1590s: of Donne, of Chapman, Marston, Jonson and the young Middleton. But this much I can say: it was a world in which human experience, thought and feeling seemed only describable in terms of *paradox*: the greatest of all, man himself'. See his *Angel with Horns*, 128. More recently, see Grady, *Shakespeare and Impure Aesthetics*, who explores an 'impure aesthetics' that focuses on an 'artwork as disunified,

as constituted by internal clashes of discourse and by the insubordination of repressed materials. ... [T]he aesthetic is intrinsically 'impure' – it is a place-holder for what is repressed elsewhere in the system; it develops as an autonomous practice but participates in the market economy, the social-status system, the political world, the religious communities, and private life' (4; 21).

5. Montaigne, 'We Taste Nothing Purely' (2.20), in *Shakespeare's Montaigne*, ed. Greenblatt and Platt. Where available, quotations from Florio's Montaigne will come from this edition; citations will be included in the text and will list, first, this edition's page number and, second, the page number of the 1603 *Essayes* (190; 389–90). For a parallel idea and phrasing, see Montaigne's 'Of Experience' (3.13): 'Our life is composed, as is the harmonie of the World, of contrarie things; so of divers tunes, some pleasant, some harsh, some sharpe, some flat, some low and some high: What would that Musition say, that should love but some one of them?' (*The Essayes*, 648–9).

6. Boas, *Shakspere and his Predecessors*, 345. See also E. K. Chambers, in his *Shakespeare: A Survey*: 'They are all [*Measure, All's Well*, and *Troilus*] unpleasant plays, the utterances of a puzzled and disturbed spirit, full of questionings, sceptical of its own ideals, looking with new misgiving into the ambiguous shadows of a world over which a cloud has passed and made a goblin of the sun' (210). Chambers's introductions to Shakespeare's plays, collected in this book, were originally published between 1904 and 1908, so we can safely assume the influence of Boas (the clustering of these three plays) and of George Bernard Shaw, whose *Plays Pleasant and Unpleasant* was published in 1898. Shaw mentioned the three Shakespearean problem plays by title – and called them 'unpopular plays' – in his preface to this collection (ix).

7. Boas, *Shakspere and his Predecessors*, 345.

8. Shakespeare, *All's Well That Ends Well*, The Arden Shakespeare, ed. Hunter, li.

9. Rossiter, *Angel with Horns*, 117. Rossiter has also called these plays 1) '**tragi-comedies** . . . inquisition[s] into human nature and humanism; and that implies an inquiry into what controls human nature: into "institutions" such as the principles of order, the essences of honour or virtue, etc. I have insisted that these inquiries are "sceptical", in the sense of relying on empirical observations, not on a priori hypotheses' (152–3); and 2) '**off-plays**': 'a piece in which the writer was aware of the off-notes, by which I mean the discords. The whole body is more than the tail-end, and there *are* off-notes throughout. In particular, though, I mean by the phrase those discords produced by playing off a harsh, disturbing human reality against conventional story-book or play-book sentimental expectations. . .' (93). E. K. Chambers, in his *Shakespeare: A Survey*, similarly speaks of *Measure for Measure* as 'broken music' (217).

10. Leggatt, *Shakespeare's Comedy of Love*, 256.

11. Engle, '*Measure for Measure* and Modernity', 89. Engle goes on to distinguish among the three plays: '*Troilus and Cressida* is more like *King Lear* or *Othello* or the first half of *The Winter's Tale* in pushing issues about doubt and belief toward an epistemological crisis, while in *All's Well That Ends Well* redescription is seen mostly as a redemptive set of opportunities, most fully seized by Helena. *Measure for Measure* sits between the two' (89). See also Kirsch, 'The Bitter and the Sweet of Tragicomedy', who – in an essay on the connections between *All's Well*, mixed genres, and Montaigne – notes that the problem plays reveal 'a continuously integrated action that finally does not purge discrepant elements . . . but incorporates them' (64).
12. See Knight, *The Crown of Life*, 127–8n1. In the introduction to their edition of *Measure for Measure*, Arthur Quiller-Couch and John Dover Wilson recognise the Problem Plays' worrying and partly incomprehensible qualities: 'concerning all three of which we feel that, however little importance we attach to division by category, if they arrive at being comedies it is through fire; while we confess moreover that they worry us and, if we are honest, that they worry us because we understand them imperfectly. What we note for the moment is that a certain new strain of thinking – call it rather of brooding, betwixt repulsion and fascination – persists through "tragedies" and "comedies" alike – and through the *Sonnets*, if we assign them to this period.' See Shakespeare, *Measure for Measure*, ed. Quiller-Couch and Wilson, xxiii. More recently, Gillian Woods has linked both plays to the 'visual indeterminacy of Catholics' and sees Shakespeare exploring the paradoxes of seeming and being through these 'unreformed fictions': 'Here the representational problem is one of visual seeming: the Catholic costumes of the pilgrim's, friar's, and nun's habits are at once highly legible and awkwardly polysemous'. See *Shakespeare's Unreformed Fictions*, 93, 23.
13. Florio, *A Worlde of* Wordes, n.p.
14. The Greek verse comes from Epicharmus, 'preserved in Xenophon's *Memorabilia*, II, i, 20'. See *The Essays of Michel de Montaigne*, trans. and ed. Zeitlin, 2:581n333.
15. Bodin, *Methodus ad facilem historiarum cognitidem*, IV, p. 63. For an English translation, see Bodin, *Method for the Easy Comprehension of History*, trans. Reynolds: 'If we seek the opinion of Tacitus about the laws and republic, what more weighty can be said than that every great example contains some injustice which is imposed upon the individuals for public advantage. Plato's opinion varies little from this. "They cut off the head of the hydra who think that all inconvenience can be removed from the laws"' (69). See also *The Essays of Michel de Montaigne*, trans. and ed. Zeitlin, 2:581n335.
16. Bodin, *The Six Bookes of a Commonweale* (1576/1606), trans. Knolles, book 6, chapter 6, p. 764.
17. Platt, *Shakespeare and the Culture of Paradox*, 95–137, esp. 115–37.

18. See Parker, 'Shakespeare's Argument with Montaigne': 'Montaigne, whose vision is never tragic, sustains a double perspective which tolerates contradiction: licentiousness is written deeply into the nature of life, but no less necessarily part of our foolish, self-tormenting condition is the impulse to suppress or regulate such energies. ... *Measure for Measure* is the play that addresses that Montaignean paradox most directly, and struggles to find an outcome for it which is other than tragic' (12).
19. See Platt, *Shakespeare and the Culture of Paradox*, 123–4.
20. See *Measure for Measure*, ed. Quiller-Couch and Dover Wilson: 'Not satisfactorily explained, and probably corrupt. v[ide] G. Johnson suggested "prompt", which in the seventeenth century spelling "promt" might be misread as "prone"; *e* and *t* are several times confused in the Qq., e.g. "about" for "aboue" (*Ham.* 2.2.126)' (122n179).
21. Greenblatt sees this as 'a major structural principle' of *1 Henry IV*. But the principle is at work in *Measure for Measure* as well: 'Its effect is not (as with straightforward parodies) to ridicule the claims of high seriousness but rather to mark them as slightly suspect and to encourage guarded skepticism'. See Greenblatt, *Shakespearean Negotiations*, 55.
22. Note the King's lamentation to Bertram about the triumph of novelty in *All's Well*:

> 'Let me not live', quoth he [Bertram's father],
> 'After my flame lacks oil, to be the snuff
> Of younger spirits, whose apprehensive senses
> All but new things disdain, whose judgements are
> Mere fathers of their garments, whose constancies
> Expire before their fashions'. This he wished. (1.2.58–63).

See also Thomas Nashe, *The Anatomy of Absurdity* (1589): 'in all things men haste unto novelties, and run to see new things, so that whatsoever is not usual, of the multitude is admired' (E1v). Quoted in *Measure for Measure*, ed. Bawcutt, 173n479.

23. For a discussion of the 'hat trick' of schemes in *Measure*, see Platt, *Shakespeare and the Culture of Paradox*, 129n98.
24. E. K. Chambers, *Shakespeare: A Survey*, nicely notes the lack of political beneficence here and serves to remind us that darker readings of the Duke were not born in the late twentieth century: 'Why does he conceal from Isabella, in her grief, the knowledge that her brother yet lives? To what purpose is the further prolongation of her agony, after his return, by the pretended disbelief of her story and the suspicion cast upon the friar, in whose person he has counselled her? These are the antics of a cat with a mouse, rather than the dispositions of a wise and beneficent ruler.' Chambers goes on to speculate about Shakespeare's 'satirical intention ... towards theories about the moral government of the universe which, for the time being at least, he does not share' (216).

25. Stephen Greenblatt has linked the Duke's plot to the production of 'salutary anxiety' found in the theatre: 'Indeed the theater is a virtual machine for deploying these techniques in a variety of registers, from the comic anxiety that leads to the clarification and release of marriage to the tragic anxiety that is at once heightened and ordered by the final solemnity of death. It is not surprising that the disguised duke of *Measure for Measure*, who fuses the strategies of statecraft and religion, has also seemed to many critics to be an emblem of the playwright' (*Shakespearean Negotiations*, 138). For Greenblatt, the Duke's plot is largely a failure because 'society at large seems singularly unaffected by the renewed exercise in anxiety. The magnificent emblems of indifference are the drunken Barnardine and the irrepressible Lucio: if they are any indication, the duke's strategy has not changed the structure of feeling or behavior in Vienna in the slightest degree' (141).
26. See Rossiter, *Angel with Horns*: 'Isabella, admirable in strength as she is, is not immune from Langland's "Chastity without Charity is chained in hell"' (121).
27. As we will see Diana do in describing Bertram in *All's Well*, Isabella uses paradox and is, in effect, claiming 'he's guilty, and he is not guilty' (5.3.286).
28. A. D. Nuttall, '*Measure for Measure*: Quid Pro Quo?', 239.
29. See Engle: 'The ending of the play, which disappoints many readers . . . is less puzzling if it is seen as the result of the sceptic's failed experiment in the invocation of the absolute. Having seen Angelo relativized, and having seen Isabella herself turning on principle to plead for him, Vincentio imposes a universal sentence (applying unexpectedly to Isabella and himself as well as others), one that illustrates the sceptic's general problem in enforcing social reform. . . . Montaigne's serenity, such as it is, comes from his explicit abjuration of leadership. Montaigne remarks at the end of "On Experience", the last of the *Essays*, that "upon the highest throne in the world, we are seated, still, upon our arses" (Montaigne 1987 [Screech]: 1269). Such a seat offers no universal foundation for the enforcement of justice, particularly if the sitter shares some of Montaigne's scepticism, as, I have argued, Vincentio does. Vincentio responds at the end by remaking Vienna as a marriage bed for himself and his subjects to lie in. Modern readers cannot imagine that this solution leads to lasting comfort, but *Measure for Measure* prefigures modernity precisely by exploring how difficult it is to repose on the instability of truth' (101; 102).
30. G. Wilson Knight, in his 'The Third Eye: An Essay on *All's Well That Ends Well*', notes that 'the play is more than a problem play like *Troilus and Cressida* and *Measure for Measure*' (102). Nonetheless, he, too, highlights the play's ambivalence and uncertainty, on many levels: 'The more important thinking here avoids questions of right and wrong as sharply opposed absolutes – the Clown is there to point the difference – and concentrates rather on a territory where exactitudes are impossible because ethical ideals and

human stuff, personal or communal, are in such conflict that some compromise, some unwritten code for living and action, must be devised' (103).
31. Kirsch, 'Sexuality and Marriage', 190.
32. Kirsch, 'Sexuality and Marriage', 194. Indeed, a central quotation from the play that Kirsch uses to establish the connection – the 'mingled yarn' passage included as an epigraph here – is explicitly linked by A. P. Rossiter to Montaigne's 'We Taste Nothing Purely' (2.20). See Kirsch, 'Sexuality and Marriage', 195. See also Rossiter, *Angel with Horns*: 'How all these intertwist is shown by a passage in Montaigne [2.20] that Shakespeare used in *All's Well*' (153). Indeed, Rossiter sees the play as impure at least partly because it evokes 'uneasiness' and 'mixed feelings, in which the fairy-tale solution we might like to believe in (and are adjured to by the title, and by the "historical method" interpreters) is in conflict with the realistic, psychological exposure – which is very much more convincing' (92; 100). 'Unease' and its variants are often used to describe this play. See William Shakespeare, *All's Well That Ends Well*, ed. Quiller-Couch and Wilson: 'But this inconsequence in its diction does not begin, or scarcely begins, to account for our uneasiness. If we take the play apart from these curiosities, that uneasiness goes right down into its artistry; and yet further down into its ethics, in which critics have endlessly boggled' (xii). See also Donaldson, '*All's Well That Ends Well*': 'There is some irony in the fact that a play which so often reminds us of the importance of ending well should itself end in a way which has given unease to many of its commentators' (34).
33. See Cosman, 'All's Well That Ends Well'.
34. See also Mack, *Reading and Rhetoric in Shakespeare and Montaigne*: 'The later Montaigne shares Shakespeare's interest in the experiences and actions of ordinary people . . . . Montaigne uses the necessity of bodily functions to equate rulers with ordinary people' (134, 135).
35. Montaigne would almost certainly agree: 'Whence it followeth, that nothing is so firmly believed, as that which a man knoweth least; nor are there people more assured in their reports, then such as tell-vs fables, as Alchumists, Prognosticators, Fortune-tellers, Palmesters, Phisitians, *id genus omne*, and such like. To which, if I durst, I would joyne a rable of men, that are ordinarie interpreters and controulers of Gods secret desseignes, presuming to finde out the causes of every accident, and to prie into the secrets of Gods divine will, the incomprehensible motives of his workes' (Montaigne, 'That a Man Ought to Meddle with Iudging of Divine Lawes' [1.32, 1.31 in Florio], *The Essayes*, 107).
36. Max Horkheimer and Theodor Adorno, in their *Dialectic of Enlightenment*, provide the same critique of 'enlightenment' that Lafeu does of 'seeming knowledge', invoking Francis Bacon as they do so: '[Knowledge's] concern is not "satisfaction, which men call truth", but "operation", the effective procedure. The "true end, scope or office of knowledge" does not consist in "any plausible, delectable, reverend or admired discourse, or any satisfactory arguments, but in effecting and working, and in discovery

of particulars not revealed before, for the better endowment and help of man's life". There shall be neither mystery nor any desire to reveal mystery. ... From now on matter was finally to be controlled without the illusion of immanent powers or hidden properties. For enlightenment, anything which does not conform to the standard of calculability and utility must be viewed with suspicion. ... The supernatural, spirits and demons, are taken to be reflections of human beings who allow themselves to be frightened by natural phenomena' (2; 3; 4).

37. Kirsch, 'Sexuality and Marriage', 195.
38. Mary Floyd-Wilson sees another doubleness at work in *All's Well* – that of proto-science and the occult. For a fascinating reading of the problems of hidden knowledge in the play, see her *Occult Knowledge, Science, and Gender on the Shakespearean Stage*.
39. Cosman, 'All's Well That Ends Well', 916.
40. Donaldson nicely notes the paradoxes and impurities of the play: 'The ending seems no ending, as the maid seems no maid, Parolles is a knave and no knave, as Bertram loved Diana and he loved her not, and as the dead wife seems suddenly and miraculously alive' ('*All's Well That Ends Well*', 51).
41. See Donaldson: '*All's Well That Ends Well* speaks constantly of an end which is not finally realized within its dramatic framework, but pushed forward beyond the play into an undramatized future. ... *All's Well*['s] ... problems of *ending* ... [are] not merely formal problems but also the problems of life itself' ('*All's Well That Ends Well*', 52; 54). See also Kay, '"To Hear the Rest Untold"', esp. 217–18.
42. See the 29 June 1572 *An Acte for the punishment of Vacabondes and for Releif of the Poore & Impotent* (14 Eliz. C. 5), in E. K. Chambers, *The Elizabethan Stage*: 'all Fencers Bearewardes Comon Players in Enterludes & Minstrels, not belonging to any Baron of this Realme or towardes any other honorable Personage of greater Degree; all Juglers Pedlars Tynkers and Petye Chapmen, shall wander abroade and have not Lycence of two Justices of the Peace at the leaste, whereof one to be of the Quorum, when and in what Shier they shall happen to wander ... shalbee taken adjudged and deemed Roges, Vacanboundes and Sturdy Beggers' (4: 270).
43. See *Hamlet*, 2.2.245–57 and 4.3.22–5, and discussion above in Chapter 2.
44. E. K. Chambers, *Shakespeare: A Survey*, 207, and Jonathan Bate, 'Introduction', *All's Well That Ends Well*, ed. Bate and Rasmussen, vii.
45. This is akin to what John O'Brien, in 'Montaigne and Antiquity', has called an 'esthetic of *non-finito*' (69).

Chapter 4

'We are both father and mother together in this generation': Physical and Intellectual Creations in 'Of the Affection of Fathers to Their Children' and *King Lear*

That Shakespeare essayed 'Of the Affection of Fathers to Their Children' (2.8) in writing *King Lear* has been noted before. Leo Salingar made the first sustained connection, arguing that 'Of the Affection' was 'particularly relevant' to the intellectual preoccupations of *King Lear*, 'which recall the frequent topics of the *Essays*, raising similar questions if not reaching the same answers'.[1] Salingar notes a greater pessimism in Shakespeare, who in *King Lear* 'is much less confident about rationality' than Montaigne in his essay.[2] Stephen Greenblatt concurs: 'Why should arguments that seem so reasonable and even ethically responsible appear in *King Lear* as the center of something horrible? Here, as in *The Tempest*, it is as if Shakespeare thought Montaigne had a very inadequately developed sense of depravity and evil.'[3] But I would suggest that the focus on the two writers solely at the locus of the linguistic parallel can obscure the deeper, less purely verbal affinities between essay and play.

On one hand, of course, it is hard to argue with these positions, especially since Shakespeare has Montaigne's claims about the need for elderly fathers to distribute their money to their children voiced by the villain Edmund. Even worse, Edmund suggests that these are his brother Edgar's ideas, using these views to convince their father, Gloucester, that Edgar has evil designs on Gloucester's wealth and indeed his life. Taking Edmund's Montaignian ideas as Edgar's, Gloucester disowns his elder son and sets off down the road to family disintegration, blindness, and tragedy.[4]

But as I have been arguing throughout, Shakespeare's negotiations with Montaigne are rarely if ever clear-cut: Shakespeare rarely fully endorses or critiques a Montaignian principle. Rather, he essays Montaigne, testing out ideas from the Frenchman's book. Here, I would argue, Montaigne is both more optimistic and more pessimistic about the love between parents and children than Shakespeare in *Lear*: he both argues for the natural bond between parents and their offspring and anatomises the treacheries and missed opportunities for achieving this bond that happen in the real world, beyond ideals. Further, the greater connection between essay and play is the shared fascination with non-bodily creations. In 'Of the Affection' Montaigne ultimately argues that 'what we engender by the mind, the fruits of our courage, sufficiency, or spirit, are brought forth by a far more noble part than the corporeal and more our own'.⁵ For Shakespeare, *King Lear* provides a sustained meditation not only on filial impiety but on the mind's engenderings: those of 'fools and madmen' (3.4.75), 'noble philosopher[s]' (3.4.160), and the theatre itself. It is a mistake, then, to stop the interrogation of the shared ideas of 'Of the Affection' and *Lear* at the verbal echoes of Montaigne and the feigning Edmund. The mind's engenderings may give us hope and possibility – but perhaps not in the world of the play, Shakespeare's world, or even our own world; these creations engendered in fiction may not be fully realised until an unknown future.⁶

* * *

Montaigne's 'Of the Affection' opens with a general meditation on his larger project. Addressing himself 'To the Lady of Estissac', he worries that 'I shall never with honesty quit this enterprise.' But he hopes that the 'fantastical' and literally para-doxical ('different from common custom') quality of the endeavour will justify his work: 'It is the only book in the world of this kind and of a wild extravagant design' (117; 222–3). Although he soon moves on to a discussion of parenthood, praising the 'worthy Lady' by noting that 'in our age we have no pattern of motherly affection more exemplary than yours' (117, 118–19; 223), it is significant to note that he begins as he will end: discussing mental and intellectual rather than bodily creations.

When Montaigne does begin discussing parents and children, he asserts that 'if there be any truly natural law', there are two parts to it: self-preservation – 'the care which each living creature hath to his preservation and to fly that doth hurt him' – and 'the affection which the engenderer beareth his offspring' (118; 223). Significantly, Montaigne notes that the latter is not a reciprocal law: 'And forsomuch as Nature seemeth to have recommended the same unto us, aiming to extend, increase, and advance the successive parts or parcels of this her frame, it is no wonder if back again it is not so great from children unto fathers' (118; 223). Since the future of the family is not at stake in children loving parents, the love 'is not so great'. What's more, 'he to whom a debt is owing loveth better than he that oweth' (119; 223). Even from the outset of the essay, then, Montaigne hints at inequalities and potential difficulties in parent–child relations.

Early in the essay, too, Montaigne is much more sympathetic to children than to fathers. The latter treat the former, especially when they are young, as 'pastimes', as pets, 'as we do apes, monkeys, or perikitoes, and not as men' (120; 224). It is important to share responsibility and possessions with one's offspring, too, rather than attempting to maintain power over children by means of hoarding wealth and property:

> I deem it a kind of cruelty and injustice, not to receive them into the share and society of our goods and to admit them as partners in the understanding of our domestical affairs (if they be once capable of it) and not to cut off and shut up our commodities to provide for theirs, since we have engendered them to that purpose. It is mere injustice to see an old, crazed, sinew-shrunken, and nigh-dead father sitting alone in a chimney-corner to enjoy so many goods as would suffice for the preferment and entertainment of many children, and in the meanwhile, for want of means, to suffer them to lose their best days and years without thrusting them into public service and knowledge of men. (120; 224)[7]

Practising what Stephen Greenblatt has called 'geriatric avarice',[8] fathers too often 'hoard up riches to no other purpose nor to have any use and commodity of them than to be honoured, respected, and suingly sought unto by his friends and kinsfolk and that, age having bereaved him of all other forces, it was the only remedy he had left to maintain himself in authority with his household and keep him from falling into contempt and disdain of all the world' (121; 224). Riches, then, are a last attempt at retaining pride and prestige. Worse, they can be the sole means of retaining the love of his offspring: 'That father may truly be said miserable that holdeth the affection of his children tied unto him by no other means than by the need they have of his help or want of his assistance, if that may be termed affection' (121; 224).

Just as true filial love should not be compelled, so the parental 'education of a young spirit' should be grounded in 'honour and liberty', not violence and tyranny: 'There is a kind of slavishness in churlish rigour and servility in compulsion; and I hold that *that which cannot be compassed by reason, wisdom, and discretion, can never be attained by force and constraint.* ... I have seen no other effects in rods but to make children's minds more remiss or more maliciously headstrong' (122; 225). Even a well-educated son has to wait his turn, however: 'There is no reason, neither is it convenient, that a gentleman of five and thirty years should give place to a son that is but twenty' (124; 226). At the same time,

> a father over-burdened with years and crazed through sickness and, by reason of weakness and want of health barred from the common society of men, doth both wrong himself and injure his [family] idly and to no use to hoard up and keep close a great heap of riches and deal of pelf. . . . As for other pomp and trash whereof he hath no longer use or need, he ought willingly to distribute and bestow them amongst those to whom by natural degree they ought to belong. It is reason he should have the use and bequeath the fruition of them, since nature doth also deprive him of them; otherwise without doubt there is both envy and malice stirring. (124; 226)

It is the wise father who, like 'the Emperour *Charles* the Fifth . . . had the discretion to know that reason commanded us to strip or shift ourselves when our clothes trouble and are too heavy for us, and that it is high time to go to bed when our legs fail us' (124–5; 226). Similarly, paternal wisdom comes in avoiding 'This fault for a man not to be able to know himself betimes and not to feel the impuissance and extreme alteration that age doth naturally bring both to the body and the mind. . . . I could willingly for their honor's sake have wished them at home about their own business, discharged from all negotiations of the commonwealth and employments of war that were no longer fit for them' (125; 226). There are moments in *King Lear*, especially in Act One, where both Lear and his eldest daughters make very similar points. In the essay, if not the play, it is a virtue both to recognise one's age-based limitations and to retire from public, as well as familial, responsibilities.

But in this section of his essay Montaigne imagines both revoking the gift if the children fail to fulfill expectations and duties and, assuming they do not fail, interacting with them, being 'a partner of their sports, mirths, and feasts' and living 'in some corner of my house, not the best and fairest in show but the most easeful and commodious' (126; 227). Montaigne imagines that family negotiations, both negative and positive, are ongoing (at least while the father is still alive): ideally, the father can monitor the affairs of the household and enjoy 'sports, mirths, and feasts' with his children.

Claims that Montaigne is naïve – especially when compared with Shakespeare's seemingly more world-weary and cynical approach to the same matters in *Lear* – do not tell the whole story, however. For Montaigne definitely sees that problems can arise in economic translations from one generation to the next. He discusses cases where elderly patriarchs are deceived by their wives and children. And, what's more, those without either wives or children are not safe, either: 'Old *Cato* was wont to say, *So many servants, so many enemies*. Note whether according to the distance that was between the purity of his age and the corruption of our times, he did not forewarn us that *wives, children, and servants are to us so many enemies*' (130; 228). It is hard to square this pessimism with claims of Montaigne's naïve idealism. Indeed, he seems to be much closer to Shakespeare in this section of the essay than usually recognised:

> Well fits it decrepitude to store us with the sweet benefit of ignorance and unperceiving facility wherewith we are deceived. If we did yield unto it, what would become of us? Do we not see that even then if we have any suits in law or matters to be decided before judges, both lawyers and judges will commonly take part with and favour our children?
>
> And if I chance not to spy or plainly perceive how I am cheated, cozened, and beguiled, I must of necessity discover in the end how I am subject, and may be cheated, beguiled, and cozened. (130; 228–9)

Friendship, when it exists, is the only bond that can possibly be free of these treacheries: 'And shall the tongue of man ever be able to express the invaluable worth of a friend in comparison of these civil bonds?' (130; 229).

Montaigne's darker tone shifts from pessimism and cynicism to sadness in the next part of the essay when he tells the story of 'The Lord of *Montluc*, late one of the Lord Marshals of *France*, having lost his son, who died in the island of *Madeira*' (131; 229). Instead of focusing on children who cozen and cheat, Montaigne describes a father who, because of his 'austere humour and continual endeavouring to hold a grim-stern-fatherly gravity over him . . . had lost the means perfectly to find and thoroughly to know his son and so to manifest unto him the extreme affection he bore him and the worthy judgement he made of his virtue' (131; 229).

The story becomes even more moving when Montaigne quotes the regretful father: '"I have forced and tormented myself to maintain this vain mask and have utterly lost the pleasure of his conversation and therewithal his good will, which surely was but faintly cold towards me, forsomuch as he never received but rude entertainment of me and never felt but a tyrannical proceeding in me towards him"' (131; 229). Playing the part of stern father in a 'vain mask', the Lord of Montluc did not show his affection and received little if any in return. And now it is too late: '"to whom did I reserve to discover that singular and loving affection which in my soul I bare unto him? Was it not he that should have had all the pleasure and acknowledgement thereof?"' (131; 229). Montaigne claims to be aware of that which the aggrieved father speaks, 'For, as I know by certain experience, there is no comfort so sweet in the loss of friends as that our own knowledge or conscience tells us we never omitted to tell them everything and expostulate all matters unto them and to have had a perfect and free communication with them' (131–2; 229). Loved ones need to be told and expostulated to; otherwise, their fate will be like that of the Lord Montluc's son: never knowing his father loved him, and never really loving his father as a result.

Montaigne finishes the essay by taking his argument in a rather surprising direction. Having spent most of the essay meditating on 'loving our children – because we have begotten them, for which we call them our other selves', he moves towards a discussion of 'another production coming from us and which is of no less recommendation and consequence. For what we engender by the mind, the fruits of our courage, sufficiency, or spirit are brought forth by a far more noble part than the corporeal and more our own' (137; 232). Disdaining, or at least de-emphasising, the body – which he celebrates elsewhere in the *Essays* – Montaigne elevates the mind.[9]

Partly, of course, this move continues the misogyny of the essay: mental engenderings are 'more of our own' because 'we are both father and mother together in this generation' (137; 232). Earlier, he had celebrated male children over female children because the former are 'not born to serve as women and [are] of a freer condition' (122; 225) and noted that 'women . . . [are] readily bent to contradict and cross their husbands' (129; 228). Similarly, women cannot be trusted with the 'dispensation of our succession unto their judgment, according to the choice they shall make of their children, which is most commonly unjust and fantastical' (135–6; 231). Indeed, women are 'wanting reasonable discourse to choose and embrace what they ought[;] they rather suffer themselves to be directed where nature's impressions are most single' (136; 231). In focusing solely on engenderings of the mind, Montaigne can factor out the unruliness and treachery of wives, children, and servants. These non-corporeal 'fruits', on the other hand, are 'more our own . . . ; of these all the beauty, all the grace, and all the worth is ours. And therefore do they represent and resemble us much more lively than others' (137; 232).

Montaigne signals his shift to 'brain-children'[10] by claiming that 'All histories being full of examples of this mutual friendship of fathers towards their children, I have not thought it amiss to set down some choice ones of this [other] kind' (137; 232). He goes on to discuss the metaphorical children of Heliodorus, Labienus, Lucan, and others. In his remarks on Epicurus and Saint Augustine, he directly compares bodily and mental creations:

> Shall we imagine that *Epicurus* who (as himself said), dying tormented with extreme pain of the colic, had all his comfort in the beauty of the doctrine which

he left behind him in the world, would have received as much contentment of a number of well-born and better-bred children (if he had had any) as he did of the production of his rich compositions? And if it had been in his choice to leave behind him a counterfeit, deformed, or ill-born child or a foolish, trivial, and idle book, not only he but all men in the world besides of like learning and sufficiency would much rather have chosen to incur the former rather than the latter mischief. It might peradventure be deemed impiety in Saint *Augustine* (for example-sake) if on the one part one should propose unto him to bury all his books, whence our religion receiveth so much good, or to inter his children (if in case he had any) that he would not rather choose to bury his children or the issue of his loins than the fruits of his mind. (139; 233)

For Montaigne, at least for the purpose of argument, the 'fruits of his mind' are more significant – to the author and to the audience – than the 'issue of his loins'.[11]

Montaigne finishes the essay by bringing this issue home: 'And I wot not well whether myself should not much rather desire to beget and produce a perfectly well-shaped and excellently-qualitied infant by the acquaintance of the muses than by the copulation of my wife' (140; 233).[12] And the fantasy of this essay (at least) is realised in the final example, as Montaigne discusses the story of Pygmalion, 'who, having curiously framed a goodly statue of a most singularly-beauteous woman, was so strange-fondly and passionately surprised with the lustful love of his own workmanship that the gods through his raging importunity were fain in favour of him to give it life' (141; 233). The non-bodily engendering becomes real, the idea becomes flesh, without any need for 'copulation' with a woman. 'As he assayed it, th'ivory softened much, / And (hardness left) did yield to fingers' touch.' These last words of Florio's translation of the essay – if not Montaigne's original, which leaves the Ovid untranslated – nicely focus on the assaying, the testing, of the ivory. Like Pygmalion, Montaigne has assayed the relationship between idea and reality, mental and physical creations, and has found a way to bridge the gap between them. The perfect engendering of the mind becomes substantial without involving anyone else's work but 'our own' (137; 232), our 'own workmanship' (141; 233). It remains to be seen what Shakespeare's assaying of Montaigne's essay will yield to the author's 'fingers' touch'.

King Lear

As I mentioned earlier, many scholars argue that *Lear* highlights Shakespeare's pessimistic take on Montaigne's more idealistic vision. Edmund, pretending to be a conniving Edgar, forges a letter claiming that 'The policy and reverence of age makes the world bitter to the best of our times; keeps our fortunes from us till our oldness cannot relish them. I begin to find an idle and fond bondage in the oppression of a tyranny; who sways, not as it hath power, but as it has suffered' (1.2.45–9). As we have seen, Montaigne says virtually the same thing, as a critique of old and greedy fathers:

> It is mere injustice to see an old, crazed, sinew-shrunken, and nigh-dead father sitting alone in a chimney-corner to enjoy so many goods as would suffice for the preferment and entertainment of many children, and in the meanwhile, for want of means, to suffer them to lose their best days and years without thrusting them into public service and knowledge of men. (120; 224)

Shakespeare's focus, it seems, is on the devious way Montaigne's practical and children-focused ideal can be abused by greedy sons. The Montaigne connection, too, seems inescapable because of Edmund's lead-in to his reading of the letter, supposedly written by Edgar: 'I hope, for my brother's justification, he wrote this as an essay or taste of my virtue' (1.2.43–4). The Norton Shakespeare notes that both 'essay' (and 'assay') and 'taste' come from metallurgy (2501n5), but even more clearly both derive from Montaigne: 'essay' is an obvious link, but, as Cotgrave's dictionary tells us and as I mentioned in my Introduction, 'essayer' could mean tries, proves, *tastes*, attempts, makes a trial of.[13]

Yet, as I have discussed earlier in this chapter, Montaigne, too, knows that children – and wives and servants – can violate this system; he is not naïve to or ignorant of the abuses surrounding inheritance. Indeed, the Montaigne who claims that *'wives, children, and servants are to us many enemies'* (130; 228) seems more a source than a site of critique for Shakespeare, creator of Goneril, Regan, Edmund, and Oswald.

The misogyny present in 'Of the Affections' also seems consonant with rather than opposed to that of *King Lear*. To be fair, there is nothing in the essay as graphic as King Lear's brutal depiction of 'yond simpering dame',

> Whose face between her forks presages snow;
> That minces virtue, and does shake the head
> To hear of pleasure's name;
> The fitchew, nor the soiléd horse, goes to't
> With a more riotous appetite.
> Down from the waist they are Centaurs,
> Though women all above.
> But to the girdle do the gods inherit.
> Beneath is all the fiends'; there's hell, there's darkness,
> Stench, consumption! Fie, fie, fie! pah! pah! (4.6.115–26)

The typical woman is depicted as both wildly sexual and duplicitous, seeming virtuous ('snow', 'virtue', 'women', 'gods') while actually being driven by 'pleasure' and 'a more riotous appetite' to behave like lustful 'fitchew[s]' and 'soiléd horse[s]', 'Centaurs', and 'fiends'. Montaigne's misogyny is less sexually based and less brutal, but, as we have seen, he portrays women as deceptive and, by nature, deeply inferior to men. And, as I will return to at the end of this chapter, Montaigne imagines that perfect creations can bypass women altogether.

But before turning to Shakespeare's equivalent of Montaigne's engenderings of the mind, I'd like to look at the play's affinities with Montaigne's meditations on unspoken and unexpressed love. Years ago, Stanley Cavell asserted that the crucial idea of *King Lear* was what he called 'the avoidance of love'.[14] The key to the tragic relationships in the play is that 'recognizing a person depends upon allowing oneself to be recognized by him', but characters are driven by 'the attempt to avoid recognition, the shame of exposure, the threat of self-revelation'.[15] This insight is very helpful in explaining Lear's refusal to recognise and be recognised by Cordelia. Even at the end, when there is a repair of his relationship with Cordelia, he refuses to see 'these daughters and these sisters' (5.3.7): 'He cannot finally face the thing he has done, and this means what it always does, that he cannot bear being seen.'[16] Cavell's model helps explain Gloucester's relationship with his sons, too, perhaps especially Edgar's remaining in disguise as Poor Tom for so long. So as Edgar reveals himself, Gloucester's heart 'Burst smilingly' (5.3.198), as he both acknowledges his son's love and ceases to exist. And even Edmund, once he recognises that 'Yet Edmund was beloved' (5.3.238) by both Regan and Goneril, 'can acknowledge it [the love] now, when it cannot be returned, now that its claim is dead'.[17]

This is a tragic vision that, I think, is a helpful way of looking at Shakespeare's play, the more so because it resonates with ideas from Montaigne's 'Of the Affection'.[18] For, as I discussed above, a crucial topic of Montaigne's essay is the way in which conventions and roles can lead to the lack of love's communication and acknowledgement. The Lord of Montluc's words haunt *King Lear*, just as they haunt Montaigne's essay: '"to whom did I reserve to discover that singular and loving affection which in my soul I bare unto him? Was it not he that should have had all the pleasure and acknowledgement thereof?"' (131; 229). Montaigne's Lord 'reserve[d] to discover' his 'loving affection' and asserts that his son should have had all of the 'pleasure and acknowledgment thereof'. The problem is the father's inability to 'discover' or reveal and acknowledge his love for his son. Again, the word 'acknowledgement' does not mean that Cavell read Montaigne's essay. But it may mean that Shakespeare did.

The first act – indeed, the first scene – focuses on fathers acknowledging, or refusing to acknowledge, their children. Gloucester playfully banters with Kent on the topic of his illegitimate son, Edmund, admitting that though he 'so often blushed to acknowledge him', 'now I am brazed to it' (1.1.9–10). In telling the story of Edmund's origins, Gloucester admits that his legitimate son, Edgar, 'yet is no dearer in my account', and because 'there was good sport at his making', 'the whoreson must be acknowledged' (1.1.21–2).

Lear's use of the word, however, is much more severe. Feeling, no doubt, that Cordelia has failed to acknowledge *his* love by refusing to play the rhetorical game that Goneril and Regan have played, Lear disowns her:

> The barbarous Scythian
> Or he that makes his generation messes
> To gorge his appetite, shall to my bosom
> Be as well neighbored, pitied, and relieved,
> As thou my sometime daughter. (1.1.116–20)

Lear dis-acknowledges Cordelia, turning her into a Scythian and cannibal. Building on the unnatural theme, Lear claims that not only he but Nature herself refuses to acknowledge Cordelia, telling France:

> For you, great king,
> I would not from your love make such a stray
> To match you where I hate; therefore beseech you
> To avert your liking a more worthier way
> Than on a wretch whom nature is ashamed
> Almost to acknowledge hers. (1.1.209–14)

Incredulous, France coins a wonderful word for what has transpired between father and daughter:

> Sure, her offense
> Must be of such unnatural degree,
> That monsters it, or your fore-vouched affection
> Fall'n into taint; which to believe of her,
> Must be a faith that reason without miracle
> Could never plant in me. (1.1.219–24)

France cannot believe that Cordelia has done something so 'unnatural' that it would 'monster' Lear's affection. Earlier, Lear has used a similar verb, claiming that she has been 'strangered with our oath' (1.1.205). Monstered and strangered by Lear, Cordelia is embraced, loved, and acknowledged by France:

> Fairest Cordelia, that art most rich, being poor;
> Most choice, forsaken; and most loved, despised!
> Thee and thy virtues here I seize upon:
> Be it lawful I take up what's cast away. (1.1.251–4)

By contrast, Lear assures France that 'we / Have no such daughter, nor shall ever see / That face of her again' (1.1.263–5).

The failure of a father to reveal and acknowledge love for his children becomes a key element of both the Lear and the Gloucester plots. Although the word 'acknowledge' does not appear in the play after 1.1, the theme is present throughout. Lear and Gloucester misattribute love to the children who – like Montaigne's problematic examples – scheme against them. The love that should be given to the devoted children, Cordelia and Edgar respectively, is withheld until it is almost too late. Unlike the Lord of Montluc, Lear is given time to apologise to, express love toward, and acknowledge Cordelia, though her death comes swiftly after their reconciliation:

> Have I caught thee?
> He that parts us shall bring a brand from the heavens,
> And fire us hence like foxes. Wipe thine eyes;
> The good-years shall devour them, flesh and fell,
> Ere they shall make us weep! We'll see 'em starved first.
> Come. (5.3.21–6)

Lear's sense of their being together until the end is very moving, but the simplicity of 'Come' is perhaps even more important, suggesting as it does Lear's tender acknowledgement of his once strangered daughter.

Edgar, too, is acknowledged just before Gloucester's death, but his story more closely adheres to the Montluc model. Like Cordelia, Edgar has been strangered, turned into the illegitimate son, with some help from Edmund:

> Strong and fast'ned villain!
> Would he deny his letter? I never got him . . .
> All ports I'll bar; the villain shall not 'scape;
> The duke must grant me that. Besides, his picture
> I will send far and near, that all the kingdom
> May have due note of him; and of my land,

> Loyal and natural boy, I'll work the means
> To make thee capable. (2.1.78–9; 81–6)

Edgar becomes the son not begotten by Gloucester – thus, a bastard – and Edmund is then the 'loyal and natural boy' who will inherit 'my land'. Edgar recognises this metamorphosis, declaring 'Edgar I nothing am' (2.3.21) and reinventing himself as Poor Tom, whom Gloucester can acknowledge only as a stranger. Although we will need to examine this reinvention in the next section, here it is important to stress that Edgar's lack of acknowledgement by his father can be seen to lead to his withholding of love and reconciliation until the very end of Gloucester's life. Once Gloucester has been blinded and has been shown Edmund's treachery, Edgar stays in his disguise, staging and participating in Gloucester's mock-suicide. Although he tells us 'Why I do trifle with his despair / Is done to cure it' (4.6.33–4), the extended refusal to acknowledge and be acknowledged seems akin to the Lord of Montluc's son, of whom his father noted, '"I have forced and tormented myself to maintain this vain mask and have utterly lost the pleasure of his conversation and wherewithal his good will, which surely was but faintly cold towards me, forsomuch as he never received but rude entertainment of me and never felt but a tyrannical proceeding in me towards him"' (131; 229). How could Edgar be more than 'faintly cold' when his father, like the Lord, 'never felt but a tyrannical proceeding in me towards him'?

But there are differences, too: in *Lear*, the son outlives the father, and it is the son who hides behind the 'vain mask'. Finally, although Edgar clearly waits too long to drop his disguise, when he does, the mutual love and acknowledgement occur (at least in Edgar's version of events):

> [I] became his guide,
> Led him, begged for him, saved him from despair;
> Never – O fault! – revealed myself unto him,
> Until some half-hour past, when I was armed:
> Not sure, though hoping, of this good success,
> I asked his blessing, and from first to last
> Told him of my pilgrimage. But his flawed heart –
> Alack, too weak the conflict to support! –
> Twixt two extremes of passion, joy and grief,
> Burst smilingly. (5.3.189–98)

If Shakespeare is drawing on the Montluc story for his meditation on the need for and difficulty of expressing love, it is hard to see him as the more pessimistic writer of the two, reworking the idealistic and naïve Montaigne. Although there is almost no time for Gloucester to appreciate the acknowledgement, he does not die, like the Lord's son, without knowing of the love. And Edgar, the survivor, though he admits his 'fault', will not be forever haunted by his own lack of love's articulation because he acknowledged it and 'revealed myself unto him'.

Perhaps the greatest affinity between 'Of the Affection' and *King Lear*, however, is in the exploration of, in Montaigne's words, 'what we engender by the mind' (137; 232). Some of the mind's engenderings in *Lear* are, of course, anything but 'the fruits of our courage, sufficiency, or spirit' (137; 232); instead, they are the imaginings of the increasingly unstable king. Lear's early treatment of Cordelia seems rash, even to Regan and Goneril, and they – to the extent that they can be trusted – suggest that this rashness has been a constant in Lear's character:

> **Regan:** 'Tis the infirmity of his age; yet he hath always slenderly known himself.
> **Goneril:** The best and soundest of his time hath been but rash; then must we look to receive from his age, not alone the imperfections of long-engraffed condition, but therewithal the unruly waywardness that infirm and choleric years bring with them.
> **Regan:** Such unconstant starts are we like to have from him as this of Kent's banishment. (1.1.291–9)

As Lear begins to doubt his own sanity, he raises the problem of physical and mental instability, though ostensibly speaking of Cornwall: 'we are not ourselves / When nature, being oppressed, commands the mind / To suffer with the body' (2.4.101–3). By the end of the scene, he laments, 'O fool, I shall go mad!' (2.4.281).

Lear's mad mental engenderings continue in the storm scenes, where Lear's 'tempest in my mind / Doth from my senses take all feeling else / Save what beats there' (3.4.13–15); his mind creates his new reality. Indeed, when he first sees Poor Tom, he imagines that he, like Lear, could only be in his current state for similar reasons:

> Has thou given all to thy two daughters? And art thou come to this? (3.4.49–50)
> What, has his daughters brought him to this pass?
> Couldst thou save nothing? And did thou give them all? (3.4.61–2)
> Now, all the plagues that in the pendulous air
> Hang fated o'er men's faults lie on thy daughters!
> Nothing could have subdued nature
> To such a lowness but his unkind daughters.

> Is it the fashion that discarded fathers
> Should have thus little mercy on their flesh?
> Judicious punishment! 't was this flesh begot
> Those pelican daughters.
> (3.4.67–72)

Despite his madness, Lear is aware that the world is made of fictions, ornaments, and mental creations. Nonetheless, he thinks Tom is an exception – a man beyond adornment and engendering, the *sui generis* thing itself:

> Is man no more than this? Consider him well. Thou owest the worm no silk, the beast no hide, the sheep no wool, the cat no perfume. Ha! Here's three on's are sophisticated! Thou are the thing itself; unaccommodated man is no more but such a poor, bare, forked animal as thou art. (3.4.95–100)

Lear's misreading shows that the seeming exception actually proves the rule: Poor Tom is yet another construction, a creation of Edgar's mind after his identity had been evacuated. Associated with fiction and theatricality earlier in the play by Edmund – 'My cue is villainous melancholy, with a sigh like Tom o' Bedlam' (1.2.123–4) – the Bedlam beggar Poor Tom is Edgar's creation of a new self:

> Whiles I may 'scape,
> I will preserve myself; and am bethought
> To take the basest and most poorest shape
> That ever penury, in contempt of man,
> Brought near to beast. My face I'll begrime with filth,
> Blanket my loins, elf all my hair in knots,
> And with presented nakedness out-face
> The winds and persecutions of the sky.
> The country gives me proof and precedent
> Of Bedlam beggars, who, with roaring voices,
> Strike in their numbed and mortified bare arms
> Pins, wooden pricks, nails, sprigs of rosemary;
> And with this horrible object, from low farms,
> Poor pelting villages, sheep-cotes, and mills,
> Sometime with lunatic bans, sometimes with prayers,
> Enforce their charity. Poor Turlygod! Poor Tom!
> That's something yet! Edgar I nothing am. (2.3.5–21)

Far from 'unaccommodated', Edgar 'take[s] the basest and poorest shape' and, 'with presented nakedness' and the props of the Bedlam beggar ('Pins, wooden pricks, nails, sprigs of rosemary' in his 'numbed and mortified bare arms'), plays the part of Poor Tom since he can no longer safely be Edgar. He creates 'something' from 'nothing'.[19]

Part of Edgar's refashioning as Poor Tom includes an autobiography that is a classic case of fictive and mental engendering:

> A serving-man, proud in heart and mind; that curled my hair, wore gloves in my cap; served the lust of my mistress' heart, and did the act of darkness with her; swore as many oaths as I spake words, and broke them in the sweet face of heaven: one that slept in the contriving of lust, and waked to do it. Wine loved I deeply, dice dearly; and in woman out-paramoured the Turk. False of heart, light of ear, bloody of hand; hog in sloth, fox in stealth, wolf in greediness, dog in madness, lion in prey. (3.4.80–7)

Edgar's creation is a 'proud', oath-breaking, lustful servant, who loved 'wine' and 'dice' and 'out-paramoured the Turk'. Edgar's true self is presumably nothing like this; indeed, Poor Tom resembles one of those untrustworthy servants that Montaigne writes about in his essay and that we see elsewhere in this play at least partly realised in the character of Oswald.

In addition to creating an alter ego *ex nihilo*, Edgar, extending the power of his theatricality, fashions an entire landscape out of a bare stage in the Dover Cliffs scene of 4.6, leading his father to a seeming suicide. Why does he do this, instead of dropping the mask and taking care of his father *as Edgar*?[20] Although Edgar's Poor Tom has a sexual past, Edgar does not seem to, and his creations are the kind Montaigne discusses in 'Of the Affection': mental engenderings that do not require any help from a woman – or anyone else, for that matter. Cavell's theory of acknowledgement is very helpful here; the disguised Edgar does not want to acknowledge or be acknowledged. What's more, his father has, in a sense, killed Edgar, and Edgar's new self does not require a father, a mother, or a wife (or sexual partner); he is both creator and created. Or, to bring back Montaigne, 'We are both father and mother together in this generation' (137; 232). His creation, like Montaigne's Pygmalion's, is 'his own workmanship' (141; 233).

Adding to his own creation of Poor Tom, Edgar convinces Gloucester that he is climbing 'that same hill' (4.6.1) because his father wants to end his life by jumping off of it. Claiming that they are at the summit, Edgar says,

> Come on, sir; here's the place. Stand still. How fearful
> And dizzy 'tis to cast one's eyes so low!
> The crows and choughs that wing the midway air
> Show scarce so gross as beetles. Halfway down

> Hangs one that gathers sampire, dreadful trade!
> Methinks he seems no bigger than his head.
> The fishermen, that walk upon the beach,
> Appear like mice; and yond tall anchoring bark,
> Diminished to her cock; her cock, a buoy
> Almost too small for sight. The murmuring surge,
> That on the unnumbered idle pebble chafes
> Cannot be heard so high. I'll look no more,
> Lest my brain turn, and the deficient sight
> Topple down headlong. (4.6.11–24)

To the blind Gloucester, Edgar gives a visual portrait in words – a kind of *ekphrasis* – that Gloucester must see in his mind's eye; his actual eyes no longer function, and he fights both scepticism and despair here: 'Methinks the ground is even' (4.6.3). Yet Edgar knows – and Shakespeare knows, too – that there should be some purpose to these embodiments of nothing. Edgar tells us, 'Why I do trifle thus with his despair / Is done to cure it' (4.6.33–4). His fiction has the goal of curing his father of his suicidal ideations. And, in pretending both to enable the suicide at the top of the cliff and to find the surviving Gloucester at the bottom, Edgar both writes and acts in a theatre of wonder and miracle:[21]

> Hadst thou been aught but gossamer, feathers, air,
> So many fathom down precipitating,
> Thou'dst shivered like an egg; but thou dost breathe;
> Hast heavy substance; bleed'st not; speak'st; art sound.
> Ten masts at each make not the altitude
> Which thou hast perpendicularly fell.
> Thy life's a miracle. Speak yet again.

The Edgar who finds Gloucester describes a man who should be dead yet lives: he 'dost breathe', has 'heavy substance; bleed'st not; speak'st; art sound'. Gloucester's existence is 'a miracle', is 'above all strangeness' (4.6.66), is part of the gods' performance of 'impossibilities' (4.6.74). Edgar's art has created several somethings from nothings: his alter ego Poor Tom; a Dover landscape; another man who finds the surviving Gloucester; a new life for his despairing father.[22] And, at least for awhile, his theatre of wonder seems to have some success. Gloucester promises the man who recovers him – whom he still does not know is his elder son – that 'Henceforth I'll bear / Affliction till it do cry out itself / "Enough, enough", and die' (4.6.75–7). Shakespeare, through Edgar, is also creating something out of nothing: the miraculous out of the everyday, a kind of recognition of and through a stranger. This is what theatre does.²³ And theatre is one of Montaigne's 'fruits of his mind' – embodied by the actor – that gives life some 'contentment'.

Although in 4.7 Lear is also recovered by his once monstered and strangered child, the play does not end with the triumph of wonder and miracle; Act 5 reverses most if not all of the comic energy of 4.6 and 4.7. And, though Edgar and Gloucester make peace, and Lear and Cordelia are reunited, the deaths of Gloucester and Cordelia – not to mention Edmund, Regan, Goneril, Lear, and presumably Kent – firmly situate the play in a tragic space. Edgar finishes on a downbeat note, telling us and any who are left to listen that 'The oldest hath borne most; we that are young / Shall never see so much, nor live so long' (5.3.324–5). Critics have noted before that the one redeeming quality of *King Lear* is that it exists at all – as a major engendering of the mind that continues to raise questions and to force its audiences into negotiations with the traumatic stories and ideas it contains.²⁴ In this play about parents and children, at least partly inspired by an essay on parents and children, the only lasting thing is what Montaigne calls 'the production of his rich compositions' (139; 233), the 'well-shaped and excellently-qualitied infant' begot 'by the acquaintance of the muses' (140; 233). And that's something yet.²⁵

Notes

1. Salingar, '*King Lear*, Montaigne and Harsnett', 109.
2. Salingar, '*King Lear*, Montaigne and Harsnett', 113.
3. Greenblatt, 'Shakespeare's Montaigne', in *Shakespeare's Montaigne*, ed. Greenblatt and Platt, xxix.
4. See Hamlin's 'Montaigne and Shakespeare' on Greenblatt's sense of the Montaigne and Shakespeare connection: 'For Greenblatt, then, Shakespeare's attitude toward Montaigne is significantly combative; it derives, in particular, from an intuition of Montaignian naïveté, and it takes definitive shape in the utterances of characters who privilege self-interest and realpolitik over compassion, generosity, and concern for the greater good' (345).
5. Montaigne, 'Of the Affection of Fathers to Their Children' (2.8), in *Shakespeare's Montaigne*, ed. Greenblatt and Platt. Where available, quotations from Florio's Montaigne will come from this edition; citations will be included in the text and will list, first, this edition's page number and, second, the page number of *The Essayes or Morall, Politike and Millitarie Discourses* (1603), 137; 232.
6. See Ryan, *Shakespeare's Universality*: 'A truly historical study of Shakespeare's plays – unlike the arid antiquarianism that has stifled students of them in recent decades – would approach them not only as documents of their day, but also as dispatches from alternative futures, whose

possibility they were historically empowered to disclose through their estranged dramatization of Shakespeare's times' (25).

7. This passage, as I will explore later in this chapter, informs both Edmund's approach to his father and, more specifically, the words that he passes off as Edgar's and that convince Gloucester that Edgar is a dishonest, greedy son.
8. Greenblatt, 'Shakespeare's Montaigne', xxvi.
9. As noted in Chapter 2, this paradoxical take on the mind and body is present in 'Of Diverting or Diversion' as well.
10. See Montaigne, *The Complete Essays*, trans. Screech, 449n34.
11. See also 'There are few men given unto poesy that would not esteem it for a greater honour to be the fathers of *Virgil's Æneidos* than of the goodliest boy in Rome and that would not rather endure the loss of the one than the perishing of the other' (140; 233).
12. In the original, Montaigne keeps the parallel – 'de l'accointance des Muses, que l'accointance de ma femme' (*Montaigne, Les Essais*, ed. Balsamo, Magnien, and Magnien-Simonin, 2.8, p. 423). Florio replaces the second 'acquaintance' with 'copulation', and our edition should have, too. Mea culpa. This is an interesting moment because, in 'Of Friendship' (1.28, 1.27 in Florio), Montaigne links his essays not to 'a perfectly well-shaped and excellently-qualitied infant' but to a monstrous birth – 'And what are these my compositions in truth other than antique works and monstrous bodies' (40; 89–90) – and early in this essay he has called his book 'fantastical' and 'of a wild extravagant design' (117; 222, 223).
13. Cotgrave, *A Dictionarie of the French and English Tongves*, n.p., italics mine.
14. Cavell, 'The Avoidance of Love'.
15. Cavell, 'The Avoidance of Love', 50, 58.
16. Cavell, 'The Avoidance of Love', 68.
17. Cavell, 'The Avoidance of Love', 70.
18. I would not claim, of course, that Cavell based his theory on a reading of this essay because Cavell draws on Montaigne very little. In general, Cavell's sense of scepticism is based on Descartes. See the excellent discussion in Hamlin, *Tragedy and Skepticism in Shakespeare's England*, esp. 144–8. Indeed, Cavell's allusion to Montaigne in his essay on *Lear* is minimal and casual. He quotes Montaigne as evidence for his claim that characters in *Lear* have a 'lack of wholeness' and reveal a 'separation from themselves' (79): 'In Montaigne: "We are, I know not how, double in ourselves, so that what we believe we disbelieve, cannot rid ourselves of what we condemn"' (79). He gets his Montaignian quotation from the epigraph to Auden's *The Double Man* and says that he could not find the context, but the quotation comes from 'Of Glory' (2.16) and, in Florio's translation, appears on page 360 of the *Essayes* (and as an epigraph to Chapter 3 above). For a slightly different modern translation, see *The Complete Essays of Montaigne*, trans. Frame, 469. So, while Montaigne's essay can

in no way be said to shape Cavell's thinking on the avoidance of love, it certainly can be said to shape *Shakespeare's* thinking on the topic, which Cavell helpfully brought to light.
19. See Woods, *Shakespeare's Unreformed Fictions*: 'the character of Edgar comes into being at the moment of his erasure. . . . Yet while Edgar may be less than what he once was, he is also very much more. Assuming the identity of a possessed beggar enables Edgar to realize the parts of himself that could never be voiced as Edgar' (144–5).
20. See Palfrey, *Poor Tom*: 'But perhaps there is nothing reprehensible about it at all. Imagine the difficulty, if the son were to reveal himself now, just as the father is about to leap, as though pulling a happy rabbit from his hat, like some gloating practical joker relishing the eleventh hour. It would be far more grotesque and sadistic than what the scene gives us: a man trapped in a fiction barely half of his own making, in a chain of fraudulence that is impossible to break without hateful indecorum' (186).
21. On the staging of the marvellous in this scene, see Kearney, '"This is Above All Strangeness"': '. . . this is not because *Lear* is a play that embraces the miraculous in a theological sense (or cynically denies such a sense of the miraculous) . . . Rather, the play seems interested – in the Poor Tom scenes particularly – in dramatizing the experience of a particular phenomenon: the alterity, the sheer strangeness, of the other person. . . . To borrow Blanchot's formulation, the marvel is simply the other person, the stranger *as* stranger certainly, but also the *son* as stranger, the *daughter* or *father* as stranger, "no less accessible, separate, and distant" than the divinity itself' (465). The Blanchot quotation is from *The Infinite Conversation*, trans. Hanson, 129.
22. See Palfrey, *Poor Tom*: 'He can murder his father, and then enjoy the thanks of having saved him, of bringing him back into life, humbled and grateful and obedient. The father will be made the child. The son has a duty of extraordinary delicacy. He must bring his father to his act of dying, and then take him away again' (170–1).
23. Stephen Greenblatt, in his 'Shakespeare and the Exorcists', in *Shakespearean Negotiations*, draws on Samuel Harsnett's critique of fraudulent exorcisms as 'miracle minting' and calls Edgar's attempt 'to create in Gloucester an experience of awe and wonder . . . a product of specifically histrionic manipulation' that serves as 'a disenchanted analysis of both religious and theatrical illusions' (118). The interpretation is compelling, and 'miracle minting' is certainly what Edgar and Shakespeare are up to, but Greenblatt sees a slightly more cynical practice at work here than I do. For Richard Strier, on the other hand, in his excellent 'Shakespeare and the Skeptics', Greenblatt is not pessimistic enough: 'Greenblatt's . . . argument seems to be that since *Lear* generates 'the hope for an impossible redemption' – which is taken to be equivalent to 'the dream of exorcism' (125) – the play validates this hope even while literally rejecting it. But why not see the play as truly rejecting the dream of magical or even providential exorcism of evil?' (187).

24. See, for example, Greenblatt, 'Shakespeare and the Exorcists': 'The force of *King Lear* is to make us love the theater, to seek out its satisfactions, to serve its interests, to confer on it a place of its own, to grant it life by permitting it to reproduce itself over generations. Shakespeare's theater has outlived the institutions to which it paid homage, has lived to pay homage to other, competing, institutions that in turn it seems to represent and empty out. This complex, limited institutional independence, this marginal and impure autonomy, arises not out of an inherent, formal self-reflexiveness but out of the ideological matrix in which Shakespeare's theater is created and re-created' (127).

25. On Edgar's connection to making something out of nothing and liberty out of abjection, see Palfrey, *Poor Tom*: 'Unless in precisely this abjection there is some curious privilege. The Edgar-part is never at liberty, and always coerced. And yet from the moment of escape into the 'happy hollow', Edgar steps out of social continuities, into an exile and destitution that is also a kind of freedom. Freedom because every moment, every itch and fidget, has to be thought and felt, has to find its own indigenous language. ... This freedom is the astonishment of life – of a life, your life, any life. The astonishment that it really may not be and might not have been: and yet, once here, that it opens onto endless magical connectivity, inevitable and obligatory, and as necessary for others as for oneself. Substance, it appears, truly is accidental' (252; 253).

Chapter 5

Custom, Otherness, and the Fictions of Mastery: 'Of the Caniballes' and *The Tempest*

To end at the beginning, I now turn to Montaigne's presence in *The Tempest*, which contains the one indisputable example of a Montaigne–Florio citation in a Shakespeare play. Although Shakespeare's direct quotations from 'Of the Caniballes' – first noted by Edward Capell in 1780 and Edmond Malone in 1790 – concern an ideal commonwealth put forth by Gonzalo in 2.1, it has long been assumed that Montaigne's essay influenced the topics if not necessarily the ideas of *The Tempest* as a whole.[1] Allan H. Gilbert was one of the first to suggest a wider influence of essay on play than just the Gonzalo passage.[2] And Kenji Go has recently pointed to more persuasive links between 'Caniballes' and *Tempest*.[3] Too, Eleanor Prosser convincingly laid out parallels between the opening passage of 'Of Crueltie' (2.11) and Prospero's reconciliation speech in 5.1.[4] Interestingly, she did not note that this same essay includes an allusion to the cannibals – and presumably his own earlier essay: 'The Canibales and savage people do not so much offend me with roasting and eating of dead bodies, as those, which torment and persecute the liuing. Let any man be executed by law, however deseruedly soever, I cannot endure to beholde the execution with an vnrelenting eye.'[5] Shakespeare clearly had cannibals – as well as themes of nature versus art, cruelty, justice, and mercy – firmly in mind when composing *The Tempest*.[6] The importance of Montaigne's essay to Shakespeare's play goes well beyond Gonzalo's borrowing.[7]

It is, of course, important that there is a 'smoking gun', found in the direct quotation of Florio's Montaigne here, and whether Shakespeare is challenging Montaigne's seeming idealism when Sebastian and Antonio mock Gonzalo's 'commonwealth' is a crucial issue.[8] Let us revisit the key passage in *The Tempest* borrowed from 'Of the Caniballes':

> Had I plantation of this isle my lord . . .
> I' the commonwealth I would by contraries

> Execute all things. For no kind of traffic
> Would I admit; no name of magistrate;
> Letters should not be known; riches, poverty,
> And use of service, none; contract, succession,
> Bourn, bound of land, tilth, vineyard, none;
> No use of metal, corn, or wine, or oil;
> No occupation; all men idle, all;
> And women too – but innocent and pure;
> No sovereignty . . .
> All things in common nature should produce
> Without sweat or endeavor. Treason, felony,
> Sword, pike, knife, gun, or need of any engine,
> Would I not have; but nature should bring forth,
> Of it own kind all foison, all abundance,
> To feed my innocent people. (2.1.142; 147–56, 159–64)

Shakespeare's inclusion of Montaigne's defense of pure, unadorned pre-civilisation – with the expected interruptive cynicism from Sebastian and Antonio – focuses us on a crucial issue of the play's attitude towards art and culture in general. Civilising new lands by bringing agriculture, governments, and the arts to them can be seen as part of the corruption of nature and natural instinct both by human reason and by an overly aggressive culture of mastery. This is Montaigne's seeming rhetorical position, as he contrasts 'fruits wild' with 'our artificial devices'.[9] But this importation of art and culture can also be seen as that which brings us beautiful poetry; that which sends us beyond the raw and natural; that which tames the Caliban in us.

Shakespeare's ambivalence with regard to Gonzalo in this scene is also an ambivalence with regard to Montaigne's central claim that there is something intrinsically better and more natural about the non-European, Brazilian Indians. Even Gonzalo knows that he is going against the doxa: he 'would by contraries / Execute all things.' Antonio and Sebastian delight in highlighting further contradictions in Gonzalo's commonwealth: all are equal, yet there needs to be a King; all is innocent, but there needs to be propagation and therefore sex. Gonzalo is clearly more embraced by the play than Antonio and Sebastian, but despite his moral integrity, Gonzalo is a bit of a windbag, and he is presented as at least a little naïve. So his cultural idealism, along with Montaigne's celebration of the proto-noble savage, is tempered.[10]

But perhaps more than any other play examined in this study, *The Tempest* shows Shakespeare essaying Montaigne in ways that go beyond the undoubtedly important verbal echoes. There is a larger tension revealed here that we see in Prospero's life even more than in Gonzalo's words and ideas: the conflict between a pure, idealised version of the world shaped by art and magic on the one hand, and the messy, realistic version of the world that art and magic ultimately cannot tame on the other. So in this chapter it will be important to look past Gonzalo's reciting of the passage from 'Of the Caniballes' and to consider other links between essay and play: the exploration of natural settings, especially islands; music and poetry; sex and marriage; and cannibals and Calibans.

Montaigne's 'Caniballes' opens with a fairly straightforward thesis in the form of a warning: 'Lo, how a man ought to take heed, lest he overweeningly follow vulgar opinions, which should be measured by the rule of reason and not by the common report' (56; 100). The challenge to 'vulgar opinions' and 'common report' that will serve as a springboard for the essay is the sense that 'there is nothing in that nation that is either barbarous or savage, unless men call that barbarism which is not common to them' (59; 101). Although I will do a close reading of the essay below, for now it should be noted that Montaigne takes on European 'common report' and, in the words of Richard Regosin, shows that 'the fruits of nature – her noble people or their customs – stand before European civilisation corrupted by artifice as components of that tension between the natural and the artificial that strains in the world of the *Essais*'.[11]

But does Shakespeare's play challenge 'vulgar opinions' and 'common reports' in a similar fashion? In his most overtly allusive use of Montaigne, Shakespeare seems to be most overtly taking on his teacher. As Stephen Greenblatt has claimed, 'Shakespeare's borrowing here, in short, is an act not of homage but of aggression.'[12] Shakespeare's response to Montaigne's essay will be the focus of this chapter, but Greenblatt gives an elegant statement of the standard view: 'the island's possessor before the arrival of the Europeans – Caliban, whose name is a kind of anagram for cannibal – is utterly unlike the proud, dignified, self-possessed cannibals of Montaigne's essay. Together with the very mixed bag of Europeans, Shakespeare's native seems designed to reveal Montaigne's vision as hopelessly naïve.'[13] Whether Shakespeare's play portrays Montaigne's take on the cannibals as naïve is something we will have to consider. But Shakespeare's scepticism does seem more thoroughgoing here: Caliban appears to be, at least initially, a more complicated character than Montaigne's 'canibal'. Some nurture sticks wonderfully; some does not. Caliban is both a lovely poet and an unrepentant, would-be rapist.

Nonetheless, I would like to argue for a more complicated Montaignian cannibal and thus for an (even) more complicated relationship between Montaigne's essay and Shakespeare's play. Although it is hard to know whether Shakespeare saw his relationship to this essay as complementary or contestatory, both essay and play are full of contradictions in their portrayal of their 'islanders'.[14] Whereas there are undoubtedly differences between 'canibal' and Caliban, neither one is entirely 'natural' or 'simple'. It may be, then, that Shakespeare is responding not to the singleness and simplicity of Montaigne's cannibals but to their doubleness and ambiguity. And the central link may be more important than the contrasts: the 'rule of reason' that triumphs over 'vulgar opinions' and 'the common report' is, for both writers, paradoxically a letting go of rational rule and an embrace, instead, of what David Quint has called 'an ethics of yielding'.[15] Perhaps Shakespeare's most important gleaning from Montaigne is the idea that intellectual and cultural mastery is fraught and capable of, at best, only partial success.

* * *

Montaigne begins 'Of the Caniballes' the way he begins the *Essays* as a whole: linking the Brazilian Indians to nakedness, simplicity, and unadorned truth. In his 'The Author to the Reader', he claims, 'My imperfections shall thus be read to the life, and my natural form discerned, so far-forth as public reverence hath permitted me. For if my fortune had been to have lived among those nations which yet are said to live under the sweet liberty of Nature's first and uncorrupted laws, I assure thee I would most willingly have portrayed myself fully and naked' (9; n.p.).[16] Similarly, early in 'Of the Caniballes', Montaigne celebrates a servant of his who

> was a simple and rough-hewn fellow: a condition fit to yield a true testimony. For subtle people may indeed mark more curiously and observe things more exactly, but they amplify and gloss them. And the better to persuade and make their interpretations of more validity, they cannot choose but somewhat alter the story. They never represent things truly but fashion and mask them according to the visage they saw them in. And to purchase credit to their judgment and draw you on to believe them, they commonly adorn, enlarge, yea, and hyperbolise the matter. Wherein is required either a most sincere reporter or a man so simple that he may have no invention to build upon and to give a true likelihood unto false devices and be not wedded to his own will. (59; 101)

For Montaigne, his servant – who had lived 'ten or twelve years ... in that other world which in our age was lately discovered' (56; 100) – stands apart from 'the subtle people' who 'amplify and gloss', 'fashion', and 'mask' as they 'represent'. These verbs are connected to artifice and unnatural adornment. As Carlo Ginzburg has claimed,

On the very threshold of the *Essais* we meet the Brazilian savages who will reappear in 'On Cannibals'. Their nakedness points at two crucial, and closely related, themes: on the one hand, the opposition between *coustume* and *nature*; on the other, the author's intention to speak of himself in the most direct, immediate, and truest way possible. Allusion to naked savages and naked truth have nothing surprising about them. But their convergence implies an intermediate link tied to one of Montaigne's boldest assumptions: the identification of tradition (*coustume*) with artificiality.[17]

'*Coustume*' is costume, not truth; the connection between custom and clothing was available at the time of *The Tempest*. Randall Cotgrave, in his *A Dictionarie of the French and English Tongves* (1611), defines '*Coustume*' not only as 'Custome, vse, vsage, wont' but also as 'guise; habit, manner; continuall fashion, or order'.[18] What we call savage is just wild and natural; it is *coustume* that is both artificial and savage: 'They are even savage, as we call those fruits wild, which nature of herself and her ordinary progress hath produced. Whereas indeed they are those which ourselves have altered by our artificial devices and diverted from their common order we should rather term savage' (60; 101–2).[19] At least in the first part of this essay, Montaigne has revalued 'savage', linking his cannibals to nature, simplicity, and truth, and 'we' to 'artificial devices' and falsehood.[20]

For these devices try and fail to represent nature's constructions: 'All our endeavours or wit cannot so much as reach to represent the nest of the least birdlet, its contexture, beauty, profit, and use, no nor the web of a seely spider' (60; 102). Similarly, European fictions of governmental perfection try and fail to capture the natural virtues of the cannibals:

> Those nations seem therefore so barbarous unto me because they have received very little fashion from human wit, and are yet near their original naturality. The laws of nature do yet command them, which are but little bastardized by ours. And that with such purity, as I am sometimes grieved the knowledge of it came no sooner to light, at what time there were men that better than we could have judged of it. I am sorry *Lycurgus* and *Plato* had it not. For me seemeth that what in those nations we see by experience doth not only exceed all the pictures wherewith licentious Poesy hath proudly embellished the golden age and all her quaint inventions to feign a happy condition of man but also the conception and desire of philosophy. They could not imagine a genuitie so pure and simple as we see it by experience; nor ever believe our society might be maintained with so little art and human combination. . . . How dissonant would he [Plato] find his imaginary common-wealth from this perfection? (60–1; 102)

Indeed, 'worthy men ... better learned than we are' – both ancient philosophers like Plato and contemporary thinkers – are connected to errant vision, curiosity, and emptiness instead of truth and substance: 'I fear me our eyes be greater than our bellies, and that we have more curiosity than capacity. We embrace all, but we fasten nothing but wind' (56; 100).

As the essay unfolds, however, the connections between the cannibals and at least the forebears of the Europeans seem more clear, and the cannibals as a result seem more problematic, less ideal, less connected to 'perfection'. As David Quint has argued, 'The customary reading of "Des cannibales" that praises Montaigne's impartial objectivity towards the New World peoples is tacitly based on the approval of them he voices in such passages as the comparison to the Golden Age – as if objectivity and approval were the same, as if the recognition of cultural difference and relativity precluded moral judgment.'[21] As Montaigne details the practices of cannibal culture, he does judge some of these practices – not, as we might imagine, the practice of cannibalism itself but its use as an act of vengeance:

> they roast and then eat him in common and send some slices of him to such of their friends as are absent. It is not, as some imagine, to nourish themselves with it (as anciently the Scythians were wont to do), but to represent an extreme and inexpiable revenge. (64; 104)

Montaigne does not excuse the cannibals' practice but also does not leave behind his critique of European values, returning to his earlier claim that 'we' are more barbarous than 'they':[22]

> I am not sorry we note the barbarous horror of such an action but grieved that, prying so narrowly into their faults, we are so blinded in ours. I think there is more barbarism in eating men alive than to feed upon them being dead; to mangle by tortures and torments a body full of lively sense, to roast him in pieces, and to make dogs and swine to gnaw and tear him in mammockes (as we have not only read, but seen very lately, yea and in our own memory, not amongst ancient enemies, but our neighbors and fellow citizens, and which is worse, under pretense of piety and religion) than to roast and tear him after he is dead. (64–5; 104)

So while European torture and 'cannibalism' reveal 'more barbarism', there is still 'a barbarous horror' to the vengeful actions of the cannibals, a culture that has, for Quint, 'as many dystopian as utopian features'.[23] Montaigne also paradoxically collapses differences between Europe's Roman forebears and the Brazilian cannibals even as he illustrates these differences.[24]

What Montaigne seems to emphasise is the problem of the rigidity and single-mindedness of both cultures – and, by extension, his own. As Quint says, 'Montaigne seems concerned to discredit religious obstinacy by differentiating it from Stoic firmness. The suspicion remains, however, that he sees both kinds of inflexibility as self-destructive. The unwillingness to relent and compromise . . . is an exasperating provocation.'[25] And in his call for a reformation of this unrelentingness, Montaigne stakes out a position that is closer to Shakespeare's in *The Tempest* than is usually recognised. But before turning to a reading of the play in terms of the essay, we need to look at the essay's complicated ending. For while Montaigne, unlike many of his critics, does not romanticise the cannibals, he continues to use – in John O'Brien's phrase – 'Brazilian culture as a form of critique'.[26]

The essay famously ends with Montaigne's recounting being in Rouen in 1562 and encountering 'three of that nation'.[27] We are told that 'some demanded their advice and would needs know of them what things of note and admirable they had observed among us' (70; 106). They had three responses, and Montaigne forgets 'the last' (70; 106).[28] The two observations that he remembers are both critical of French society. First, '*they found it very strange*' that the French people '*would submit themselves to obey a beardless child*' – Charles IX was around twelve at the time – instead of obeying one of the Swiss Guards protecting the King: '*many tall men with long beards, strong and well armed*' (70; 106). Second, and more disturbing, they cannot imagine why the disenfranchised accept being less than equals and why they do not violently revolt:

> *they had perceived there were men amongst us full gorged with all sorts of commodities and others which, hunger-starven and bare with need and poverty, begged at their gates. And found it strange these moieties so needy could endure such an injustice and that they took not the others by the throat or set fire on their houses.* (70; 106)

Montaigne tells us that 'they have a manner of phrase whereby they call men but a moiety of men from others' (70; 106) – in other words, they speak of men as halves of each other. But the split is not done equally, and the poor are halves-not as well as have-nots.

Montaigne's ending takes another slight digression, though, temporarily away from a critique of European culture, as he tells us that 'I talked a good while with one of them.' This encounter was far from harmonious for several reasons. First, there was literally a problem of translation: 'I had so bad an interpreter, who did so ill apprehend my meaning and who through his foolishness was so troubled to conceive my imaginations, that I could draw no great matter from him' (70; 106).[29] Second, what matter he *could* glean seemed to underscore the complicated, less-than-ideal portrait of cannibal culture discussed earlier. When Montaigne asks the man, 'what good he received by the superiority he had amongst his countrymen . . .

> he told me, it was to march foremost in any charge of war. . . . Moreover, I demanded, if when wars were ended, all his authority expired? He answered that he had only this left him, which was that when he went on progress and visited the villages depending on him, the inhabitants prepared paths and highways athwart the hedges of their woods for him to pass through at ease. (70–1; 106–7)

These rewards for superiority seem grounded narrowly in their military culture and, ultimately, appear very weak and limited. The essay's celebration of the cannibal peters out just as the cannibal's superior status does.

Montaigne's final paragraph switches directions one last time, adding another layer of irony and reminding us of the smug sense of superiority that Europeans have towards the likes of the Brazilians: 'All that is not very ill; but what of that? They wear no kind of breeches or hose' (71; 107). The essay's last section, then, finishes by accentuating the folly inherent in a sense of superiority and mastery of any kind, *in any culture*.[30] That is the great levelling idea, the true relativism of the essay: ideas of superiority deriving from human makings – human cultures – are both limited and fleeting.[31]

* * *

Caliban, Shakespeare's 'canibal', is the obvious link between Montaigne's essay and Shakespeare's play, and Caliban, like Montaigne's cannibal, is portrayed in deep ambivalence. And through Caliban we get access to the shared perspectives on the difficulties of human systems and mastery. But before looking at Caliban, I would like to examine some other echoes and resonances from 'Of the Caniballes' that make their way into *The Tempest*. For although I will be examining different parts of the essay than Kenji Go did, I agree with his central claim that 'Shakespeare's borrowing from Montaigne–Florio's essay is far more substantial than a few verbal parallels.'[32]

The setting of Shakespeare's play and the site for Prospero's and the Italians' encounter with Caliban are greatly contested topics.[33] What is interesting is that physical descriptions of geographical sites and especially islands in 'Of the Caniballes' are similarly complex. The so-called new world hovers around both essay and play, and though the islands in each are not specifically anchored there – one could argue are specifically *not* anchored there – both essay and play offer – indeed, almost require – the comparison.

Reading Shakespeare's source text in terms of *The Tempest*, one is struck by the prominence of islands in the essay's early pages.[34] Montaigne starts by discussing the man who lives with him and who for 'ten or twelve years had dwelt in that other world which in our age was lately discovered in those parts where *Villegaignon* first landed and surnamed *Antartike France*' (56; 100), near present-day Rio de Janeiro. Thoughts of Brazil lead him to discuss

> a great island called *Atlantis*, situated at the mouth of the strait of *Gibraltar*, which contained more firm land than *Africa* and *Asia* together. And that the kings of that country – who did not only possess that island but had so far entered into the mainland that of the breadth of *Africa* they held as far as *Egypt*; and of *Europe's* length, as far as *Tuscany* – and they that undertook to invade Asia and to subdue all the nations that compass the Mediterranean Sea, to the gulf of *Mare-Maggiore* and to that end they traversed all *Spain*, *France*, and *Italy*, so far as *Greece*, where the Athenians made head against them. But that awhile after both the Athenians themselves and that great island were swallowed up by the Deluge. (56–7; 100)

Montaigne goes on to meditate on the likelihood that this 'extreme ruin of waters' – a deluge, a tempest – 'wrought strange alterations in the habitations of the earth, as some hold that the sea hath divided *Sicily* from *Italy* . . . *Cyprus* from *Soria* [Syria], the island of *Negroponte* from the mainland of *Beotia*, and in other places joined lands that were sundered by the sea, filling with mud and sand the channels between them' (57; 100). This is the world of *The Tempest* – Africa, the Mediterranean, Italy, 'strange alterations' (sea changes, even), worlds 'sundered' and 'joined'. And, like the island in *The Tempest* – though issues surrounding 'that other world' (56; 100) inevitably come to mind – 'there is no great appearance the said island should be the new world we have lately discovered' (57; 100), which, after all, 'our modern navigations have now almost discovered that it is not an island, but rather firm land, and a continent' (57; 101). Montaigne's essay, though, allows the comparison between this ruined African–European island and the new world, and *The Tempest* can do so, too.

Montaigne next discusses the 'certain motions in these vast bodies', even in 'my river of Dordogne', which in the past twenty years 'hath overwhelmed and carried away . . . many foundations of diverse houses . . . ; I confess it to be an extraordinary agitation' (58; 101).

Ongoing meditations on 'changes and alterations' by water lead him back to islands, specifically one mentioned in the pseudo-Aristotelian book of wonders, 'to which some will refer this discovery' of the new world (58; 101). The details here are even more evocative of *The Tempest*, enough that Go claims this passage 'appears to provide ... the source of ... the mysterious location of Prospero's island'.[35] Pinning down a firm source is always difficult, but, again, the resonances are deep:

> certain *Carthaginians*, having sailed athwart the Atlantic Sea without the strait of Gibraltar, after long time discovered a great fertile island – all replenished with goodly woods and watered with great and deep rivers, far-distant from all land; and that both they and others, allured by the goodness and fertility of the soil, went thither with their wives, children, and household, and there began to habituate and settle themselves. The lords of *Carthage* seeing their country by little and little to be dispeopled, made a law and express inhibition that upon pain of death no more men should go thither and banished all that were gone thither to dwell, fearing (as they said) that in success of time, they would so multiply as they might one day supplant them and overthrow their own estate. (58–9; 101)

It is hard to encounter the 'fertile island'; the references to Carthage (that so vex critics of *The Tempest*);[36] the location of the island between Carthage and Gibraltar; and the island as a site of banishment, and not think of *The Tempest*. But although he continues to connect these European–African islands to the new world, Montaigne concludes this section by sounding like a cranky Shakespeare critic who reminds us – usually to defuse any discussion of colonialist themes – that Shakespeare's island is *not* in the new world: 'This narration of *Aristotle* hath no reference unto our new-found countries' (59; 101). Montaigne's 'fertile island' and Caliban's 'fresh springs, brine-pits, barren place and fertile' (1.2.341) at once suggest and resist new-world comparisons.

Music provides another fruitful connection between 'Of the Caniballes' and *The Tempest*. This is significant because music in both essay and play complicates the 'savagery' of cannibal and Caliban. The role of music in *The Tempest* has been well documented,[37] but the links to Montaigne's essay have been less explored. For Montaigne does stress the importance of both a cannibal song and a cannibal canzonet, telling us that he possesses

> a song made by a prisoner, wherein is this clause: 'Let them boldly come altogether and flock in multitudes to feed on him. For, with him they shall feed upon their fathers and grandfathers, that heretofore have served his body for food and nourishment. These muscles' (saith he), 'this flesh, and these veins

are your own. Fond men as you are, know you not that the substance of your forefathers limbs is yet tied unto ours? Taste them well, for in them shall find the relish of your own flesh': An invention that hath no show of barbarism. (68; 105–6; quotation marks added)

This time cannibalism is not linked to valour through vengeance but instead to valour through cultural history: to eat a countryman is to be sustained by the bravery and the 'substance' of the past. Consistent with his thesis, Montaigne also emphasises the aesthetic power of the song, 'an invention that hath no show of barbarism'. Yet again, the cannibals are distinguished from the barbaric but, this time, with the reference to the song as an 'invention', linked to the cultured more than the natural.

Montaigne highlights the sophistication of their songs even more in his discussion of the canzonet:

> Besides what I have said of one of their warlike songs, I have another amorous canzonet, which begins in this sense: *Adder stay, stay good adder, that my sister may, by the pattern of thy parti-coloured coat, draw the fashion and work of a rich lace, for me to give unto my love; so may thy beauty, thy nimbleness, or disposition be ever preferred before all other serpents.* The first couplet is the burden of the song. (69; 106)

Again, Montaigne remarks on the craft, the 'invention' of the canzonet and its lack of savagery: 'I am so conversant with poesy that I may judge this invention hath no barbarism at all' (69; 106). He goes even further this time, eliding the barriers between cannibal and European poetry by claiming that the song is 'altogether Anacreontike. Their language is a kind of pleasant speech and hath a pleasing sound, and some affinity with the Greek terminations' (69; 106).[38]

This elision of musical barriers is also characteristic of *The Tempest*. Ariel is the famous link to music and song, and this is one of the many ways Ariel has been distinguished from Caliban, a creature 'which any print of goodness wilt not take' (1.2.351) and 'on whose nature / Nurture can never stick' (4.1.188–9). And yet Caliban is arguably more musical than any other character, spontaneously providing a playful song of liberation – ''Ban, 'Ban, Ca-Caliban / Has a new master – get a new man!' (2.2.179–80) – and a beautiful lament for music found and lost:

> Be not afeard, the isle is full of noises,
> Sounds and sweet airs, that give delight and hurt not.
> Sometimes a thousand twangling instruments
> Will hum about mine ears, and sometime voices

> That, if I then had waked after long sleep,
> Will make me sleep again, and then in dreaming
> The clouds methought would open and show riches
> Ready to drop upon me, that when I waked
> I cried to dream again. (3.2.133–41)

It is too simplistic to say that this is not a crafted song, that Caliban is merely a 'natural' poet who discovers music in the sounds of the island.[39] He does, of course, find music in nature, but like Montaigne's cannibal, there is invention here – and European poetic form: Caliban's elegy is in iambic pentameter. Music, then, in both essay and play becomes another site of ambiguity, a place where opposites blur if not disappear.[40]

The same slippery connection can be found in the role of marriage in 'Of the Caniballes' and *The Tempest*, another site where the tensions between nature and culture, between the unadorned and the customary, are central. Montaigne reports that 'some of their old men ... preach in common to all the household, walking from one end of the house to the other, repeating one self-same sentence many times, till he hath ended his turn (for their buildings are a hundred paces in length) he commends but two things unto his auditory: *First, valor against their enemies, then lovingness unto their wives*' (62; 103). Interestingly, these are the two areas covered by the cannibal songs that Montaigne mentions. The first is not surprising, given what we know about the culture of battle among the cannibals, but the second may be more so. Indeed, there is an ongoing refrain that puts 'men in mind of this duty', though the focus is on domestic devotion rather than on what we might think of as 'lovingness': 'it is their wives which keep their drink lukewarm and well-seasoned' (62; 103). And significantly, when thinking about husbands and wives in terms of *The Tempest*, it is important to note that cannibal marriage is not built on monogamy and sexual fidelity – in fact, just the opposite:

> Their men have many wives, and by how much more they are reputed valiant, so much the greater is their number. The manner and beauty in their marriages is wondrous strange and remarkable. For, the same jealousy our wives have to keep us from the love and affection of other women, the same have theirs to procure it. Being more careful for their husbands' honour and content than of anything else, they endeavor and apply all their industry to have as many rivals as possibly they can, forasmuch as it is a testimony of their husbands' virtue.
>
> Our women would count it a wonder, but it is not so. It is a virtue properly matrimonial, but of the highest kind. (69; 106)

Montaigne highlights distinction between the cultures, revealing that *they* are not *we*. As he says right before the discussion of cannibal polygamy, 'there is a wondrous difference between their form and ours' (69; 106). What we might call a 'wonder', or even a monstrosity, is actually 'a virtue properly matrimonial'.

Yet even here the cannibals are closer to us than we might think; Montaigne's ambivalent and paradoxical portrait reappears:

> And in the Bible, *Leah, Rachel, Sarah*, and *Jacob's* wives brought their fairest maiden-servants unto their husbands' beds. And *Livia* seconded the lustful appetites of *Augustus* to her great prejudice. And *Stratonica*, the wife of King *Deiotarus*, did not only bring a most beauteous chambermaid, that served her to her husband's bed, but very carefully brought up the children he begot on her, and by all possible means aided and furthered them to succeed in their father's royalty. (69; 106)

This practice of showing devotion to one's husband by providing him with other women to sleep with is not just an exotic practice of the Other – or, if it is, the concept of the Other has to include famous classical and biblical women. As he does throughout the essay, Montaigne sets up binaries and then complicates them, especially when exploring the world of *coustume*.

Prospero clearly does not share Montaigne's permissiveness, and he and Miranda have shunned Caliban since his rape attempt. But, as Stephen Orgel reminds us, the information about the 'sanction[ed] adultery' in Shakespeare's source text 'is especially relevant, because the practice of free love in the New World is regularly treated as an instance not of the lust of the savages but of their edenic innocence; and it helps to explain why Caliban is not only unrepentant for his attempt on Miranda, but incapable of seeing that there is anything to repent for'.[41] Prospero's betrothal masque, too, shows his obsession with chastity and virginity, his attempt to counter Calibanism. Before the masque begins, he warns Ferdinand

> If thou dost break her virgin-knot before
> All sanctimonious ceremonies may
> With full and holy rite be ministered,
> No sweet aspersion shall the heavens let fall
> To make this contract grow; but barren hate,
> Sour-eyed disdain, and discord shall bestrew
> The union of your bed with weeds so loathly
> That you shall hate it both. Therefore, take heed,
> As Hymen's lamps shall light you. (4.1.13–23)

This is a conceptual world utterly foreign to Caliban, and he and his iconographical surrogates – Cupid and Venus – are banned from the ceremony.

But the binary cannot hold: the 'country footing' (4.1.138)[42] of the dancers reminds us that Eros cannot be excluded for long, and Caliban lurks outside, plotting to kill Prospero; when the magus remembers him, the virginal dream-masque comes to an end. Orgel reminds us, too, that the ideal of European virginity on a larger scale was never completely separate from Calibanesque rapacity:

> In the potential of virginity lay not only civilization but the promise of infinite bounty within a hegemonic order. But the epithet expresses as well the darker truth of imperial ambitions. Ralegh's designs on the virgin land, appropriately carried out on the authority of the new Dido, were as much Caliban's as Prospero's.[43]

Virginity and bounty are as connected to rapine and conquest as they are to civilisation and culture. As the title of a Montaigne essay that we have already examined tells us, 'we taste nothing purely'. The relationship between 'Of the Caniballes' and *The Tempest* on the topic of marriage – as on so many topics – is more complementary than contestatory.

And yet Shakespeare's Caliban is usually distinguished from, rather than linked to, Montaigne's 'canibal': the former is ambivalent, paradoxical, and contradictory, while the latter is simple, singular, and 'natural'. On a purely verbal level, however, Caliban's name is virtually an anagram of 'cannibal', especially in the spelling of the day that used a single *n*. (This is the case with all four of Shakespeare's First-Folio instances of the term, as well as Florio's spellings in his dictionaries and in his translation of Montaigne.[44]) Whereas there is no textual evidence that Caliban is actually a cannibal, his name suggests, perhaps playfully, that Montaigne's essay provides at least one of his textual origins.

Further, even though Shakespeare's Caliban is not Montaigne's cannibal,[45] both are deeply connected to ambivalence: both cannot be pinned down, and both call attention to the difficulty of pinning things down.[46] As Michel de Certeau has argued,

> The cannibal is only a variant of this general difference [between name and thing], but a typical one since he is supposed to demarcate a boundary line. Therefore when he sidesteps the identifications given him, he causes a disturbance that places the entire symbolic order in question. The global delimitation of 'our' culture in relation to the savage concerns the entire gridding of the system that brushes up against the boundary and presupposes, as in

Ars Memoriae, that there is a *place* for every *figure*. The cannibal is a figure on the fringe who leaves the premises, and in doing so jolts the entire topographical order of language. (70–1)[47]

It is this aspect that Caliban shares with Montaigne's cannibal and the one that I will turn to now. For Caliban both *is distinguished and divided* from the rest of the characters by his status as an islander and a 'monster' and *distinguishes and divides*, blends, and mingles, as he breaks up logical wholes and standard assumptions. In their important and exhaustive study of the sources and historical interpretations of Caliban, Alden and Virginia Vaughan assert that the safest way to summarise the Caliban effect – whether he is taken as an Indian, a wild man, or a gypsy – is as a character who 'violates the order of things' and symbolises 'a general unruliness in society and in nature. . . .'[48] Similarly, Peter Holbrook uses the term 'Calibanism' to describe the presence of a restless and anarchic 'theory of liberty' in Shakespeare.[49] Caliban is a character, then, who troubles the status quo, and thus both is hard to read and forces a reexamination of categories and knowledge.[50]

We see Caliban's disturbing the order of things early in Act Two when Trinculo tries to find the cause behind the effect that is Caliban:[51]

> What have we here? a man or a fish? dead or alive? A fish, he smells like a fish; a very ancient and fish-like smell; a kind of not-of-the-newest poor-John. A strange fish! Were I in England now (as once I was) and had but this fish painted, not a holiday fool there but would give a piece of silver. There would this monster make a man; any strange beast there makes a man. When they will not give a doit to relieve a lame beggar, they will lay out ten to see a dead Indian. Legg'd like a man; and his fins like arms! Warm, o' my troth! I do now let loose my opinion, hold it no longer: this is no fish, but an islander, that hath lately suffer'd by a thunderbolt. (24–37)

Before deciding that Caliban is an islander, Trinculo first thinks that he has encountered a 'strange beast', a man-fish with leg-arms who is not clearly dead or alive – in short, a 'monster'.[52] Indeed, by the end of his speech, the paradoxical monster has caused Trinculo, comically, to reevaluate his earlier position – about the very status of the monster, no less: 'I do now let loose my opinion, hold it no longer: this is no fish, but an islander, that hath lately suffer'd by a thunderbolt.'

Trinculo also says that in England a monster makes a man. And whereas Trinculo clearly imagines a monster bringing economic profit – 'any strange beast there makes a man. When they will not give a doit to relieve a lame beggar, they will lay out ten to see a dead Indian' – we see that monsters can bring a more Horatian kind of profit, too. Monsters can make – or re-make – a man (a group of men, women, human beings) in a more substantial, less economic way as well. For just as the islander helps Trinculo let loose his opinion, Caliban – in all of his liminality – forces the audience to reconsider many of the seemingly stable binary relationships in *The Tempest*. To determine, as Prospero does, that Caliban is one 'on whose nature / Nurture can never stick' (4.1.188–9) is to be too confident and too certain. Indeed, Prospero ends the play having reevaluated – with Caliban's help – another binary: that of self and other. Seeing Caliban late in the play, the magician remarks, 'This thing of darkness I/ Acknowledge mine.'

In that wonderful moment at the line break, Prospero can be seen as a 'thing of darkness' himself ('This thing of darkness I'). When he goes on to acknowledge Caliban as this 'thing', he still accepts responsibility for Caliban's creation.[53] Prospero is recognising his role in the usurpation of the island: gleaning Caliban's harvest (as Caliban had gleaned 'pig-nuts' [2.1.162]) and inheriting his possessions, Prospero is a raiding outsider. Like Montaigne's Europeans in the 'Caniballes' essay, he alters 'fruits wild' with 'our artificial devices' and diverts them 'from their common order'. Letting go of his power at play's end is part of his larger recognition, his yielding of mastery: 'Now I want / Spirits to enforce, art to enchant' (Epilogue, 13–14).[54] What's more, as Prospero acknowledges, the magician is not utterly separate from the things of darkness; his art not only fails to alter Caliban and Antonio but cannot even mend himself.

And where does this leave Shakespeare, essaying Montaigne's cannibal? Shakespeare's position may not be that far from Montaigne's after all.[55] Both essay and play seem to establish firm boundaries between barbarism and civilisation, nature and art, only to collapse them.[56] Both expose the shaky quality of European triumphalism and highlight the potential for beauty and integrity in their 'canibals'.[57] But neither gives an unequivocal upper hand to the natural and unadorned elements of their Calibans, either.[58] Finally, Montaigne's essay and Shakespeare's play at once celebrate art and human makings and show the limitations and evanescence of these cultural formations: government and 'commonwealth'; agriculture and 'tilth'; 'letters', 'songs', and 'canzonets'; marriage; magic and 'pageants'.[59] Human constructions can lead to great beauty but also to tremendous violence, to both joy and sadness.[60] They can last forever, providing possibility and hope for future generations and audiences, or they can fade, signifying nothing. Given this transience and instability, both writers suggest that it is better to admit to the fragility of claims to mastery than to assert them as unyielding truths: 'We embrace all, but we fasten nothing but wind'; 'Yea, all which it inherit, shall dissolve, / And like this insubstantial pageant faded, / Leave not a rack behind.'[61]

Notes

1. For a radical departure from usual readings, see Warren Boutcher's 'Montaigne in England and America': 'When Shakespeare borrows from Florio he is not alluding to Montaigne, but developing a comically self-undercutting declamation on the Platonic and Ovidian theme of the golden age and its restoration. He is doing so in a particular dramatic context that is itself in conversation with a prior dramatic scenario developed via Montaigne's handling of the same theme by another playwright (Daniel [in his 1605 *The Queenes Arcadia*]) who was drawing mainly on Italian sources' (324). This may be true, but I hope this chapter will convincingly prove that the allusion is to Montaigne and his essay as well as to Daniel's use of Montaigne.
2. Gilbert, 'Montaigne and *The Tempest*'.
3. Go, 'Montaigne's "Cannibals" and *The Tempest* Revisited'.
4. Prosser, 'Shakespeare, Montaigne, and the Rarer Action'.
5. Montaigne, *The Essayes, or Morall, Politike and Millitarie Discourses* (1603), 248.
6. See Paster, 'Montaigne, Dido, and *The Tempest*': 'Prosser's discovery also underscores a curious fact – that only in *The Tempest* are echoes from Montaigne so clear as to be unmistakable. While writing this play, if not while writing any other, Shakespeare seems to have had Florio's translation at his elbow' (91).
7. See de Gooyer, '"Their Senses I'll Restore"': 'But comparisons [between Florio's Montaigne and Shakespeare] have continued nonetheless, shifting gradually to questions of how Shakespeare employed the *Essais* rather than what exactly he borrowed. . . . *Can we find areas of common concern? or associations of ideas that take us beyond the devoted straining of ears for verbal echoes?*' (512; 513, emphasis mine).
8. Jonathan Bate interestingly claims, in his *Shakespeare and Ovid*, that 'Though Shakespeare imitated [Gonzalo's Utopian vision] from Montaigne, his audience would have been more likely to identify it with Montaigne's source,' which is Book One of Ovid's *Metamorphoses*. Bate, then, sees a negotiation not just between Shakespeare and Montaigne but between both authors and Ovid, as they encounter a falling away from a Golden Age and imagine how to avoid the 'craft, treason, violence, envy, pride, lust, the parceling out of land (Gonzalo's "plantation") which was previously held in common, and family quarrels. . . . All the dark elements in *The Tempest* are of the Iron Age' (255, 256).

9. Montaigne, 'Of the Caniballes', in *Shakespeare's Montaigne*, ed. Greenblatt and Platt. Where available, quotations from Florio's Montaigne will come from this edition; citations will be included in the text and will list, first, this edition's page number and, second, the page number of the 1603 *Essayes* (60; 101–2).
10. For a very different view of the tension, see Boutcher, *The School of Montaigne in Early Modern Europe: Volume II, The Reader–Writer*: 'In *Tempest* 2.1, we see the discussion, circulation, and application of the themes of an idle pastoral lecture lose direction and spin out of control, because the noble master on stage (King Alonso) does not command and protect the process and its outcome. This almost results in regicide, as two other lords turn Gonzalo's Arcadian theme in politic, conspiratorial directions' (271).
11. Regosin, *The Matter of My Book*, 37. See most recently the indispensable contextualising of Montaigne's meeting with and writing about the cannibals in Philippe Desan, *Montaigne: A Life*, 155–82. See also Lestringant, *Cannibals*, esp. 94–111, who suggests that the essay should be considered as a literary paradox, akin to Erasmus's *Praise of Folly*: 'Here and there an apparently humorous remark may point to a profound truth. The comic overtones, which are felt, in particular, at the conclusion of the essay, are intended to put the reader in a questioning frame of mind' (95).
12. Greenblatt, 'Shakespeare's Montaigne', in *Shakespeare's Montaigne*, ix–xxxiii, p. xxviii.
13. Greenblatt, 'Shakespeare's Montaigne', xxviii. Jean-Marie Maguin, in his '*The Tempest* and Cultural Exchange', is less severe: 'The confrontation between Shakespeare and Montaigne, as I see it, is anything but a head-on collision. It is rather in the nature of an abrasion of Montaigne's philosophy by Shakespeare concerning the point of knowing whether the savages' existence is perfect or not. At first sight, we might have thought primarily of Gonzalo as a man hopelessly exposed, a sort of *enfant perdu* shot at by his own camp. . . . Instead we discover that Gonzalo is, practically speaking, a mask from behind which Shakespeare is vigorously teasing Montaigne for his radicalism' (153).
14. Fred Parker captures the ambivalence beautifully in his 'Shakespeare's Argument with Montaigne': 'The real interest of the comparison [between 'Of the Caniballes' and *The Tempest* passage] lies, however, in the divergence it reveals. For the Montaignean vision of radical naturalness, of unaccommodated man, both fascinates certain of Shakespeare's characters, and generates a kind of recoil. Thoughts which Montaigne embraces as salutary and humane, as fostering a profound toleration of the nature of human life, become in their Shakespearean context radically destabilizing, markers of an intolerable distress, often associated with cynicism or disgust. . . . Shakespeare translates Montaigne's vision sympathetically, in that he gives it to the good Gonzalo, but also exposes it to sceptical voices. The result is an unstable ambivalence' (3).

15. Quint, *Montaigne and the Quality of Mercy*, 99. The chapter on 'Of the Caniballes' was originally published as 'A Reconsideration of Montaigne's *Des Cannibales*'. See also Cavell, *Disowning Knowledge*: 'How do we learn that what we need is not more knowledge but the willingness to forgo knowing?' (95).
16. See Reiss, 'Montaigne, the New World, and Precolonialisms', who compares the two pieces as follows: 'And, as in "Of cannibals", right after explaining the need for the simplest sensible knowing of direct experience, he turns to Americans' (207).
17. Ginzburg, 'Montaigne, Cannibals, and Grottoes', 35.
18. Cotgrave, *A Dictionarie of the French and English Tongves*, n.p.
19. See de Certeau, 'Montaigne's "Of Cannibals"': 'What Montaigne ponders in this essay is precisely the status of the strange: Who is "barbarian"? What is "savage"? In short, what is the place of the other?' (67). In his 'The *Essays* and the New World', Tom Conley has similarly noted, 'Montaigne writes in a manner that welcomes the arrival of the "other", of the native inhabitants of the Americas, in a context where they would otherwise be estranged' (77). More recently, Timothy Reiss has seen Montaigne's interest in 'Americans' as primarily about self-definition: 'No reader, I think, has seen in Montaigne's paean further self-appraisal, less of his critical thinking than of being, as if imagining not alterity but real others were basic to knowing oneself, explicitly *not* as another' ('Montaigne, the New World, and Precolonialisms', 197).
20. Carlo Ginzburg has noted that Montaigne shifts from using a 'purely relative meaning of *barbarous*' to one with a 'negative connotation. Given that we, civilized people, are more cruel than cannibals, we are the true barbarians' (52).
21. Quint, *Montaigne and the Quality of Mercy*, 78.
22. See John O'Brien, 'A Fantasy of Justice': 'In particular, of course, Montaigne uses the polyvalence of the term 'barbarie' in order to highlight the barbarity of the French Wars of Religion – the real cannibals are already in France, not outside it' (254). See also Todorov, 'L'Etre et L'Autre: Montaigne': 'Montaigne would like to have his cake and eat it too; barbarism does not exist, and besides we are more barbarous than the others. The polysemy of the word is the price of such a paradoxical position' (126).
23. Quint, *Montaigne and the Quality of Mercy*, 85. See also Hartle, *Michel de Montaigne*: 'Montaigne describes the life of the cannibals' captive: he is treated well so as to make his life more dear to him and he is constantly threatened with his approaching horrible death, all for the purpose of making him show terror, of forcing him to acknowledge that his heart and his will have been subdued. And the act of cannibalism is not, as is often thought, for the sake of nourishment, but rather to manifest an extreme vengeance. So, in some ways, the cannibals are just as bad as we are, and nature is not sweet, innocent, and gentle' (45).

24. Quint's helpful contribution is to show that Montaigne disapproves of aspects of cannibal culture for the same reason that he disapproves of aspects of classical Roman culture: 'At the center of both the Brazilian and Roman cultures is a ritualized spectacle of bravery – is it the means or the end, the true raison d'être, of their warfare? The defeated cannibal and gladiator demonstrate their refusal to give in to their conquerors or to the prospect of death. . . . In 'Des cannibales', Montaigne further demonstrates the wider political consequences of this culture by attributing its Stoic postures and martial values to the cannibals and by observing how they turn the cannibals' otherwise idyllic existence into a constant state of warfare and revenge. Montaigne depicts the cannibals as perfect Stoics, so perfect that they call Stoicism itself into question' (*Montaigne and the Quality of Mercy*, 88–9).
25. Quint, *Montaigne and the Quality of Mercy*, 94.
26. O'Brien, 'A Fantasy of Justice', 254. 'The superabundant fertility of the New World that Montaigne highlights earlier in "Des Cannibales" is not a neutral description of a natural state; rather, it passes judgement on the inequalities of the Old World, in the same way that the lack of division of New World goods condemns Occidental distributions, however secured in the judicial system. The premises of Western equity are thereby questioned and their inadequacies revealed . . .' (257).
27. Most scholars now agree that the encounter happened in Bordeaux in 1565. See Desan, *Montaigne: A Life*, 155–82, esp. 167–75, and Reiss, 'Montaigne, the New World, and Precolonialisms', 207n46, 214. Elizabeth Guild, in her chapter on 'Des Cannibales' in *Unsettling Montaigne*, still assumes the meeting happened in Rouen in 1562. She also provides several reasons why this date would matter to Montaigne and his first readers, including the publication that year of Henri Estienne's Latin translation of Sextus Empiricus's *Hypotyposes* (*Outlines of Pyrrhonism*) and the death a year later of Montaigne's beloved Etienne de La Boétie, whose *De la servitude volontaire* she sees resonating with the ideas of Montaigne's essay.
28. Hoffmann, 'Anatomy of the Mass', has provocatively suggested that the forgotten – repressed? suppressed? – third term is religion. Antoine Compagnon, in his *A Summer with Montaigne*, claims the third topic is 'transubstantiation' (95).
29. See Duval, 'Lessons of the New World': 'What makes the interpreter inadequate is precisely what made the eyewitness so reliable. But the natural quality that had previously been given a positive value in the word "*simple*" is now condemned as *bestise* ['stupidity'], and the mental activity that had previously been condemned in "*fines gens*" as "*inventions fauces*" (205 [152]) is now presented in a more favorable light as "*mes imaginations*"' (101).
30. See Quint, *Montaigne and the Quality of Mercy*: 'Montaigne, the real-life negotiator between Catholic and Protestant forces, asserts that it takes more, not less, courage to yield, to seek compromise and dialogue with

one's adversary rather than dominate or be dominated. The desire for conquest that the *Essais* show to be identical with a desire for self-destruction in the stoical martyr, the tyrant, the man of honour is, in fact, Montaigne claims, the product of a pathological fear of mortality. Even more, it is a fear of living itself' (xv).

31. See Duval, 'Lessons of the New World': '"Art" and "nature" can be as slippery and mutable as "barbare" and "sauvage" as criteria for judging the Old World, the New World, or any world at all' (103). See also Guild: 'Historicized, the erstwhile symbolic cannibal is a means of problematizing the reader's desire for the full knowledge associated both with supposed symbolic universalism and with the turning to a supposed site of origins or pure truth. . . . Montaigne plays with the potential of the cannibal to function as a figure of the truth (as in the earlier part of the chapter) to put, now, instead, other truths, plural, into circulation and to encourage us to question our desire for there to be a locus of truth. Here we shall be left to find a way to enjoy more partial and contingent understanding' (*Unsettling Montaigne*, 43, 67).
32. Go, 'Montaigne's "Cannibals" and *The Tempest* Revisited', 457.
33. See especially, Orgel, Introduction, *The Tempest*, 31–6; Skura, 'Discourse and the Individual'; and Kastan, '"The Duke of Milan / And His Brave Son"'.
34. The mention of islands in Montaigne's essay certainly struck Edmond Malone as relevant to *The Tempest*: 'Whoever shall take the trouble to turn to the old translation here quoted, will, I think, be of the opinion that, in whatsoever novel our author might have found the *fable* of *the Tempest*, he was led by the perusa[l] of this book to make the *scene* of it an unfrequented island' (*The Plays and Poems of William Shakespeare*, vol. 1, part 2, pp. 38–9).
35. Go, 'Montaigne's "Cannibals" and *The Tempest* Revisited', 457.
36. See Paster, who convincingly links the Dido reference to 'Of Diverting or Diversion' (3.4) but strangely does not draw on the reference to Carthage in 'Of the Caniballes'.
37. See Orgel's claim in his edition of *The Tempest* that 'No Shakespeare play calls for more music, and of more various kinds, than *The Tempest*' (220). See also Lindley, *Shakespeare and Music*, esp. 218–33; Duffin, *Shakespeare's Songbook*; and Kott, *The Bottom Translation*, 93–102.
38. Reiss, 'Montaigne, the New World, and Precolonialisms', sees the songs as a place of potential communality between cultures: 'These songs fit easily into European traditions, and could be ready sites of exchange' (214). See also Hendrick, 'Montaigne, Florio, and Shakespeare', who attributes the emphasis on a cultured sense of the cannibals more to Florio than to Montaigne: 'Florio is more concerned with the aesthetic, stylistic nature of his text, even if in the process he creates a more refined and polished image of the natives than had appeared in the French text which he was translating' (124).
39. See Fiedler, *The Stranger in Shakespeare*: 'There is, moreover, a kind of music in Caliban's speech, one is tempted to say a "natural rhythm", quite

remote from Shylock's tone; for the Jew is postulated as an enemy of all sweet sound, whereas the New World savage is a singer of songs and a maker of poems, especially when he remembers the virginal world he inhabited before the coming of patriarchal power' (235).

40. Although he is much quicker to judge Caliban and praise Prospero than I am, Gilbert does make the important link between the beautiful 3.2 speech of Caliban and the songs of Montaigne's cannibals (362).
41. Orgel, 'Shakespeare and the Cannibals', 42.
42. 'Country footing' is rustic dancing. But the pun on 'cunt' – see Hamlet's 'Do you think I meant country matters?' (*Hamlet*, 3.2.105) – is almost surely present here as well. For a cautionary tale on finding obscenity in 'country matters' – and thus in 'country footing', I imagine – see Lesser, *Hamlet After Q1*, 72–113.
43. Orgel, 'Shakespeare and the Cannibals', 66.
44. Edmund Malone was perhaps the first to link Florio's Montaigne to Shakespeare's Caliban, just as he was the first to link Florio's Montaigne to the Gonzalo passage in *The Tempest*, though he gives 'Dr Farmer' credit for the Canibal/Caliban link: 'The title of the chapter, which is – *"Of the Canniballes"*, evidently furnished him with the name of one of his characters. In his time almost every proper name was twisted into an anagram. Thus, *"I moyl in law,"* was the anagram of the laborious William Noy, Attorney General to Charles I. By inverting this process, and transposing the letters of the word *Canibal*, Shakespeare (as Dr Farmer long since observed) formed the name of *Caliban*' (*The Plays and Poems of William Shakespeare*, vol. 1, part 2, p. 39). See also Go, 'Montaigne's "Cannibals" and *The Tempest* Revisited', who notes that 'no fewer than ten out of its [the *OED*'s] twelve earliest citations ranging between 1553 and 1607 are spelled with a single *n*, of which six are spelled "Canibals"' (468).
45. See Orgel, 'Shakespeare and the Cannibals': 'Caliban has almost nothing in common with the prelapsarian savages described by Montaigne' (54).
46. See Guild, *Unsettling Montaigne*: 'But the cannibal of Montaigne's famous chapter is not barbaric, and also exposes how much greater is "our own" barbarism. He is nonetheless a cannibal: this ambiguity acts to maximize the unsettling interpretative openness and challenge to habits of thought of this – ambiguously – figurative and existent other. Montaigne's unbarbaric cannibal unsettles the discourse of barbarism used so aggressively at the time' (32).
47. Compare Desan, *Montaigne: A Life*: 'the outside observer can only give his *impressions* of these societies. Montaigne maintains the critical distance that relativizes his assessments of these peoples. Description is ephemeral, an exercise – or an "essay" – that has to be constantly repeated when talking about others. "There are peoples where . . ." remains an unfinished painting, always waiting for another brushstroke, another touch, a new example. The Cannibal is permanently under construction' (158).

48. Vaughan and Vaughan, *Shakespeare's Caliban*, xv. Jan Kott, *The Bottom Translation*, connects Caliban's 'hybrid nature' to doubleness everywhere in *The Tempest*. Caliban's monstrosity, Prospero's magic, and the island's being 'simultaneously a Mediterranean island of metamorphosis and penitence and a new plantation of the coast of America' are all part of its 'mythical code'. Drawing on Edmund Leach, Kott sees these elements of the play, as 'in every myth system', mediating 'the paired categories .... Mediation (in this sense) is always achieved by introducing a third category which is abnormal or anomalous in terms of ordinary rational categories' (70, 74; see Edmund Leach, *Genesis as Myth and Other Essays*, 11).
49. Holbrook, *Shakespeare's Individualism*, 208.
50. Drawing on the Cuban critic Roberto Fernández Retamar, Edward Said argues, in his *Culture and Imperialism*, that 'it is Caliban himself, and not Ariel, who is the main symbol of hybridity, with his strange and unpredictable mixture of attributes. This is truer to the Creole, or *mestizo* composite of the new America' (213).
51. I have explored some of these ideas in a different context in my *Shakespeare and the Culture of Paradox*, 202–3.
52. Based in the Latin *monstrare* (to show), monsters were thought to point to and de*monstrate* aspects of the world that would otherwise be unknown. Isidore of Seville famously noted that monsters and portents do not 'arise contrary to nature but contrary to what nature is understood to be'. Isidore of Seville, *Etymologiae* 11.3.1–2; cited in Williams, *Deformed Discourse*, 13. See also Vaughan and Vaughan, *Shakespeare's Caliban*: '"monster" appears in the text some forty times, usually with a pejorative adjective: "shallow", "weak", "credulous", "most perfidious and drunken", "puppy-headed", "scurvy", "abominable", "ridiculous", "howling", "ignorant", and "lost". Only "brave", used twice, might be a favourable modifier, and it is almost certainly meant sarcastically. More neutral are "servant-monster", "man-monster", "lieutenant-monster", and "poor monster". To the extent that "monster" implies physical deformity, as it did generally but not exclusively in Shakespeare's time, these abundant reminders strengthen the notion of Caliban as grotesque. They do nothing, however, to specify the deformity. Nor does Alonso's quip that "This is a strange thing as e'er I looked on" (V.i.289). The text tells us that Caliban had long nails to dig pignuts (II.ii.162); otherwise his physical deformities are unspecified' (14).
53. See Greenblatt, Introduction to *The Tempest*, The Norton Shakespeare, second edition: 'The words need only be a claim of ownership, but they seem to hint at a deeper, more disturbing link between father and monster, legitimate ruler and savage, judge and criminal' (3061).
54. Part of Prospero's yielding is his willingness to forgive, especially Antonio and Caliban. See de Gooyer, '"Their Senses I'll Restore"': 'Insofar as we see Prospero's forgiveness as tied to the difficult acceptance of his own mortal condition, we can perhaps see Shakespeare giving dramatic substance to another important theme of Montaigne's.... [T]hey both recognize at the

end that old age will . . . mortify us with our most human limitations. And they both beg for its indulgence' (528).

55. See Lestringant, who considers '"Of Cannibals" . . . an essay in the most literal sense of the word, an experiment, both playful and rigorous, in the exercise of a shocking degree of freedom' (*Cannibals*, 99). Hendrick, again, suggests that the ambivalence may come from Shakespeare's negotiations not directly with Montaigne but instead with *Florio's* Montaigne: 'Florio continues to interpret the situation from his own perspective, that of the European considering the strangeness of the barbarians. . . . [T]he translation of *Des Cannibales* betrays, in some sections, elements of colonial discourse, whether implied or explicit, and . . . these elements were not present in the original French text. . . . [W]e may reasonably argue that the discourse of colonialism in *The Tempest* does not derive directly from *Des Cannibales*, which is one of the great anti-colonial texts of literature, but that it may well adopt some of the perceptions and attitudes that find their expression in Florio's translation' ('Montaigne, Florio, and Shakespeare', 132; 133).

56. See the fascinating recent take on the collapse of the nature/culture binary by John Kerrigan, who – in his '*The Tempest* to 1756', from *Shakespeare's Originality* – sees the two writers' shared focus on *both* unadorned nature *and* the positive aspects of agriculture as deriving from a mutual engagement with Virgil's *Georgics*: 'It is as though natural fecundity and the life of man within it cannot be thought about for Montaigne without a georgic dimension. Much the same . . . could be said of *The Tempest*' (88–9). See also Ramachandran, *The Worldmakers*: 'Montaigne thus plays a double-edged game: his essay dwells on the essential otherness of the New World, as European rhetoric typically presented it, even as it works to undermine those assumptions of distance and difference. Because Europeans do not fully understand the futility of drawing absolute ontological distinctions between self and other, New and Old Worlds, Catholic and Huguenot, they are locked in violent battles that stem from their desire to assert radical difference where there is none' (85).

57. Reiss, 'Montaigne, the New World, and Precolonialisms', argues that Montaigne invokes the Americans to show 'the reality that we are all one under the skin, and that we should act accordingly. Doff clothes and custom and we can no longer talk of "others" (far less Others). . . . The infinite variety in and of our reason and its constant inconstancy is the essence of humanity' (207). In the end, though, Europeans 'stop any communal dialogue of equals in its tracks, establishing in its place barbarous destruction of difference' (214).

58. See Reiss, 'Montaigne, the New World, and Precolonialisms': Montaigne gave the Americans a 'local habitation and a voice', but they were 'by no means always "noble": they also sacrifice humans, fight bloody wars, and gratify evil customs' (200). Jan Kott, drawing on Erwin Panofsky, also sees an inescapable dualism at work in *The Tempest*'s approach to nature

more generally: 'These two Arcadias, the idyllic and the barbaric, are both notions of "nature" in a pure state' (*The Bottom Translation*, 81).

59. In his 'Eating Montaigne', Paul Yachnin also links rather than separates the two writers: 'Montaigne helped induct Shakespeare and afterwards generations of Shakespeare's readers into an experience of reading as a form of incorporation and communion and also helped make the play a valuable source-text. Is there any work in literature more cannibalized than *The Tempest*? ... [W]e are interested in knowing what the playwright thinks about the essayist, just as we are interested to know what the essayist thinks about Plato, Seneca, Plutarch, and the other writers that he ate' (170–1).

60. Building on de Certeau, Lestringant sees Montaigne's cannibals as being ultimately more about speaking than eating: 'The prisoner's flesh resolves itself into words: defiance, insult or song of death and revenge. This yields not only the true meaning, but also the true purpose of the cannibal exchange. The Brazilian Cannibal is raised to the status of an orator and philosopher, a free and fraternal citizen of a back-to-nature utopia: as such, he no longer provokes horror. By gracing him with an abundance of words, Montaigne ... has successfully cleansed anthropophagy from the stigma of the flesh' (*Cannibals*, 110–11).

61. Montaigne, 'Of the Caniballes', 56; 100; Shakespeare, *The Tempest*, 4.1.154–6. See also a parallel sense of the futility of mastery in Montaigne's other 'new-world' essay, 'Of Coaches' (3.6): 'We go not, but rather creep and stagger here and there; we go our pace. I imagine our knowledge to be weak in all senses: *we neither discern far-forward, nor see much backward*. It embraceth little and liveth not long. It is short, both in extension of time and in ampleness of matter or invention' (291; 543–4).

Epilogue: Shakespeare before the *Essays*

It is fair to ask, after reading this book, what a pre-Montaignian Shakespeare would look like. One could reasonably argue that even in his pre-1603 plays Shakespeare was interested in the mutability of the self; the multiplicity of truth claims and scepticism in a variety of forms; and a fascination with cultural others. There is no question that these interests and patterns were present in Shakespeare's earlier work; indeed, they can be seen as intellectual through-lines of his plays. But I think the difference is that the encounter with Montaigne gave Shakespeare a new set of tools for essaying these issues and changed his approach to them in his later dramas.

If soliloquies are a gauge of inwardness, the pre-1603 soliloquies are less concerned with exploring self-knowledge than they are with getting the soliloquist in touch with the audience, akin to the way the character of the medieval Vice did.[1] For example, in his opening soliloquy, Richard III is much more interested in talking with us – seducing us the way he will seduce Anne in the next scene – than he is in exploring the intricacies of his 'inner life':

> But I, that am not shaped for sportive tricks,
> Nor made to court an amorous looking-glass,
> I that am rudely stamped, and want love's majesty
> To strut before a wanton ambling nymph,
> I that am curtailed of this fair proportion,
> Cheated of feature by dissembling nature,
> Deformed, unfinished, sent before my time
> Into this breathing world scarce half made up,
> And that so lamely and unfashionable
> That dogs bark at me as I halt by them –
> Why, I in this weak piping time of peace,
> Have no delight to pass away the time,
> Unless to spy my shadow in the sun

> And descant on mine own deformity:
> And therefore, since I cannot prove a lover,
> To entertain these fair well-spoken days,
> I am determinèd to prove a villain
> And hate the idle pleasures of these days.²

There is a cynical self-knowledge here but not a questing one, and Richard wants us to align ourselves with his 'unfashionable' self and pity his being 'Cheated of feature by dissembling nature' and reduced to 'descant[ing] on [his] own deformity'.

Contrast this speech with those speeches of Iago, a later, post-1603 creation whose roots are also often traced to the medieval Vice. Iago is cynical, too, but his cynicism directly addresses the problem of knowledge of a self – and of self-knowledge. In a private speech to Roderigo, Iago admits that he is not knowable:

> In following him I follow but myself.
> Heaven is my judge, not I for love and duty,
> But seeming so for my peculiar end.
> For when my outward action doth demonstrate
> The native act and figure of my heart
> In compliment extern, 'tis not long after
> But I will wear my heart upon my sleeve
> For daws to peck at. I am not what I am. (1.1.58–65)

What Iago seems is not what he is; further, he *is not* what he is.

Iago also highlights the instability of the self because he can make and unmake not only himself but others. We find out in an Act Two soliloquy that Iago is confident that he can use Desdemona's goodness against her and re-make her into someone who seems evil:

>   Divinity of hell:
> When devils will the blackest sins put on,
> They do suggest at first with heavenly shows,
> As I do now; for whiles this honest fool
> Plies Desdemona to repair his fortune,
> And she for him pleads strongly to the Moor,
> I'll pour this pestilence into his ear:
> That she repeals him for her body's lust,
> And by how much she strives to do him good
> She shall undo her credit with the Moor.
> So will I turn her virtue into pitch,
> And out of her own goodness make the net
> That shall enmesh them all. (2.3.224–36)

He turns Desdemona's attempt 'to do him [Cassio] good' into her undoing. Earlier in the speech, Iago has mentioned that Othello's love for Desdemona is such 'That she may make, unmake, do what she list' (320). It is the fluidity of the self – his self, other selves – that Iago manipulates to his advantage in *Othello*.

Other Shakespearean characters have meditated on this problem, and some of them were in pre-1603 plays. Richard II, imprisoned late in Act 5, has learned that he is not one self but many selves:

> Thus play I in one person many people,
> And none contented. Sometimes am I king;
> Then treasons make me wish myself a beggar,
> And so I am. Then crushing penury
> Persuades me I was better when a king.
> Then am I kinged again, and by and by
> Think that I am unkinged by Bolingbroke,
> And straight am nothing. But whate'er I be,
> Nor I nor any man that but man is
> With nothing shall be pleased till he be eased
> With being nothing. (5.5.31–41)

There is no doubt that this speech interrogates both the multiplicity and the instability of selves. Using the theatrical metaphor, Richard notes that a self is not something solid but something that is played, acted, performed. And he, like Iago later, also uses negations to highlight the mutability: 'kinged ... unkinged', 'Nor I nor any man', 'nothing'. So the Montaignian Shakespeare by no means has a monopoly on self-conscious meditations on the self-in-flux.

But I maintain that there is something different in Hamlet's and Antony's meditations on the complexities of selfhood – both noted earlier in this book. Hamlet is especially intriguing because his famous, self-conscious 'To be or not to be' soliloquy is so very different in its pre-Montaignian, Q1 form. As I explored extensively in Chapter 2, there is by no means critical consensus on the Q1 *Hamlet* being a Shakespearean first draft. But two elements from the famous soliloquy are interesting if we posit a post-Montaignian revision. First, the often mocked first line of the Q1 speech – 'To be, or not to be, I there's the point' – is changed to foreground the questing after the meaning of being that has led so many to assume that *Hamlet* is a Montaignian play: 'To be, or not to be, that is the Question' [F spelling]. Second, utterly absent from Q1 are the five lines that close the speech and that highlight the tension between thought and action:

> And thus the native hue of resolution
> Is sicklied o'er with the pale cast of thought,
> And enterprises of great pith and moment
> With this regard their currents turn awry,
> And lose the name of action. (3.1.86–90)

This addition deepens the speech and turns it from one primarily about suicide to one about the potentially killing properties of thought, intellect, and philosophy: thinking makes one pale and sickly and saps the life out of the 'native hue of resolution', forcing one to 'lose the name of action'.³ Instead of leading to self-knowledge, 'thought' can lead to an alteration – even a figurative annihilation – of self. Montaigne's *Essays* are full of just such warnings, as Montaigne often cautions against the very philosophical, thought-ful practice he is employing.⁴

As we briefly explored in Chapter 1, Antony's meditations on the instability of the self are technically not part of a soliloquy – *Antony and Cleopatra* has very few such solo speeches – but the extreme nature of his portrayal of the insubstantial self reveals how different his perspective is from that of Richard II. For Antony goes beyond the sense of the self as a performance, portraying it as something akin to vapours. Discussing cloud formations with Eros, he claims, 'That which is now a horse even with a thought / The rack distains, and makes it indistinct / As water is in water' (4.15.9–11). These dissolving clouds are Antony: 'My good knave Eros, now thy captain is / Even such a body. Here I am Antony, / Yet cannot hold this visible shape, my knave' (4.15.12–14). Whereas Richard imagined his flux as that between a king and a beggar, or between something and nothing, Antony imagines a once-strong, discernible self that 'cannot hold this visible shape', becoming 'as water is in water'. Or, as Montaigne would have it, 'We have no communication with being, for every human nature is ever in the middle between being born and dying, giving nothing of itself but an obscure appearance and shadow, and an uncertain and weak opinion. And if perhaps you fix your thought to take its being, it would be even as if one should go about to [grasp] the water: for how much the more he shall close and press that which by its own nature is ever gliding, so much the more he shall lose what he would hold and fasten.'⁵

Just as Shakespeare explored the multiplicity of the self in his earlier plays, Shakespeare's Montaignian plays are not the only ones to evince scepticism, to worry about the limitations of human knowledge. As in the case of the self, though, I would argue that the post-1603 meditations are more overt, self-conscious, and central. The case of a very early Shakespearean comedy, *The Comedy of Errors*, is instructive. A sceptical approach to the world is certainly revealed, especially by the Syracusan Antipholus and Dromio when they arrive in Ephesus and encounter its seeming mysteries. Antipholus notes that

> They say this town is full of cozenage,
> As nimble jugglers that deceive the eye,
> Dark-working sorcerers that change the mind,
> Soul-killing witches that deform the body,
> Disguisèd cheaters, prating mountebanks,
> And many such-like liberties of sin. (1.2.97–102)

When the characters encounter the inexplicable, the default position is to blame witches – and their fraudulent counterparts, 'jugglers' and 'mountebanks'. Later in the play, the critique of this same group is expanded to include exorcists, and Dr Pinch is most certainly mocked as a fraudulent example of this profession. There is no question, then, that this approach to scepticism – encountering doubt and resolving it by recourse to magic, witchcraft, demonism, and exorcism – is one that we are mostly supposed to laugh with and at. Indeed, Shakespeare seems to let us in on the joke, replacing one kind of scepticism with another, taking a position that Richard Strier calls 'totally skeptical about witchcraft, about demonic possession as an account of madness, and about exorcism. What is needed in *Errors* is neither faith nor ritual but ordinary common sense.'[6] In later plays, Shakespeare will certainly deepen his examination of what happens when characters encounter the ineffable. But even here, I would argue, are the seeds of the later plays' warnings: there are more things in heaven and earth than are dreamt of in our cynical, withering, sceptical philosophy.[7] We laugh at the characters in *Errors* – and their attempts to sort out their world – at our peril.[8]

And this is where Montaigne comes in, giving Shakespeare tools that allowed him to deepen his exploration of scepticism – showing the limitations of both too much credulity and too much doubt. Will Hamlin's formulation is extremely helpful here: 'I propose that total scepticism amounts to casting doubt not only towards credulous assumptions but towards rational attempts to dismiss them . . . ; we must not too hastily equate scepticism with sustained ratiocination.'[9] The key-text for this resistance to both extreme credulity and extreme doubt is Montaigne's 'It is Follie to Referre Truth or Falsehood to Our Sufficiencie' (1.27, 1.26):

> We must judge of this infinite power of nature with more reverence and with more acknowledgement of our own ignorance and weakness. How many things of small likelihood are there, witnessed by men, worthy of credit

whereof if we cannot be persuaded, we should at least leave them in suspense? For to deem them impossible is by rash presumption to presume and know how far possibility reacheth. (36; 88)

It is rash to presume that we can 'know how far possibility reacheth'. Montaigne and Shakespeare share this conception of knowledge and of doubt.[10]

Warnings against this kind of rashness are present throughout the canon, but they get foregrounded when Shakespeare essays Montaigne. As we have seen in Chapter 3, *All's Well*'s Helena reminds herself that, just because something has not happened yet does not mean that it cannot happen: 'Impossible be strange attempts to those / That weigh their pains in sense and do suppose / What hath been cannot be' (1.1.207–9). And when Helena is able to cure the king after the wise doctors of France have failed to do so, Lafeu sounds like someone who has just put down his copy of 'It is Follie': 'They say that miracles are past, and we have our philosophical persons to make modern and familiar things supernatural and causeless. Hence it is that we make trifles of terrors, ensconcing ourselves into seeming knowledge when we should submit ourselves to an unknown fear' (2.3.1–5). It is folly, says Lafeu, to assume that you can turn the 'supernatural and causeless' into something 'modern and familiar'. Significantly, he chides 'philosophical persons' as the ones most likely to attempt to achieve this 'seeming knowledge'.

Shakespeare's very last plays – with their focus on wonder – further resist making trifles of terrors and are founded on the need to embrace unknowing.[11] In *Cymbeline*, King Cymbeline and Posthumus both undergo changes with respect to knowledge and certainty. Once so confident in the banishment of Posthumus and the punishment of his daughter, Imogen, Cymbeline is eventually forced to accept that he does not understand much of what has happened in his life. Shakespeare forces his king into an interrogative mood:

Does the world go round?

* * *

When shall I hear all through? This fierce abridgment
Hath to it circumstantial branches which
Distinction should be rich in. Where? How lived you?
And when came you to serve our Roman captive?
How parted with your brothers? How first met them?
Why fled you from the court? And whither? These,
And your three motives to the battle, with
I know not how much more, should be demanded,

>   And all the other by-dependences,
>   From chance to chance. But nor the time nor place
>   Will serve our long inter'gatories. (5.6.232, 383–93)

Cymbeline knows that he does not know, and knows that he will need more questioning, further 'inter'gatories', to get closer to knowledge.

Posthumus's intellectual journey is slightly different: from certainty to an acceptance of possible unknowns rather than to a need for questions. But the effect is the same: having been vicious in his misogynistic confidence that Imogen had betrayed him, Posthumus displays a new-found patience with unknowing that, had he practised it earlier, might have prevented the (seeming) death of his wife. Reading a tablet left for him by Jupiter late in the play, Posthumus expresses a cognitive humility – a scepticism very different from the nihilistic version revealed in Act 2:

>   'Tis still a dream, or else such stuff as madmen
>   Tongue, and brain not; either both, or nothing,
>   Or senseless speaking, or a speaking such
>   As sense cannot untie. Be what it is,
>   The action of my life is like it, which I'll keep,
>   If but for sympathy. (5.5.238–43)

Posthumus's remarks after reading the tablet reveal his new appreciation for wonder-based scepticism: a questing inquiry – note the four *or*'s – that nonetheless recognises the inevitability of ignorance and uncertainty in the world.

Moving from a similar kind of misogynistic sceptical certainty to a peace with unknowing is *The Winter's Tale*'s Leontes. For the king in this play is certain that his wife, Hermione, has been unfaithful with his best friend, Polixenes. Doubting all whom he loved best, he orders Hermione to stand trial and sends his new-born daughter, Perdita, to death-by-banishment. After the oracle is presented at the trial, clearing all suspects, Leontes initially rejects the divine pronouncement. Immediately afterward we hear news of the death of his son, Mamillius, and Hermione collapses, seemingly in death. No one – including us – has any evidence that Hermione is alive. Leontes chides himself for his error and misplaced certainty: 'I have too much believed mine own suspicion' (3.2.149).

Although neither Mamillius nor Antigonus – eaten by a bear when he was doing Leontes's bidding and removing Perdita from Sicilia – returns from death, both Perdita and Hermione appear sixteen years later, and a comic ending accompanies a different approach to knowledge. Leontes accepts Paulina's dictum that 'It is required / You do awake your faith' (5.3.94–5). And upon seeing the statue of the seeming-dead Hermione come to life, he succumbs to unknowing and – like Cymbeline – goes off stage to ask more questions and gain more knowledge:

> Good Paulina,
> Lead us from hence, where we may leisurely
> Each one demand and answer to his part
> Performed in this wide gap of time since first
> We were dissevered. (5.3.152–6)

Unlike our experience of *The Comedy of Errors* and even *Cymbeline*, we are not in possession of the knowledge that Leontes will gain. Among many things, we do not know how Hermione survived, what was put in her coffin, or why Leontes was able to accept her as dead. We must awake our faith, too, and must embrace a very Montaignian approach to questions and knowledge:

> There is no end in our inquisitions. Our end is in the other world. It is a sign his wits grow short when he is pleased, or a sign of weariness. No generous spirit stays and relies upon himself; he ever pretendeth and goeth beyond his strength. He hath some vagaries beyond his effects. If he advance not himself, press, settle, shock, turn, wind, and front himself, he is but half alive. His pursuits are termless and formless. His nourishment is admiration, questing, and ambiguity. Which *Apollo* declared sufficiently, always speaking ambiguously, obscurely, and obliquely unto us, not feeding, but busying and amusing us. It is an irregular uncertain motion, perpetual, patternless, and without end. His inventions enflame, follow, and interproduce one another. ('Of Experience', 3.13, 321; 635–6)

Like his interests both in the complexity of the self and in scepticism and the limits of knowledge, Shakespeare's concern with the outsider or 'Other' runs throughout his work. But the presentation of this type of character deepens after 1603. Aaron, from the very early *Titus Andronicus*, is not a completely stereotypical stage Moor, but there is a strong sense that Aaron thrives on evil and connects his evil to his blackness:

> O, how this villainy
> Doth fat me with the very thoughts of it!
> Let fools do good, and fair men call for grace:
> Aaron will have his soul black like his face. (3.1.201–4)

And Aaron does not repent in the slightest; indeed, the only regrets he claims to have are based in not committing more evil deeds and in potentially committing 'one good deed':

> Ah, why should wrath be mute and fury dumb?
> I am no baby, I, that with base prayers
> I should repent the evils I have done.
> Ten thousand worse than ever yet I did
> Would I perform, if I might have my will.
> If one good deed in all my life I did
> I do repent it from my very soul. (5.3.183–9)

Yet Shakespeare, even in this early play, gives a sense of what he will more fully realise later: a cultural outsider who brings a different perspective to the views of the dominant culture. After Tamora has become Empress and has given birth to an illegitimate child with Aaron, the Nurse brings the black baby to Aaron so that he can kill his offspring. Instead, Aaron praises the child for the very blackness that horrifies Tamora, her sons, and the Nurse:

> What, what, ye sanguine, shallow-hearted boys,
> Ye whitelimed walls, ye alehouse painted signs,
> Coal-black is better than another hue,
> In that it scorns to bear another hue;
> For all the water in the ocean
> Can never turn the swan's black legs to white,
> Although she lave them hourly in the flood.
> Tell the empress from me, I am of age
> To keep mine own, excuse it how she can.

* * *

> Why, there's the privilege your beauty bears:
> Fie, treacherous hue, that will betray with blushing
> The close enacts and counsels of the heart!
> Here's a young lad framed of another leer.
> Look, how the black slave smiles upon the father,
> As who should say 'Old lad, I am thine own.'
> He is your brother, lords, sensibly fed
> Of that self-blood that first gave life to you,
> And from that womb where you imprisoned were
> He is enfranchisèd and come to light.
> Nay, he is your brother by the surer side,
> Although my seal be stampèd in his face. (4.2.96–104, 115–26)

Aaron challenges the supremacy of the white face, calling attention to its ability both to be changeable and to blush and give itself away. Blackness, from Aaron's perspective, is the colour of stability and courage. Although Shakespeare ultimately does not let Aaron transcend his stereotype, there are hints here of the more powerful outsider critics to come – those who destabilise the assumptions of the natural and normative in the dominant society.

Shylock is another such critic of his culture who both provides an alternative perspective on Venice and is subject to its – and arguably the play's – prejudices. Shylock has been abused by Antonio and others in the past, and we see him abused in this play. But Shakespeare does not let Shylock – or arguably himself – off the hook, either; Shylock reacts to his daughter, Jessica's departure by focusing as much on lost ducats as on lost daughter, even saying, 'I would my daughter were dead at my foot and the jewels in her ear!' (3.1.74–5). The daughter/ducat tension is developed further later in the scene:

> **Tubal:** Your daughter spent in Genoa, as I heard, one night four score ducats.
> **Shylock:** Thou stick'st a dagger in me. I shall never see my gold again. Fourscore ducats at a sitting? Fourscore ducats?

Shylock goes on to find comfort in the potential financial ruin of Antonio, when he also gets news from Tubal that Antonio 'hath an argosy cast away coming from Tripolis' and 'There came divers of Antonio's creditors that swear he cannot choose but break' (3.1.85, 94–5). In his seeming privileging of ducats over daughter and his glee at Antonio's misfortune – 'I am very glad of it. I'll plague him, I'll torture him. I am glad of it' (3.1.96–7) – we are shown Shylock at his worst.

But this is the same scene that ends with Shylock's tender reminiscences of his dead wife Leah. When he hears from Tubal that Jessica has exchanged a ring of his for a monkey, Shylock responds, 'It was my turquoise. I had it of Leah when I was a bachelor. I would not have given it for a wilderness of monkeys' (3.1.100–2). And, of course, this is the scene that both presents Shylock at his most humane and reveals his take on the hypocrisy of his Christian colleagues:

> He hath disgraced me, and
> hindered me half a million; laughed at my losses,
> mocked at my gains, scorned my nation, thwarted my
> bargains, cooled my friends, heated mine
> enemies; and what's his reason? – I am a Jew. Hath

> not a Jew eyes? Hath not a Jew hands, organs,
> dimensions, senses, affections, passions; fed with
> the same food, hurt with the same weapons, subject
> to the same diseases, healed by the same means,
> warmed and cooled by the same winter and summer, as
> a Christian is? If you prick us, do we not bleed?
> If you tickle us, do we not laugh? If you poison
> us, do we not die? And if you wrong us, shall we not
> revenge? If we are like you in the rest, we will
> resemble you in that. If a Jew wrong a Christian,
> what is his humility? Revenge. If a Christian
> wrong a Jew, what should his sufferance be by
> Christian example? Why, revenge. The villainy you
> teach me, I will execute, and it shall go hard but I
> will better the instruction. (3.1.46–61)

Although the Christians fancy themselves the merciful ones, Shylock shows that they have, in fact, taught him a vengeful 'villainy' that he will try to outdo by bettering their 'instruction'. The speech begins with a somewhat tender universalism and ends with a bitter one: everyone bleeds, laughs, and dies, but everyone also returns a wrong with revenge. Through Shylock, Shakespeare destroys the sense of a strict Christian/Jewish, Mercy/Revenge binary, troubling expectations and assumptions.

This paradoxical – literally, challenging the *doxa* or received teachings – and binary-busting approach is characteristic of Shakespeare's Others. We have seen in Chapter 5 how Caliban extends and deepens this tendency, and I hope there is little doubt that Montaigne shaped both Shakespeare's 'canibal' and *The Tempest* as a whole. But another post-Montaignian outsider who is shaped by Montaigne is Cleopatra. Even more than Caliban – and certainly more than Aaron and Shylock – Cleopatra and her perspectives seem more celebrated than condemned by the play (if not necessarily by the characters in it).

There are, of course, plenty of anti-Cleopatra and anti-Egyptian sentiments expressed by the play's Roman characters. In the very first scene, Philo refers to Antony's 'devotion' to 'a tawny front' and his becoming 'the fan / To cool a gipsy's lust' (1.1.5, 6, 9–10). Shakespeare's Rome is masculine, single-minded, rational, and constant, then, while his Egypt is feminine (or emasculated); multiple and ambiguous; sensual and passionate; and mutable and shifting. Again, it is important to remember that most of the misogyny directed towards Cleopatra and Egypt comes via the largely unsympathetic Romans, whose world most – in the play and in the audience – are happy to leave for Egypt.

The counter-view of Egypt is presented not only by Cleopatra and her attendants but also by one of the most cynical Romans, Enobarbus. Responding to his compatriots' requests for details of Cleopatra, Enobarbus eschews a detailed description of feasting and focuses instead on Cleopatra's first appearance in front of Antony at Cydnus, which he describes as a multi-sensual performance of aesthetic beauty and marvellous creations. Significantly, Cleopatra is portrayed not as Nature – as Shakespearean Others often are and to some degree Caliban is – but as a triumphant artist: Cleopatra is described as 'O'er-picturing that Venus where we see / The fancy outwork nature' (2.7.206–7). At first glance, Enobarbus would seem to suggest that she tops fancy and art; she is better than the imaginative creation of Venus that 'outwork[ed] nature'. But Shakespeare cleverly troubles this seeming triumph of – and link of Cleopatra to – nature by having Enobarbus's verb form of victory be 'o'er-picturing'. The blurring of art and nature is clear, and this is a very Montaignian move – both, as we have seen, in 'Of the Caniballes' and in the *Essays* in general:

> They are even savage, as we call those fruits wild, which nature of herself and her ordinary progress hath produced. Whereas indeed they are those which ourselves have altered by our artificial devices and diverted from their common order we should rather term savage. . . . And if notwithstanding, in diverse fruits of those countries that were never tilled, we shall find that in respect of ours they are most excellent and as delicate unto our taste, there is no reason art should gain the point of honour of our great and puissant mother Nature. We have so much, by our inventions, surcharged the beauties and riches of her works that we have altogether over-choked her. Yet wherever her purity shineth, she makes our vain and frivolous enterprises wonderfully ashamed. ('Of the Caniballes' [1.31, 1.30], 60; 101–2)

This blurring of art and nature comes back late in the play, when Cleopatra is recounting her dream of the dead Antony to Dolabella. Just as Cleopatra's barge-pageant seemed at first to give nature a hard-fought win over fancy, so Cleopatra wonders whether her Antony might actually reverse the norm:

> Nature wants stuff
> To vie strange forms with fancy; yet t'imagine
> An Antony were nature's piece against fancy,
> Condemning shadows quite. (5.2.98–9)

But just as nature's victory was compromised by 'o'er-pictured' in 2.2, so 'nature's piece against fancy' is mitigated here by 't'imagine'. Both set pieces posit the triumph of nature over 'fancy', imagination, and art, only to suggest that nature is always already artificial and constructed. Shakespeare's Other in *Antony and Cleopatra*, just like that in *The Tempest*, raises the issues of prejudice that we saw with Aaron and Shylock but moves beyond these to meditate on the relationship between artifice and nature, a tension that was crucial to the work of Montaigne. Whether one sees Shakespeare challenging the celebration of the 'natural' cannibal and Other in Montaigne or sharing his forbear's sense of the instability of the natural/artificial binary, Shakespeare's encounter with Montaigne was transformational.

Like his interest in the multiple self and in scepticism, Shakespeare's interest in the outsider is present in his pre-Montaignian plays but gets deepened and expanded after 1603. He read the *Essays* and learned to essay – both Montaigne's writings themselves and the ideas that constantly intrigued him. Finally, I think it is safest to say that – whereas Montaigne did not provide Shakespeare with the topics of discontinuous selfhood, of partial knowledge, and of the cultural Other – Shakespeare's essaying the *Essays* gave him the material with which to challenge his own, and sometimes Montaigne's, ideas about the very nature of the world he scrutinised on stage. To essay human experience is to continue to learn, probe, and try – to be a life-long apprentice and never to resolve: 'There is no end in our inquisitions. Our end is in the other world. . . . If he advance not himself, press, settle, shock, turn, wind, and front himself, he is but half alive. His pursuits are termless and formless.'[12]

Notes

1. See Weimann, *Shakespeare and the Popular Tradition in the Theater*, 112–60, esp. 158–60. Weimann conceives of Richard III as a liminal figure, between 'the traditional convention of vicious [Vice-like] self-expression' and 'a newly mimetic and characterizing function. . . . The dramatic paradox is that Gloucester, *because* he is made to assert the psychological realism of an 'unfashionable' Duke of York, can (out of and beyond the mimetic requirements of a *locus*-oriented royal personage) still assert the ritual heritage of an amoral inversion – even from within the world and the values he both shares and destroys. . . . The first great artistic portrait of a nascently tragic figure as central to the drama develops from a character – the Vice – deeply rooted in the popular tradition and now turned distinctively to a modern representation of reality' (160).
2. Shakespeare, *Richard III*, 1.1.14–31, in *The Norton Shakespeare*, second edition. Unless otherwise noted, all further citations from the plays of Shakespeare are to this edition and are annotated within the text.

3. See Bruster, *To Be or Not to Be*: 'Q1 is shorter and simpler in its vocabulary, and it is also less dedicated to what we have earlier called "thought". Many of the traditional version's "thought" words (words concerning the intellect, the imagination, and point of view) are missing in Q1. The latter keeps the words **conscience, dream,** and **know** – and even adds <u>sense</u> and two <u>hopes</u> (for **wish**) – but omits the words **mind, question, regard, resolution, respect,** and **thought**. In its substitution of <u>brain</u> for **mind**, in fact, we can see the larger tendency of Q1 to simplify the abstractions it encountered in the traditional soliloquy. A <u>brain</u> is a physical part of the body; **the mind** is a concept' (95). Note, however, that Bruster sees Q1 as a revision of the 'traditional version' and not the other way around; he assumes the 'memorial reconstruction' version of the relationship between Q1 and the standard texts discussed in Chapter 2. I would like instead to posit a post-Montaignian *Hamlet adding* the issues and language of 'thought' to the speech.
4. See Frampton, '"To Be, or Not to Be"', for an extended analysis of how Shakespeare's reading of Montaigne changed the 'To be or not to be' speech.
5. Montaigne, 'An Apologie of Raymond Sebond' (2.12), in *Shakespeare's Montaigne*, ed. Greenblatt and Platt. Where available, quotations from Florio's Montaigne will come from this edition; citations will be included in the text and will list, first, this edition's page number and, second, the page number of *The Essayes, or Morall, Politike and Millitarie Discourses* (1603) (350; 197).
6. Strier, 'Shakespeare and the Skeptics'.
7. In his 'Scepticism in Shakespeare's England', William H. Hamlin deems 'vulgar scepticism' the kind practised by those, like the characters in *The Comedy of Errors*, who respond to the unknown with 'a dogmatic induction, committing what Pierre Charron calls "precipitation of judgement", and therefore abandoning the standard Pyrrhonian thought trajectory' (296).
8. Graham Bradshaw, in his *Shakespeare's Scepticism*, carves out two types of scepticism that he sees operating in Shakespeare's plays: '*dogmatic* scepticism, as represented by the terminal, materialistic nihilism of a Thersites, Iago, or Edmund, and *radical* scepticism, which turns on itself – weighing the human need to affirm values against the inherently problematic nature of all acts of valuing' (39). Though Bradshaw connects the latter type to Montaigne, he also adds that 'Shakespeare's scepticism is radical in this sense, long before there is evidence of his reading Montaigne' (39). Among several interesting examples Bradshaw provides is the contrast between *Midsummer*'s Theseus – whom Bradshaw links to dogmatic scepticism in his speech on reason and imagination in Act 5 – and Hippolyta, whom Bradshaw claims can, unlike Theseus, 'countenance the "strange" and suspend judgment – like the radical sceptic – at that point where certainty is unattainable' (39, 43).

9. Hamlin, *Tragedy and Scepticism in Shakespeare's England*, 134. For a very succinct and helpful survey of the terrain, see Hamlin, 'Scepticism in Shakespeare's England'.
10. Hamlin's two key 'sceptical values' – versions of which were discussed in Chapter 1 – are relevant here: 'the modesty, diffidence and intellectual humility consequent upon recognition of the profound limitations of human perception and reason' and 'coupled with this humiliation of reason and mockery of intellectual hubris is an exhilarating though chastened sense of the liberating possibilities of open-minded enquiry' ('Scepticism in Shakespeare's England', [300]). See also his 'What Did Montaigne's Skepticism Mean to Shakespeare and His Contemporaries?': '[Skepticism] was an antidote rather than a substitute for dogmatism; it promoted the avoidance of rash judgment and a heightened sensitivity to epistemological questions, distinctions, and anxieties. . . . [W]hat attracts him to both the Pyrrhonian and Academic outlooks is their common utility in combating intolerance, fanaticism, closed-mindedness, and dogmatic pronouncement' (199, 209).
11. See Platt, *Reason Diminished*.
12. On the influence of Montaigne on Shakespeare, see Anzai, *Shakespeare and Montaigne Reconsidered*: 'the consequence will be the most fruitful kind of influence: the actualization of potentiality already latent in the receiver's mind awaiting the impact as, so to speak, an ignition or catalyst' (85).

Works Cited

Anzai, Tetsuo, *Shakespeare and Montaigne Reconsidered* (Tokyo: The Renaissance Institute, 1986).
Aristotle, *The Complete Works of Aristotle*, Revised Oxford Translation, ed. Jonathan Barnes, 2 vols (Princeton: Princeton University Press, 1984).
Auerbach, Eric, 'Montaigne the Writer', in *Time, History, and Literature: Selected Essays of Erich Auerbach*, edited with an introduction by James I. Porter and trans. Jane O. Newman (Princeton and Oxford: Princeton University Press, [1932] 2014), 200–14.
Auerbach, Eric, *Mimesis: The Representation of Reality in Western Literature*, trans. Willard R. Trask (Princeton: Princeton University Press, 1953).
Barnes, Jonathan, 'Introduction to Sextus Empiricus', in Sextus Empiricus, *Outlines of Scepticism*, ed. Julia Annas and Jonathan Barnes (Cambridge: Cambridge University Press, [1994] 2000), xi–xxxi.
Bate, Jonathan, *Shakespeare and Ovid* (Oxford: Oxford University Press, 1993).
Bate, Jonathan, 'Montaigne and Shakespeare: Two Great Writers of One Mind', review of Stephen Greenblatt and Peter G. Platt (eds), *Shakespeare's Montaigne*, New Statesman, 10 July 2014, <http://www.newstatesman.com/culture/2014/07/montaigne-and-shakespeare-two-great-writers-one-mind> (last accessed 18 March 2020).
Belsey, Catherine, 'Iago the Essayist: Florio between Montaigne and Shakespeare', in A. Höfele and W. von Koppenfels (eds), *Renaissance Go-Betweens* (Berlin: de Gruyter, 2005), 262–78.
Belsey, Catherine, 'Psychoanalysis and Early Modern Culture: Lacan with Augustine and Montaigne', in Lena Cowen Orlin (ed.), *Center or Margin: Revisions of the English Renaissance in Honor of Leeds Barroll* (Selinsgrove: Susquehanna University Press, 2006), 257–78.
Berlin, Isaiah, 'Fathers and Children: Turgenev and the Liberal Predicament', in Isaiah Berlin, *Russian Thinkers*, ed. Henry Hardy and Aileen Kelly (London: Penguin, [1978] 1994), 261–305.

Blanchot, Maurice, *The Infinite Conversation*, trans. Susan Hanson (Minneapolis: University of Minnesota Press, 1993).

Boas, Frederick S., *Shakspere and his Predecessors* (London: John Murray, [1896] 1947).

Bodin, Jean, *Methodus ad facilem historiarum cognitidem* (Paris, 1566).

Bodin, Jean, *The Six Bookes of a Commonweale*, trans. Richard Knolles, edited with an introduction by Kenneth Douglas McRae (Cambridge, MA: Harvard University Press, [1576/1606] 1962).

Bodin, Jean, *Method for the Easy Comprehension of History*, trans. Beatrice Reynolds (New York: W. W. Norton and Company, Inc., [1945] 1969).

Borges, Jorge Luis, *Labyrinths: Selected Stories and Other Writings*, ed. Donald A. Yates and James E. Irby (New York: New Directions, 1964).

Bourus, Terri, *Young Shakespeare's Young Hamlet: Print, Piracy, and Performance* (New York: Palgrave Macmillan, 2014).

Boutcher, Warren, 'Marginal Commentaries: The Cultural Transmission of Montaigne's *Essais* in Shakespeare's England', in Jean-Marie Maguin (ed.), *Shakespeare et Montaigne: Vers un Nouvel Humanisme* (Paris: Société Française Shakespeare, 2003), 13–27.

Boutcher, Warren, 'Butchering the Cannibals: *Essais* I.31 Dismembered for Florio's Modern Readers', in Neil Kenny, Richard Scholar, and Wes Williams (eds), *Montaigne in Transit: Essays in Honor of Ian Maclean* (Cambridge: Legenda, 2016), 107–32.

Boutcher, Warren, 'Montaigne in England and America', in Philippe Desan (ed.), *The Oxford Handbook of Montaigne* (Oxford: Oxford University Press, 2016), 306–27.

Boutcher, Warren, *The School of Montaigne in Early Modern Europe: Volume I, The Patron–Author* (Oxford: Oxford University Press, 2017).

Boutcher, Warren, *The School of Montaigne in Early Modern Europe: Volume II, The Reader–Writer* (Oxford: Oxford University Press, 2017).

Bradshaw, Graham, *Shakespeare's Scepticism* (Ithaca: Cornell University Press, 1987).

Bradshaw, Graham, and Thomas Bishop (eds), *The Shakespearean International Yearbook 6: Special Section, Shakespeare and Montaigne Revisited* (Aldershot and Burlington, VT: Ashgate, 2006).

Bradshaw, Graham, Thomas Bishop, and Mark Turner (eds), *The Shakespearean International Yearbook 4: Shakespeare Studies Today* (Aldershot and Burlington, VT: Ashgate, 2004).

Brandes, George, *William Shakespeare: A Critical Study*, trans. William Archer, Mary Morison, and Diana White (London: Heinemann, [1898] 1905).

Bruster, Douglas, *To Be or Not to Be* (London and New York: Continuum, 2007).

Burnyeat, Myles (ed.), *The Skeptical Tradition* (Berkeley, Los Angeles and London: University of California Press, 1983).

Burrow, Colin, 'Frisks, Skips and Jumps', *The London Review of Books* 25.21, 6 November 2003.

Burrow, Colin, 'Why Shakespeare is Not Michelangelo', in William Poole and Richard Scholar (eds), *Thinking with Shakespeare: Comparative and Interdisciplinary Essays for A. D. Nuttall* (London: Legenda, 2007), 9–22.

Burrow, Colin, 'Montaignian Moments: Shakespeare and the *Essays*' in Neil Kenny, Richard Scholar, and Wes Williams (eds), *Montaigne in Transit: Essays in Honor of Ian Maclean* (Cambridge: Legenda, 2016), 239–52.

Capell, Edward, *Notes and Various Readings to Shakespeare*, volume II (London, 1780).

Cave, Terence, 'Imagining Scepticism in the Sixteenth Century', *Journal of the Institute of Romance Studies* 1 (1992): 193–205.

Cavell, Stanley, *Disowning Knowledge in Six Plays of Shakespeare* (Cambridge: Cambridge University Press, 1987).

Cavell, Stanley, 'The Avoidance of Love: A Reading of *King Lear*', in *Disowning Knowledge in Seven Plays of Shakespeare*, updated edition (Cambridge: Cambridge University Press, 2003), 39–123.

Chambers, E. K., *The Elizabethan Stage*, 4 vols (Oxford: Clarendon Press, 1923).

Chambers, E. K., *Shakespeare: A Survey* (London: Sidgwick & Jackson, Ltd., 1925).

Chambers, E. K., *William Shakespeare: A Study of Facts and Problems*, 2 vols (Oxford: Clarendon Press, 1930).

Chambers, R.W., *Man's Unconquerable Mind: Studies of English Writers from Bede to A. E. Housman and W. P. Ker* (London and Toronto: Jonathan Cape, 1939).

Chappuit, Jean-François, 'Introduction' ('Avant-Propos'), in Jean-Marie Maguin (ed.), *Shakespeare et Montaigne: Vers un Nouvel Humanisme* (Paris: Société Française Shakespeare, 2003), 3–6.

Chasles, Philarète, *L'Angleterre au seizième siècle* (Paris: G. Charpentier, 1879).

Clayton, Thomas (ed.), *The Hamlet First Published (Q1, 1603): Origins, Form, Intertextualities* (Newark: University of Delaware Press, 1992).

Clayton, Thomas, Susan Brock, and Vicente Forés (eds), *Shakespeare and the Mediterranean: The Selected Proceedings of the International Shakespeare Association World Congress, Valencia, 2001* (Newark: University of Delaware Press, 2004).

Collins, J. Churlton, *Studies in Shakespeare* (Westminster: Archibald Constable and Co, Ltd., 1904).

Compagnon, Antoine, *A Summer with Montaigne*, trans. Tina Kover (New York: Europa Editions, 2019).

Conley, Tom, 'The *Essays* and the New World', in Ulrich Langer (ed.), *The Cambridge Companion to Montaigne* (Cambridge: Cambridge University Press, 2005), 74–95.

Cornwallis [the Younger], Sir William, *Essayes* (London, 1600).
Cornwallis [the Younger], Sir William, *Essayes*, ed. Don Cameron Allen (Baltimore: Johns Hopkins University Press, 1946).
Cosman, Bard C., 'All's Well That Ends Well: Shakespeare's Treatment of Anal Fistula', *Diseases of Colon and Rectum* 41.7 (1998): 914–24.
Cotgrave, Randle, *A Dictionarie of the French and English Tongves* (London, 1611).
Daniel, Samuel, 'To my deere friend M. *Iohn Florio,* concerning *his translation of* Montaigne', in *The Essayes*, ed. John Florio, sig. ¶r–v.
De Certeau, Michel, 'Montaigne's "Of Cannibals": The Savage "I"' [1981], in *Heterologies: Discourse on the Other*, trans. Brian Massumi (Minneapolis: University of Minnesota Press, 1986), 67–79.
De Gooyer, Alan, '"Their Senses I'll Restore": Montaigne and *The Tempest* Reconsidered', in Patrick M. Murphy (ed.), The Tempest: *Critical Essays* (New York and London: Routledge, 2001), 509–31.
Defaux, Gérard (ed.), *Montaigne: Essays in Reading*, special issue of *Yale French Studies* 64 (1983).
Desan, Philippe (ed.), *Dictionnaire de Michel de Montaigne* (Paris: Honoré Champion, 2004).
Desan, Philippe (ed.), *The Oxford Handbook of Montaigne* (Oxford: Oxford University Press, 2016).
Desan, Philippe, *Montaigne: A Life*, trans. Steven Rendall and Lisa Neal (Princeton and Oxford: Princeton University Press, 2017).
Dessen, Alan C., 'Weighing the Options in Q1', in Thomas Clayton (ed.), *The* Hamlet *First Published (Q1, 1603): Origins, Form, Intertextualities* (Newark: University of Delaware Press, 1992), 65–78.
DiPietro, Cary, 'The Shakespeare Edition in Industrial Capitalism', *Shakespeare Survey* 59 (2006): 147–56.
Donaldson, Ian, '*All's Well That Ends Well*: Shakespeare's Play of Endings', *Essays in Criticism* 27.1 (1977): 34–55.
Duffin, Ross W., *Shakespeare's Songbook* (New York: W.W. Norton & Company, 2004).
Dutton, Richard, *Shakespeare, Court Dramatist* (Oxford: Oxford University Press, 2016).
Duval, Edwin, 'Lessons of the New World: Design and Meaning in Montaigne's "Des Cannibales" [I:31] and "Des Coches" [III:6]', in Gérard Defaux (ed.), *Montaigne: Essays in Reading*, special issue of *Yale French Studies* 64 (1983), 95–112.
Eliot, T. S., 'Hamlet and His Problems', *Athenaeum* 4665 [26 September 1919]: 940–1.
Eliot, T. S., *The Sacred Wood* (London: Methuen and Co., 1920).
Eliot, T. S., 'Shakespeare and Montaigne', *Times Literary Supplement*, 24 December 1925: 895.
Eliot, T. S., *Selected Essays: 1917–1932* (London: Faber and Faber, 1932).

Ellrodt, Robert, 'Self-Consciousness in Montaigne and Shakespeare', *Shakespeare Survey* 28 (1975): 37–50.
Ellrodt, Robert, 'Self-Consistency in Montaigne and Shakespeare', in Tom Clayton, Susan Brock, and Vicente Forés (eds), *Shakespeare and the Mediterranean: The Selected Proceedings of the International Shakespeare Association World Congress, Valencia, 2001* (Newark: University of Delaware Press, 2004), 135–50.
Ellrodt, Robert, *Montaigne and Shakespeare: The Emergence of Modern Self Consciousness* (Manchester: Manchester University Press, 2015).
Elton, William R., and John M. Mucciolo (eds), *Shakespeare International Yearbook 2: Where are We Now in Shakespeare Studies?* (Aldershot and Burlington, VT: Ashgate, 2002).
Elze, Karl, *Essays on Shakespeare*, trans. L. Dora Schmitz (London, [1865] 1874).
Elze, Karl, *Life of Shakespeare*, trans. L. Dora Schmitz (London, [1872] 1888).
Empson, William, '*Hamlet* When New', *The Sewanee Review* 61.1 (1953): 15–42.
Engle, Lars, '*Measure for Measure* and Modernity: The Problem of the Sceptic's Authority', in Hugh Grady (ed.), *Shakespeare and Modernity: Early Modern to Millennium* (London and New York: Routledge, 2000), 85–104.
Engle, Lars, 'Shakespearean Normativity in *All's Well That Ends Well*', in Graham Bradshaw, Thomas Bishop, and Mark Turner (eds), *The Shakespearean International Yearbook 4: Shakespeare Studies Today* (Aldershot and Burlington, VT: Ashgate, 2004), 264–78.
Engle, Lars, 'Sovereign Cruelty in Montaigne and *King Lear*', in Graham Bradshaw and Thomas Bishop (eds), *The Shakespearean International Yearbook 6: Special Section, Shakespeare and Montaigne Revisited* (Aldershot and Burlington, VT: Ashgate, 2006), 119–39.
Engle, Lars, Patrick Gray, and William M. Hamlin (eds), *Shakespeare and Montaigne* (Edinburgh: Edinburgh University Press, 2021).
Feis, Jacob, *Shakspere and Montaigne: An Endeavour to Explain the Tendency of 'Hamlet' from Allusions in Contemporary Works* (London: Kegan Paul, Trench, & Co., 1884).
Ferrari, Emiliano, 'Continental Skepticism and American Pragmatism: Transatlantic Views from Montaigne to Richard Rorty', *Montaigne Studies* 31.1–2 (2019): 83–96.
Fiedler, Leslie, *The Stranger in Shakespeare* (New York: Stein and Day, 1972).
Florio, John, *A Worlde of* Wordes, *Or Most copious, and exact* Dictionarie *in Italian and* English, collected by *Iohn Florio* (London, 1598).
Floyd-Wilson, Mary, *Occult Knowledge, Science, and Gender on the Shakespearean Stage* (Cambridge: Cambridge University Press, 2013).

Foucault, Michel, 'Nietzsche, Genealogy, History', in Paul Rabinow (ed.), *The Foucault Reader* (New York: Pantheon Books, 1984), 76–100.

Foucault, Michel, 'Structuralism and Post-Structuralism', in James D. Faubion (ed.), *Aesthetics, Method, and Epistemology: Essential Works of Foucault, 1954–1984*, volume II (New York: The New Press, 1998), 433–58.

Frampton, Saul, '"To Be, or Not to Be": *Hamlet* Q1, Q2 and Montaigne', *Critical Survey* 31.1/2 (2019): 101–12.

Friedrich, Hugo, *Montaigne*, ed. Philippe Desan, trans. Dawn Eng (Berkeley, Los Angeles, Oxford: University of California Press, [1949] 1991).

Frye, Roland Mushat, *The Renaissance Hamlet: Issues and Responses in 1600* (Princeton: Princeton University Press, 1984).

Furnivall, F. J., 'Is the Character of Hamlet Shakspere's Creation or Not?', *Academy* 431 (7 August 1880): 101.

Garber, Marjorie (ed.), *Cannibals, Witches, and Divorce: Estranging the Renaissance* (Baltimore and London: Johns Hopkins University Press, 1987).

Gilbert, Allan H., 'Montaigne and *The Tempest*', *The Romanic Review* 5 (1914): 357–63.

Ginzburg, Carlo, 'Montaigne, Cannibals, and Grottoes', in Carlo Ginzburg, *Threads and Traces: True False Fictive*, trans. Anne C. Tedeschi and John Tedeschi (Berkeley, Los Angeles, and London: University of California Press, 2012), 34–53.

Go, Kenji, 'Montaigne's "Cannibals" and *The Tempest* Revisited', *Studies in Philology* 109.4 (2012): 455–73.

Gollancz, Israel (ed.), *A Book of Homage to Shakespeare* (Oxford: Oxford University Press, 1916).

Grady, Hugh, *Shakespeare, Machiavelli, and Montaigne: Power and Subjectivity from* Richard II *to* Hamlet (Oxford: Oxford University Press, 2002).

Grady, Hugh (ed.), *Shakespeare and Modernity: Early Modern to Millennium* (London and New York: Routledge, 2000).

Grady, Hugh, 'Afterword: Montaigne and Shakespeare in Changing Cultural Paradigms', in Graham Bradshaw and Thomas Bishop (eds), *The Shakespearean International Yearbook 6: Special Section, Shakespeare and Montaigne Revisited* (Aldershot and Burlington, VT: Ashgate, 2006), 170–81.

Grady, Hugh, *Shakespeare and Impure Aesthetics* (Cambridge: Cambridge University Press, 2009).

Gray, Patrick, '"HIDE THY SELFE": Montaigne, Hamlet and Epicurean Ethics', in Patrick Gray and John D. Cox (eds), *Shakespeare and Renaissance Ethics* (Cambridge: Cambridge University Press, 2014), 213–36.

Gray, Patrick, and John D. Cox (eds), *Shakespeare and Renaissance Ethics* (Cambridge: Cambridge University Press, 2014).

Greenblatt, Stephen, *Shakespearean Negotiations* (Berkeley and Los Angeles: University of California Press, 1988).
Greenblatt, Stephen, 'Shakespeare's Montaigne', in Montaigne, *Shakespeare's Montaigne: The Florio Translation of the Essays*, ed. Stephen Greenblatt and Peter G. Platt, trans. John Florio (New York: New York Review Books, 2014), ix–xxxiii.
Grossman, Marshall (ed.), *Reading Renaissance Ethics* (New York and London: Routledge, 2007).
Guild, Elizabeth, *Unsettling Montaigne: Poetics, Ethics and Affect in the* Essais *and Other Writings* (Cambridge: D. S. Brewer, 2014).
Hales, Steven D., and Robert C. Welshon, 'Truth, Paradox, and Nietzschean Perspectivism', *History of Philosophy* 11.1 (1994): 101–19.
Hamlin, William M., 'A Lost Translation Found? An Edition of *The Sceptick* (c. 1590) Based on Extant Manuscripts [with text]', *English Literary Renaissance* 31.1 (2001): 34–51.
Hamlin, William M., 'Scepticism in Shakespeare's England', in John M. Mucciolo and William R. Elton (eds), *The Shakespearean International Yearbook 2: Where are We Now in Shakespeare Studies?* (Aldershot and Burlington, VT: Ashgate, 2002), 290–304.
Hamlin, William M., *Tragedy and Scepticism in Shakespeare's England* (Houndmills and New York: Palgrave Macmillan, 2005).
Hamlin, William M., 'What Did Montaigne's Skepticism Mean to Shakespeare and His Contemporaries?', *Montaigne Studies* 17 (2005): 195–210.
Hamlin, William M., 'The Shakespeare–Montaigne–Sextus Nexus: A Case Study in Early Modern Reading', in Graham Bradshaw and Thomas Bishop (eds), *The Shakespearean International Yearbook 6: Special Section, Shakespeare and Montaigne Revisited* (Aldershot and Burlington, VT: Ashgate, 2006), 21–36.
Hamlin, William M., *Montaigne's English Journey: Reading the* Essays *in Shakespeare's Day* (Oxford: Oxford University Press, 2013).
Hamlin, William M., 'Montaigne and Shakespeare', in Philippe Desan (ed.), *The Oxford Handbook of Montaigne* (Oxford: Oxford University Press, 2016), 328–46.
Harmon, Alice, 'How Great was Shakespeare's Debt to Montaigne?' *PMLA* 57.4 (1942): 988–1008.
Hartle, Ann, *Michel de Montaigne: Accidental Philosopher* (Cambridge: Cambridge University Press, 2003).
Hartle, Ann, *Montaigne and the Origins of Modern Philosophy* (Evanston: Northwestern University Press, 2013).
Hazlitt, William, *The Collected Works of William Hazlitt*, ed. A. R. Waller and Arnold Glover, 12 vols (London: J. M. Dent, 1902–4).
Hazlitt, William Carew, *Shakespear[e]* (London: Bernard Quaritch, 1902).
Hendrick, Philip, 'Montaigne, Florio, and Shakespeare: The Mediation of Colonial Discourse', in Jean-Marie Maguin (ed.), *Shakespeare*

et Montaigne: Vers un Nouvel Humanisme (Paris: Société Française Shakespeare, 2003), 117–33.

Hill, W. Speed (ed.), *New Ways of Looking at Old Texts II: Papers of the Renaissance English Text Society, 1992–1996* (Tempe, AZ: Medieval and Renaissance Texts and Studies in Conjunction with Renaissance English Text Society, 1998).

Hodgen, Margaret, 'Montaigne and Shakespeare Again', *The Huntington Library Quarterly* 16.1 (1952): 23–42.

Höfele, A., and W. von Koppenfels (eds), *Renaissance Go-Betweens* (Berlin: de Gruyter, 2005).

Hoffmann, George, 'Anatomy of the Mass: Montaigne's "Cannibals"', *PMLA* 117.2 (2002): 207–21.

Holbrook, Peter, *Shakespeare's Individualism* (Cambridge: Cambridge University Press, 2010).

Holbrook, Peter, 'Shakespeare, Montaigne and Classical Reason', in Patrick Gray and John D. Cox (eds), *Shakespeare and Renaissance Ethics* (Cambridge: Cambridge University Press, 2014), 261–83.

Honan, Park, *Shakespeare: A Life* (Oxford: Oxford University Press, 1998).

Hooker, Elizabeth R., 'The Relation of Shakespeare to Montaigne', *PMLA* 17 (ns 10) (1902): 312–66.

Horkheimer, Max, 'Montaigne and the Function of Skepticism' [1938], in Max Horkheimer, *Between Philosophy and Social Science: Selected Early Writings*, trans. G. Frederick Hunter, Matthew S. Kramer, and John Torpey (Cambridge, MA and London: MIT Press, 1993), 265–311.

Horkheimer, Max, and Theodor Adorno, *Dialectic of Enlightenment: Philosophical Fragments* [1944/1947], ed. Gunzelin Schmid Noerr, trans. Edmund Jephcott (Stanford: Stanford University Press, 2002).

Irace, Kathleen, 'Origins and Agents of Q1 *Hamlet*', in Thomas Clayton (ed.), *The* Hamlet *First Published (Q1, 1603): Origins, Form, Intertextualities* (Newark: University of Delaware Press, 1992), 90–122.

Irace, Kathleen (ed.), *The First Quarto of Hamlet*, The Early Quartos (Cambridge: Cambridge University Press, 1998).

Jolly, Margrethe, '*Hamlet* and the French Connection: The Relationship of Q1 and Q2 *Hamlet* and the Evidence of Belleforest's *Histoires Tragiques*', *Parergon* 29.1 (2012): 83–105.

Jonson, Ben, *Ben Jonson*, ed. C. H. Herford, Percy Simpson, and Evelyn Simpson, 11 vols (Oxford: Clarendon Press, 1925–52).

Jourdan, Serena, *The Sparrow and the Flea: The Sense of Providence in Shakespeare and Montaigne* (Salzburg: Institut für Anglistik und Amerikanistik, 1983).

Kastan, David Scott, '"His semblable is his mirror": *Hamlet* and the Imitation of Revenge', *Shakespeare Studies* 19 (1987): 111–24.

Kastan, David Scott, '"The Duke of Milan / And His Brave Son": Old Histories and New in *The Tempest*', in David Scott Kastan, *Shakespeare after Theory* (London and New York: Routledge, 1999), 183–97.

Kastan, David Scott, *A Will to Believe: Shakespeare and Religion* (New York: Oxford University Press, 2014).
Kay, Dennis, '"To Hear the Rest Untold": Shakespeare's Postponed Endings', *Renaissance Quarterly* 37.2 (1984): 207–27.
Kearney, James, '"This is Above All Strangeness": *King Lear*, Ethics, and the Phenomenology of Recognition', *Criticism* 54.3 (2012): 455–67.
Keats, John, *The Letters of John Keats: 1814–1821*, ed. Hyder Edward Rollins, 2 vols (Cambridge, MA: Harvard University Press, 1958).
Kenny, Neil, Richard Scholar, and Wes Williams (eds), *Montaigne in Transit: Essays in Honor of Ian Maclean* (Cambridge: Legenda, 2016).
Kerrigan, John, *Shakespeare's Originality* (Oxford: Oxford University Press, 2018).
King, Walter N., *Hamlet's Search for Meaning* (Athens: University of Georgia Press, 1982).
Kirsch, Arthur, 'Sexuality and Marriage in Montaigne and *All's Well That Ends Well*', *Montaigne Studies* 9.1–2 (1997): 187–202.
Kirsch, Arthur, 'Virtue, Vice, and Compassion in Montaigne and *The Tempest*', *Studies in English Literature* 37.2 (1997): 337–52.
Kirsch, Arthur, 'The Bitter and the Sweet of Tragicomedy: Shakespeare's *All's Well That Ends Well* and Montaigne', *Yale Review* 102.2 (2014): 63–84.
Kliman, Bernice W., and Paul Bertram (eds), *The Three-Text-Hamlet: Parallel Texts of the First and Second Quartos and First Folio*, second edition (New York: AMS Press, Inc., 2003).
Knight, G. Wilson, *The Crown of Life: Essays in Interpretation of Shakespeare's Final Plays* (London: Methuen & Co. Ltd., [1947] 1965).
Knight, G. Wilson, 'The Third Eye: An Essay on *All's Well That Ends Well*', in *The Sovereign Flower: On Shakespeare as the Poet of Royalism together with Related Essays and Indexes to Earlier Volumes* (New York: Macmillan, 1958), 93–160.
Knowles, Ronald, '*Hamlet* and Counter-Humanism', *Renaissance Quarterly* 52.4 (1999): 1046–69.
Kott, Jan, *The Bottom Translation: Marlowe and Shakespeare and the Carnival Tradition*, trans. Daniela Miedzyrzecka and Lillian Vallee (Evanston: Northwestern University Press, 1987).
Kristeva, Julia, 'Word, Dialogue, and Novel', [1966/1969], in Julia Kristeva, *Desire in Language: A Semiotic Approach to Literature and Art*, ed. Leon S. Roudiez, trans. Thomas Gora, Alice Jardine and Leon S. Roudiez (Oxford: Basil Blackwell, 1980), 64–91.
Kritzman, Lawrence D., *The Fabulous Imagination: On Montaigne's Essays* (New York: Columbia University Press, 2009).
Lacan, Jacques, *The Four Fundamental Concepts of Psycho-analysis*, ed. Jacques-Alain Miller, trans. Alan Sheridan (New York: Norton, 1977).
Lacan, Jacques, 'Presentation on Psychical Causality', in Jacques Lacan, *Écrits: The First Complete Edition in English*, trans. Bruce Fink (New York and London: W.W. Norton and Company, 1999), 123–60.

Langer, Ulrich (ed.), *The Cambridge Companion to Montaigne* (Cambridge: Cambridge University Press, 2005).

Leach, Edmund, *Genesis as Myth and Other Essays* (London: Jonathan Cape, 1969).

Lee, John, '"A Judge That Were No Man": Montaigne, Shakespeare, and Imagination', in Graham Bradshaw and Thomas Bishop (eds), *The Shakespearean International Yearbook 6: Special Section, Shakespeare and Montaigne Revisited* (Aldershot and Burlington, VT: Ashgate, 2006), 37–55.

Leggatt, Alexander, *Shakespeare's Comedy of Love* (London and New York: Routledge, [1973] 1990).

Lesser, Zachary, *Renaissance Drama and the Politics of Publication: Readings in the English Book Trade* (Cambridge: Cambridge University Press, 2004).

Lesser, Zachary, *Hamlet after Q1: An Uncanny History of the Shakespearean Text* (Philadelphia: University of Pennsylvania Press, 2015).

Lestringant, Frank, *Cannibals: The Discovery and Representation of the Cannibal from Columbus to Jules Verne*, trans. Rosemary Morris (Berkeley and Los Angeles: University of California Press, 1997).

Levin, Harry, *The Question of Hamlet* (New York: Oxford University Press, 1959).

Lewis, Rhodri, *Hamlet and the Vision of Darkness* (Princeton and Oxford: Princeton University Press, 2017).

Lindley, David, *Shakespeare and Music*, Arden Critical Companions (London and New York: Bloomsbury, 2006).

Lodge, Thomas, *VVits Miserie, and the vvorlds madnesse discouering the devils incarnate of the age* (London, 1596).

Longworth de Chambrun, Clara, *Giovanni Florio: un apôtre de la Renaissance en Angleterre à l'époque de Shakespeare* (Paris: Payot, 1921).

Lyotard, Jean-François, *The Postmodern Condition: A Report on Knowledge*, trans. Geoff Bennington and Brian Massumi (Minneapolis: University of Minnesota Press, 1984).

McCarthy, Dennis, and June Schlueter, *'A Brief Discourse of Rebellion and Rebels' by George North: A Newly Uncovered Manuscript Source for Shakespeare's Plays* (Cambridge: D. S. Brewer, 2018).

Mack, Peter, *Reading and Rhetoric in Shakespeare and Montaigne* (New York: Bloomsbury Academic, 2010).

Mack, Peter, 'Montaigne and Shakespeare: Source, Parallel, or Comparison?', *Montaigne Studies* 23 (2011): 151–80.

Mack, Peter, 'Madness, Proverbial Wisdom and Philosophy in *King Lear*', in Patrick Gray and John D. Cox (eds), *Shakespeare and Renaissance Ethics* (Cambridge: Cambridge University Press, 2014), 284–302.

Madden, Sir Frederic, 'Observations on an Autograph of Shakspere, and the orthography of his Name', *Archaeologia* 27 (1838): 113–23.

Maguin, Jean-Marie, '*The Tempest* and Cultural Exchange', *Shakespeare Survey* 48 (1995): 147–54.
Maguin, Jean-Marie (ed.), *Shakespeare et Montaigne: Vers un Nouvel Humanisme* (Paris: Société Française Shakespeare, 2003).
Maguire, Laurie (ed.), *How to Do Things with Shakespeare: New Approaches, New Essays* (Oxford: Wiley-Blackwell, 2008).
Marino, James J., *Owning William Shakespeare: The King's Men and Their Intellectual Property* (Philadelphia: University of Pennsylvania Press, 2011).
Matthiessien, F. O., *Translation: An Elizabethan Art* (New York: Octagon Books, Inc., [1931] 1965).
Menzer, Paul, *The* Hamlets: *Cues, Qs, and Remembered Texts* (Newark: University of Delaware Press, 2008).
Merleau-Ponty, Maurice, 'Reading Montaigne', in Maurice Merleau-Ponty, *Signs*, trans. and with an introduction by Richard C. McCleary (Evanston: Northwestern University Press, 1964), 198–210.
Mommsen, Tycho, '"Hamlet", 1603; and "Romeo and Juliet", 1597', *The Athenaeum* 1528 (7 February 1857): 182.
Montaigne, Michel de, *The essayes or morall, politike and millitarie discourses*, trans. John Florio (London: Valentine Simmes for Edward Blount, 1603).
Montaigne, Michel de, *The Essays of Michel de Montaigne*, trans. and ed. Jacob Zeitlin, 3 vols (New York: Alfred A. Knopf, 1934–6).
Montaigne, Michel de, *The Complete Essays of Montaigne*, trans. Donald M. Frame (Stanford: Stanford University Press, [1958] 1965).
Montaigne, Michel de, *The Complete Essays*, trans. M. A. Screech (Harmondsworth: Penguin, 1991).
Montaigne, Michel de, *Les Essais*, ed. Jean Céard et al. (Paris: Livre de Poche, 2001).
Montaigne, Michel de, *Les Essais*, ed. Jean Balsamo et al. (Paris: Gallimard, 2007).
Montaigne, Michel de, *Shakespeare's Montaigne: The Florio Translation of the Essays*, ed. Stephen Greenblatt and Peter G. Platt, trans. John Florio (New York: New York Review Books, 2014).
Murphy, Patrick M. (ed.), The Tempest: *Critical Essays* (New York and London: Routledge, 2001).
Nashe, Thomas, *Works*, ed. Ronald B. McKerrow, 3 vols (London: A. H. Bullen, 1904–5).
Nicholl, Charles, *The Lodger Shakespeare: His Life on Silver Street* (New York: Viking, 2008).
Nietzsche, 'Richard Wagner in Bayreuth' [1876], in *Untimely Meditations*, trans. R. J. Hollingdale (Cambridge: Cambridge University Press, 1983), 195–254.
Nowotny, Helen, *The Cunning of Uncertainty* (Cambridge and Malden, MA: Polity Press, 2016).

Nuttall, A. D., '*Measure for Measure*: Quid Pro Quo?', *Shakespeare Studies* 4 (1968): 231–51.

O'Brien, John, 'A Fantasy of Justice', in Jean-Marie Maguin (ed.), *Shakespeare et Montaigne: Vers un Nouvel Humanisme* (Paris: Société Française Shakespeare, 2003), 245–58.

O'Brien, John, 'Montaigne and Antiquity: Fancies and Grotesques', in Ulrich Langer (ed.), *The Cambridge Companion to Montaigne* (Cambridge: Cambridge University Press, 2005), 53–73.

O'Brien, John, 'The Humanist Tradition and Montaigne', in Philippe Desan (ed.), *The Oxford Handbook of Montaigne* (Oxford: Oxford University Press, 2016), 58–77.

Orgel, Stephen, 'Shakespeare and the Cannibals', in Marjorie Garber (ed.), *Cannibals, Witches, and Divorce: Estranging the Renaissance* (Baltimore and London: Johns Hopkins University Press, 1987), 40–66.

Orlin, Lena Cowen (ed.), *Center or Margin: Revisions of the English Renaissance in Honor of Leeds Barroll* (Selinsgrove, PA: Susquehanna University Press, 2006).

Page, Frederic, 'Shakespeare and Florio', *Notes and Queries* 184 (1943): 283–5.

Page, Frederic, 'Shakespeare and Florio', *Notes and Queries* 185 (1943): 42–4 and 107–8.

Palfrey, Simon, *Poor Tom: Living* King Lear (Chicago and London: University of Chicago Press, 2014).

Palfrey, Simon, *Shakespeare's Possible Worlds* (Cambridge: Cambridge University Press, 2014).

Parker, Fred, 'Shakespeare's Argument with Montaigne', *The Cambridge Quarterly* 28.1 (1999): 1–18.

Paster, Gail Kern, 'Montaigne, Dido, and *The Tempest*: "How Came That Widow In?"' *Shakespeare Quarterly* 35.1 (1984): 91–4.

Pierce, Robert B., 'Shakespeare and the Ten Modes of Scepticism', *Shakespeare Survey* 46 (1994): 145–58.

Platt, Peter G., *Reason Diminished: Shakespeare and the Marvelous* (Lincoln: University of Nebraska Press, 1997).

Platt, Peter G., *Shakespeare and the Culture of Paradox* (Farnham and Burlington, VT: Ashgate, 2009).

Pollard, Tanya, 'What's Hecuba to Shakespeare?', *Renaissance Quarterly* 65 (2012): 1060–93.

Pollard, Tanya, *Greek Tragic Women on Shakespearean Stages* (Oxford: Oxford University Press, 2017).

Poole, William, and Richard Scholar (eds), *Thinking with Shakespeare: Comparative and Interdisciplinary Essays for A. D. Nuttall* (London: Legenda, 2007).

Popkin, Richard, *The History of Scepticism from Savonarola to Bayle*, revised and expanded edition (Oxford: Oxford University Press, 2003).

Prosser, Eleanor, 'Shakespeare, Montaigne, and the Rarer Action', *Shakespeare Studies* 1 (1965): 261–4.
Quint, David, 'A Reconsideration of Montaigne's *Des Cannibales*', *Modern Language Quarterly* 51 (1990): 459–89.
Quint, David, *Montaigne and the Quality of Mercy* (Princeton: Princeton University Press, 1998).
Quintilian, *Institutio oratoria*, trans. H. E. Butler, 4 vols (London: William Heinemann, 1921–2).
Ramachandran, Ayesha, *The Worldmakers: Global Imagining in Early Modern Europe* (Chicago and London: University of Chicago Press, 2015).
Regosin, Richard L., *The Matter of My Book: Montaigne's* Essais *as the Book of the Self* (Berkeley, Los Angeles and London: University of California Press, 1977).
Reiss, Timothy J., 'Montaigne, the New World, and Precolonialisms', in Philippe Desan (ed.), *The Oxford Handbook of Montaigne* (Oxford: Oxford University Press, 2016), 196–214.
Robertson, J. M., *Montaigne and Shakespeare, and Other Essays on Cognate Questions* (London: Adam & Charles Black, 1909).
Rossiter, A. P., 'Hamlet', in A. P. Rossiter, *Angel with Horns: Fifteen Lectures on Shakespeare*, ed. Graham Storey (London and New York: Longman, [1961] 1989), 171–88.
Rossiter, A. P., 'The Problem Plays', in A. P. Rossiter, *Angel with Horns: Fifteen Lectures on Shakespeare*, ed. Graham Storey (London and New York: Longman, [1961] 1989), 108–28.
Ryan, Kiernan, *Shakespeare's Universality: Here's Fine Revolution* (London and New York: Bloomsbury Arden Shakespeare, 2015).
Said, Edward, *Culture and Imperialism* (New York: Alfred A. Knopf, 1994).
Salingar, Leo, '*King Lear*, Montaigne and Harsnett', in Leo Salingar, *Dramatic Form in Shakespeare and the Jacobeans: Essays by Leo Salingar* (Cambridge: Cambridge University Press, 1986), 107–39.
Scholar, Richard, 'French Connections: The *Je-Ne-Sais-Quoi* in Montaigne and Shakespeare', in Laurie Maguire (ed.), *How to Do Things with Shakespeare: New Approaches, New Essays* (Oxford: Wiley-Blackwell, 2008), 11–33.
Schmitt, C. B., 'The Rediscovery of Ancient Skepticism', in Myles Burnyeat (ed.), *The Skeptical Tradition* (Berkeley, Los Angeles and London: University of California Press, 1983), 225–51.
Sextus Empiricus, *Outlines of Scepticism*, ed. Julia Annas and Jonathan Barnes (Cambridge: Cambridge University Press, [1994] 2000).
Shakespeare, William, *The Plays and Poems of William Shakespeare*, ed. Edmond Malone, 10 vols (London: 1790).
Shakespeare, William, *Hamlet*, ed. Horace Howard Furness, in *A New Variorum Edition of Shakespeare*, volume 4 (Philadelphia: J. B. Lippincott & Co, [1871] 1877).

Shakespeare, William, *Hamlet, Prince of Denmark*, The Clarendon Shakespeare, ed. William George Clark and William Aldis Wright (Oxford: Clarendon Press, 1872).

Shakespeare, William, *Measure for Measure*, ed. Arthur Quiller-Couch and John Dover Wilson (Cambridge: Cambridge University Press, [1922] 1969).

Shakespeare, William, *All's Well That Ends Well*, ed. Arthur Quiller-Couch and John Dover Wilson (Cambridge: Cambridge University Press, 1929).

Shakespeare, William, *All's Well That Ends Well*, The Arden Shakespeare, ed. G. K. Hunter (London and New York: Routledge, [1959] 1991).

Shakespeare, William, *Hamlet*, The Arden Shakespeare, ed. Harold Jenkins (London and New York: Methuen, 1982).

Shakespeare, William, *The Tempest*, The Oxford Shakespeare, ed. Stephen Orgel (Oxford: Oxford University Press, 1987).

Shakespeare, William, *The Norton Shakespeare*, second edition, ed. Stephen Greenblatt et al. (New York and London: W.W. Norton and Company, 2008).

Shapiro, James, *A Year in the Life of Shakespeare: 1599* (New York: Harper Perennial, 2005).

Sherman, Anita Gilman, 'The Aesthetic Strategies of Skepticism: Mixing Memory and Desire in Montaigne and Shakespeare', in Graham Bradshaw and Thomas Bishop (eds), *The Shakespearean International Yearbook 6: Special Section, Shakespeare and Montaigne Revisited* (Aldershot and Burlington, VT: Ashgate, 2006), 99–118.

Simon, David Carroll, *Light without Heat: The Observational Mood from Bacon to Milton* (Ithaca and London: Cornell University Press, 2018).

Sisson, C. J., 'The Mythical Sorrows of Shakespeare', *Proceedings of the British Academy* 20 (1934): 45–70.

Skinner, Quentin, *Forensic Shakespeare* (Oxford: Oxford University Press, 2014).

Skura, Meredith Anne, 'Discourse and the Individual: The Case of Colonialism in *The Tempest*', *Shakespeare Quarterly* 40.1 (1989): 42–69.

Spencer, Theodore, *Shakespeare and the Nature of Man* (New York: Macmillan, 1949).

Starobinski, Jean, *Montaigne in Motion*, trans. Arthur Goldhammer (Chicago: University of Chicago Press, [1982] 1985).

Stedefeld, G. F., *Hamlet: ein Tendenzdrama Sheakspeare's* [sic] *gegen die skeptische und kosmopolitische Weltanschauung des Michael de Montaigne* (Berlin, 1871).

[Sterling, John], 'Art. IV', review of 'Observations on an Autograph . . . ', *London and Westminster Review* 31.2 (1838): 321–52.

Stern, Tiffany, 'Sermons, Plays, and Note-Takers: *Hamlet* Q1 as a "Noted" Text', *Shakespeare Survey* 66 (2013): 1–23.

Strier, Richard, 'Shakespeare and the Skeptics', *Religion and Literature* 32.2 (2000): 171–96.

Taylor, Charles, *Sources of the Self: The Makings of the Modern Identity* (Cambridge, MA: Harvard University Press, 1989).
Taylor, Gary, 'Judgment', in W. Speed Hill (ed.), *New Ways of Looking at Old Texts II: Papers of the Renaissance English Text Society, 1992–1996*, 91–9.
Taylor, Gary, and Gabriel Egan (eds), *The New Oxford Shakespeare: Authorship Companion* (Oxford: Oxford University Press, 2017).
Taylor, George Coffin, *Shakspere's Debt to Montaigne* (Cambridge, MA: Harvard University Press, 1925).
Taylor, George Coffin, 'The Date of Edward Capell's *Notes and Various Readings to Shakespeare, Volume II*', *Review of English Studies* 5 (1929): 317–19.
Taylor, George Coffin, 'Montaigne-Shakespeare and the Deadly Parallel', *Philological Quarterly* 22 (1943): 330–7.
Todorov, Tzvetan, 'L'Etre et L'Autre: Montaigne', in Gérard Defaux (ed.), *Montaigne: Essays in Reading*, special issue of *Yale French Studies* 64 (1983), 113–44.
Todorov, Tzvetan, *Imperfect Garden: The Legacy of Humanism*, trans. Carol Cosman (Princeton and Oxford: Princeton University Press, 2002).
Toulmin, Stephen, *Cosmopolis: The Hidden Agenda of Modernity* (Chicago: University of Chicago Press, [1990] 1992).
Toulmin, Stephen, *Return to Reason* (Cambridge, MA: Harvard University Press, 2001).
Urkowitz, Steven, *Shakespeare's Revision of* King Lear (Princeton: Princeton University Press, 1980).
Urkowitz, Steven, '"Well-sayd olde Mole": Burying Three *Hamlet*s in Modern Editions', in Georgianna Ziegler (ed.), *Shakespeare Study Today* (New York: AMS Press, 1986), 37–70.
Urkowitz, Steven, 'Back to Basics: Thinking about the *Hamlet* First Quarto', in Thomas Clayton (ed.), *The* Hamlet *First Published (Q1, 1603): Origins, Form, Intertextualities* (Newark: University of Delaware Press, 1992), 257–91.
Van Es, Bart, *Shakespeare in Company* (Oxford: Oxford University Press, 2013).
Vaughan, Alden T., and Virginia Mason Vaughan, *Shakespeare's Caliban: A Cultural History* (Cambridge: Cambridge University Press, 1991).
Villey, Pierre, 'Montaigne et Shakespeare', in Israel Gollancz (ed.), *A Book of Homage to Shakespeare* (Oxford: Oxford University Press, 1916), 417–20.
Villey, Pierre, 'Montaigne et les poètes dramatiques anglais du tempes de Shakespeare', *Revues d'histoire littéraire de la France* 24 (1917): 357–93.
Webster, John, *The White Devil*, ed. Benedict S. Robinson (London: The Arden Shakespeare, 2019).

Weimann, Robert, *Shakespeare and the Popular Tradition in the Theater: Studies in the Social Dimension of Dramatic Form and Function*, ed. Robert Schwartz (Baltimore and London: The Johns Hopkins University Press, 1978).

Williams, David, *Deformed Discourse: The Function of the Monster in Medieval Thought and Literature* (Montreal: McGill-Queen's University Press, 1996).

Wilson, F. W., *Elizabethan and Jacobean* (Oxford: Clarendon Press, 1945).

Wilson, John Dover, *The Essential Shakespeare: A Biographical Adventure* (Cambridge: Cambridge University Press, [1932] 1964).

Woods, Gillian, *Shakespeare's Unreformed Fictions* (Oxford: Oxford University Press, 2013).

Woolf, Virginia, 'Montaigne', in *The Common Reader* (New York: Harcourt, Brace, and Company, 1925), 87–100.

Woolf, Virginia, *A Room of One's Own* (New York: Harcourt, Brace, and Company, 1929).

Yachnin, Paul, 'Eating Montaigne', in Marshall Grossman (ed.), *Reading Renaissance Ethics* (New York and London: Routledge, 2007), 157–72.

Yates, Frances, *John Florio: The Life of an Italian in Shakespeare's England* (New York: Octagon Books, Inc., [1934] 1968).

Zalloua, Zahi, 'Essaying Trouble: Montaigne and Judith Butler', *Montaigne Studies* 31.1–2 (2019): 161–72.

Ziegler, Georgianna (ed.), *Shakespeare Study Today* (New York: AMS Press, 1986).

Index

Academica (Cicero), 25
Adorno, Theodor, 12–13, 22n66, 42n37, 107n36
All's Well That Ends Well (Shakespeare), 94–102
  ambition in, 95
  culture-nature tension in, 98
  doubleness of, 77–8, 108n38
  ending of, 100–2, 107n32, 108n40
  Engle on, 104n11
  Kirsch on, 104n11
  mixture in, 96–100, 107n32
  Montaignists of, 100
  on novelty, 105n22
  paradoxes in, 95, 108n38
  as problem play, 78, 103n6, 106n29
  on rash presumptions of knowledge, 29, 99, 159
  scepticism in, 29, 98, 99, 107n36
  self-conscious title of, 94–5, 101
  sexuality in, 99–100
  shiftingness of, 102n4
  'the web of our life is of a mingled yarn', 77
  theatricality in, 101–2
  'Upon Some Verses of Virgil' linked to, 95, 100
  visual indeterminacy linked to, 104n12
  'We Taste Nothing Purely' linked to, 10–11, 95, 100, 107n32
ambition
  in *All's Well That Ends Well*, 95
  in *Hamlet*, 67–8

'Of Diverting or Diversion' on, 56, 66–7
Amyot, Jacques, 33
anamorphic painting, 28
Anatomy of Absurdity, The (Nashe), 105n22
Antony and Cleopatra (Shakespeare), 32–3, 157, 164–6
Anzai, Tetsuo, 14n6, 69n5, 168n12
'Apologie of Raymond Sebond, An' (Montaigne), 17n34, 24, 26, 33–4, 42n33, 45, 51, 157, 167n5
As You Like It (Shakespeare), 42n34
Auerbach, Eric, 22n64, 39n3

Barnes, Jonathan, 25, 26
Bate, Jonathan, 9, 11, 145n8
Belleforest, François de, 71n27
Belsey, Catherine, 43n48
Berger, Harry, 92
Berlin, Isaiah, 9
Blanchot, Maurice, 127n21
Blount, Edward, 3
Boas, F. S., 78, 103n6
Bodin, Jean, 81, 104n15
Borges, Jorge Luis, 9
Bourus, Terri, 49, 50, 62, 71n27, 71n29, 71n32, 75n58
Boutcher, Warren, 8, 14n6, 74n50, 145n1, 146n10
Bradshaw, Graham, 167n8
Brandes, George, 68n5
'Brief Discourse of Rebellion and Rebels, A' (McCarthy and Schlueter), 21n62

186   *Shakespeare's Essays*

Bruster, Douglas, 167n3
Burrow, Colin, 13n3, 20n60, 21n63, 43n50

cannibals
 'Of Crueltie' alludes to, 129
 in 'Of the Caniballes', 131, 133–6, 138–9, 140–1, 142, 148n24, 149n31, 150n46, 150n47, 153n60
 in *The Tempest*, 11, 129, 131, 136, 142–3
Capell, Edward, 2, 3–4, 5, 14n7, 129
Cave, Terence, 40n9
Cavell, Stanley, 40n10, 117, 118, 123, 126n18, 147n15
certainty
 Cartesian modernity's rage for, 38, 40n10
 in *Cymbeline*, 159–60
 in *Measure for Measure*, 82, 84, 86, 88
 Montaigne on difficulty of obtaining, 31
 Montaigne on philosophers and, 26
 in *The Winter's Tale*, 160–1
 see also uncertainty
Chambers, E. K., 70n18, 103n6, 103n9, 105n24
Chappuit, Jean-François, 5
Charles IX (king of France), 135
Chasles, Philarète, 5
chastity, 90, 141
Cicero, 25, 81
Clarendon Shakespeare, 48
Clark, William George, 48, 49
Collier, John Payne, 47–8, 49, 70n13
Collins, J. Churlton, 6, 16n29
Comedy of Errors, The (Shakespeare), 157–8, 161, 167n7
Conley, Tom, 147n19
'contrarieties', 28, 31, 36, 42n33
Coriolanus (Shakespeare), 5
Cornwallis, Sir William, 46, 69n5, 69n6
Cosman, Bard, 100
Cotgrave, Randall, 2, 14n4, 22n64, 116, 133
critical theory, 30

culture versus nature
 in *All's Well That Ends Well*, 98
 in *Antony and Cleopatra*, 165–6
 in 'Of the Caniballes', 130, 133–4, 140, 144, 152n56, 165
 in *The Tempest*, 130, 140, 144, 152n56, 165, 166
Cymbeline (Shakespeare), 159–60, 161
cynicism
 in *All's Well That Ends Well*, 102
 in 'An Apologie de Raymond Sebond', 18n37
 in *Antony and Cleopatra*, 165
 in *Hamlet*, 18n37
 in *King Lear*, 112, 127n21, 127n23
 in 'Of Diverting or Diversion', 60
 in 'Of the Affection of Fathers to Their Children', 112, 113
 in *Othello*, 155
 in problem plays, 78
 in *The Tempest*, 130, 146n14

Daniel, Samuel, 3, 145n1
De Certeau, Michel, 142, 147n19
De Gooyer, Alan, 20n58, 145n7, 151n54
death
 in *Hamlet*, 65–6
 in *Measure for Measure*, 89–90, 91, 92
 in 'Of Diverting or Diversion', 55–6
 in *The Winter's Tale*, 160, 161
 see also mourning
Desan, Philippe, 14n4, 150n47
Descartes, René, 36, 38, 40n10, 43n48, 43n50
Dessen, Alan C., 72n35
Dictionarie of the French and English Tongves, A (Cotgrave), 2, 116, 133
Diogenes Laertius, 25
DiPietro, Cary, 71n18
disintegrationism, 48–9, 70n18
diversions
 change associated with, 57
 functions of, 45
 in *Hamlet*, 10, 55, 64, 65, 66, 77
 Montaigne's ambivalence toward, 10, 53, 57–60, 64, 66, 77
 revenge contrasted with, 56
 theatricality linked to, 45, 57

Donaldson, Ian, 107n32, 108n38, 108n40
Dutch Courtesan, The (Marston), 3, 15n12
Dutton, Richard, 19n54
Duval, Edwin, 148n29, 149n31

Eliot, T. S.
  'Hamlet and His Problems', 17n34
  on Montaigne as stimulant for Shakespeare, 7, 17n34
  on Taylor on Montaigne-Shakespeare connection, 7, 51–2, 53
  on words and phrases in Shakespeare and Florio's translation of Montaigne, 7, 12
Ellrodt, Robert
  exploration of shared ideas of Montaigne and Shakespeare, 12
  on language in 'Of the Caniballes' and *The Tempest*, 5
  Montaigne and Shakespeare: The Emergence of Modern Self-Consciousness, 8, 42n44
  on Montaigne and Shakespeare and relativism, 42n44
  on self-consciousness in Montaigne and Shakespeare, 35
  on self-consistency in Montaigne, 35–6
emotion, feigning versus true, 62–3
Empson, William, 73n43
Engle, Lars, 9, 29, 78, 104n11, 106n29
Epaminondas, 55
Epicurus, 55, 114–15
equipollence, 26, 30
Essayes or morall, politike and millitarie discourses, The (Montaigne)
  Blount as publisher of, 3
  'canibal' in, 142
  'Epistle Dedicatorie', 71n32
  Hamlet influenced by, 69n7, 50–2, 62, 73n43
  Harmon on Shakespeare and, 7
  Montaigne's cannibals in, 149n38
  playwrights make use of, 3, 15n12
  Prosser on Shakespeare and, 17n36
  publication of, 1, 52
  Shakespeare influenced by, 9
  Shakespeare linked to language of, 5, 6–7, 12, 47
  Shakespeare's knowledge of, 1, 2, 17n35
  Shakespeare's possible pre-1603 access to, 46, 69n5, 69n6
  The Tempest linked to, 4, 17n36, 129, 136, 145n6, 145n7, 150n44, 152n55
  see also essays by name
'Essaying Trouble' (Zalloua), 22n66, 43n48
essays
  as corrosive, 10
  Montaigne's and Shakespeare's compared, 2
  plays contrasted with, 9–10
  post-structuralism and, 43n48
  soliloquies compared with, 9–10, 19n52, 74n43
  transgress orthodoxy of thought, 12–13, 22n66
  see also Montaigne's essays
Estienne, Henri, 25

Fabulous Imagination, The (Kritzman), 22n65, 42n45
Feis, Jacob, 5–6, 30, 50–1, 72n38
Fiedler, Leslie, 149n39
First Folio (F)
  'A little more then kin, and lesse then kind' in, 71n32
  Blount as publisher of, 3
  'canibal' in, 142
  Hamlet in, 48, 49, 50, 61, 65, 156
First Quarto (Q1) *Hamlet*
  'A little more then kin, and lesse then kind' not in, 71n32
  borrowings from Belleforest in, 71n27
  on death, 65–6
  gains in anger and focus on theatricality in Q2, 60–1, 62, 63–4
  growing sophistication seen between two Quartos, 70n15

First Quarto (Q1) *Hamlet* (*cont.*)
  as memorial reconstruction, 70, 70n13, 72n33, 167n3
  Montaignian echoes in, 68n5
  Montaignian nature of post-Q1 *Hamlet*, 10, 156
  seen as Elizabethan, 19n54
  as shorter and simpler than traditional version, 71n27, 167n3
  textual history of the play, 47–51
  'to be, or not to be' soliloquy, 156
  two-track approach to, 72n35
Fleay, F. G., 48
Florio, John
  Montaigne's essays transformed by, 12
  translation of Montaigne's *Essais*, 1
  A Worlde of Wordes, 67
  see also Essayes or morall, politike and millitarie discourses, The (Montaigne)
Floyd-Wilson, Mary, 108n38
Foucault, Michel, 38, 47
Frampton, Saul, 21n63
Friedrich, Hugo, 17n35, 36–7
friendship, 113
Frye, Roland Mushat, 61, 62
Furnivall, F. J., 48

Gilbert, Allan H., 129, 150n40
Ginzburg, Carlo, 132–3, 147n20
Go, Kenji, 129, 136, 138, 150n44
Grady, Hugh
  on dates of Shakespeare's encounter with Montaigne, 46–7
  on discursive dynamics, 12, 46–7
  exploration of shared ideas of Montaigne and Shakespeare, 12
  on French and German scholars on Montaigne–Shakespeare connection, 15n21
  on getting bogged down in source hunting, 21n61
  on impure aesthetics, 102n4
  on scepticism of Montaigne and Shakespeare, 18n40, 34, 42n37, 44n56
  on Shakespeare and Montaigne on instrumental reason, 23n68

Shakespeare, Machiavelli, and Montaigne, 8, 42n37, 44n56
  on shift in Anglo-American scholarship on Montaigne–Shakespeare linkage, 18n43
Gray, Patrick, 72n38
Greenblatt, Stephen
  on anticipatory, or proleptic, parody, 85, 105n21
  attitude toward Montaigne, 125n4
  on geriatric avarice, 111
  on *King Lear* and the theatre, 128n24
  on *Measure for Measure*, 106n25
  on miracle minting in *King Lear*, 127n23
  on 'Of the Affection of Fathers to Their Children' and *King Lear*, 109
  on Prospero-Caliban relationship, 151n53
  on Shakespeare's borrowing as act of aggression, 131
Guarini, Giambattista, 3
Guild, Elizabeth, 22n65, 148n27, 149n31, 150n46

Hamlet (Shakespeare), 60–8
  ambition in, 67–8
  Claudius's soliloquy, 19n52
  dating of, 10, 45, 69n5
  on death, 65–6
  discontinuous self in, 32
  on diversions, 10, 55, 64, 65, 66, 77
  Eliot on, 17n34
  in First Folio (F), 48, 49, 50, 61, 65, 156
  Florio's translation of Montaigne as influence on, 69n7, 50–2, 62, 73n38
  Graveyard scene, 65–6
  Hamlet compared with Montaigne, 5–6, 51, 65, 72n38
  Harmon's misreading of, 17n37
  Hecuba in, 63, 64, 74n49
  as most Montaignian of Shakespeare's plays, 10, 45–6, 52–3, 68n2, 68n5, 156
  obscene pun in, 150n42

'Of Diverting or Diversion' linked to, 45, 60, 62–3, 65–6
Pyrrhus episode, 63
'quintessence of dust' speech, 75n70
revenge and, 66, 67
scepticism in, 29
selfhood in, 32, 156–7
textual history of, 47–53
theatricality, 10, 53, 60, 62–5
'To be, or not to be' soliloquy, 156–7, 167n3
Ur-Hamlet, 48, 49, 50, 66
see also First Quarto (Q1) *Hamlet*; Second Quarto (Q2) *Hamlet*
'Hamlet and His Problems' (Eliot), 17n34
'*Hamlet* When New' (Empson), 73n43
Hamlin, William M.
  'A Lost Translation Found?', 42n33
  on 'contrarieties', 42n33
  on English playwrights reading Florio's translation of Montaigne, 15n12
  exploration of shared ideas of Montaigne and Shakespeare, 12
  on Greenblatt on Montaigne-Shakespeare connection, 110
  on influence, 21n61
  on Montaignean constellation, 39n5
  on Montaigne and Pyrrhonism, 26
  'Montaigne and Shakespeare', 12, 125n4
  Montaigne's English Journey, 8, 69n6
  on sceptical values, 27, 168n10
  Scepticism in Shakespeare's England, 15n12, 40n10, 167n7, 168n10
  on *The Sceptick* fragment, 27
  on Shakespeare and Montaigne on systematic thinking, 21n60
  'The Shakespeare–Montaigne–Sextus Nexus', 21n60, 21n61, 38, 39n5
  on Shakespeare's knowledge of Montaigne before 1603, 69n6
  on skeptical paradigm, 40n14
  on total scepticism, 158
  Tragedy and Scepticism in Shakespeare's England, 15n12, 40n14

on vulgar scepticism, 167n7
weaker thesis of synchronic affinity, 12
'What Did Montaigne's Skepticism Mean to Shakespeare and His Contemporaries?', 40n14, 168n10
Harmon, Alice, 7, 17n36, 17n37
Hartle, Ann, 22n67, 26–7, 44n57, 147n23
Harvey, Gabriel, 50
Hazlitt, William Carew, 19n46, 46
Hendrick, Philip, 149n38, 152n55
Henry IV (king of France), 56
Henry V (Shakespeare), 46
Hodgen, Margaret, 7–8
Hoffmann, George, 148n28
Holbrook, Peter, 35, 39n4, 40n5, 143
Hooker, Elizabeth R., 6
Horkheimer, Max, 29–30, 31, 41n29, 42n37, 107n36
'How Great was Shakespeare's Debt to Montaigne?' (Harmon), 7
Hunter, George, 78

International Shakespeare World Congress (2001), 8
intertextuality, 20n57
Irace, Kathleen, 49, 50, 72n33
Isidore of Seville, 151n52
'It is Follie to Referre Truth or Falsehood to Our Sufficiencie' (Montaigne), 158–9

James I (king of England), 1, 98
Jenkins, Harold, 67, 69n7, 76n71
Jolly, Margarethe, 71n27
Jonson, Ben, 3, 15n12, 36, 57
Jourdan, Serena, 18n41, 21n61, 39n5
justice
  injustice of the problem plays, 78
  in *Measure for Measure*, 85, 86, 93, 106n29
  'We Taste Nothing Purely' on, 80–1, 82

Kastan, David, 66, 74n55
Kearney, James, 127n21
Keats, John, 9
Kerrigan, John, 152n56

King Lear (Shakespeare), 115–25
  avoidance of love in, 117
  Dover Cliffs scene, 123–4
  elements in shaping of, 1
  fathers refusing to acknowledge
    their children in, 118–21, 123
  Lear's madness, 121–2
  on mental engenderings, 11, 110,
    121–3
  misogyny of, 116–17
  Montaigne's influence on *Hamlet*
    and, 10, 46
  'Of the Affection of Fathers to Their
    Children' linked to, 11, 109–10,
    112, 116, 117–18, 121, 123
  theatricality in, 11, 123, 124–5,
    128n24
  as tragedy, 125
  Troilus and Cressida compared with,
    104n11
  two versions of, 49
Kirsch, Arthur, 8, 95, 100, 104n11,
  107n32
Knight, Charles, 47–8, 49, 70n15
Knight, G. Wilson, 106n30
knowledge
  contrariety in, 28, 36
  in *Cymbeline*, 159–60
  instability of, 1, 2
  quest for self and quest for, 35–8
  rash presumptions of, 29, 99, 159
  self-knowledge, 36, 154, 155, 157
  see also certainty; scepticism
Knowles, Ronald, 69n5
Kott, Jan, 151n48, 152n58
Kristeva, Julia, 20n57
Kritzman, Lawrence, 10, 22n65,
  42n45, 44n56

La Boétie, Etienne, 56–7
Lacan, Jacques, 36, 38, 43n48
law
  in *Measure for Measure*, 84–5, 93
  'We Taste Nothing Purely' on, 80–1
  see also justice
Leggatt, Alexander, 78
Lesser, Zachary, 48–9, 70n18
Lestringant, Frank, 146n11, 152n55,
  153n60

Levin, Harry, 19n52, 64, 73n43
Lewis, Rhodri, 73n38
Life of Pyrrho (Diogenes Laertius), 25
Livy, 81
Lodge, Thomas, 50, 66
'Lost Translation Found?, A' (Hamlin),
  42n33
love, diversion and, 56
Lyotard, Jean-François, 43n48

McCarthy, Dennis, 21n62
Mack, Peter
  exploration of shared ideas of
    Montaigne and Shakespeare, 12
  on Montaigne and necessity of
    bodily functions, 107n34
  on Montaigne and Shakespeare on
    thinking ethically, 39n5
  *Reading and Rhetoric in
    Shakespeare and Montaigne*, 8,
    19n52
  on soliloquies, 19n52
Madden, Sir Frederic, 5, 15n18
Maguin, Jean-Marie, 146n13
Malone, Edmund, 4, 129, 149n34,
  150n44
Marino, James, 49, 50
marriage
  in *Measure for Measure*, 93–4,
    106n29
  in 'Of the Caniballes', 140–1, 144
  in *The Tempest*, 141–2, 144
Marston, John, 3, 15n12
Matthiessien, F. O., 16n27
Measure for Measure (Shakespeare),
  82–94
  absence of purity in, 82–3, 89,
    92, 93
  anticipatory, or proleptic, parody in,
    85, 105n21
  certainty in, 82, 84, 86, 88
  darker readings of the Duke, 92,
    105n24
  on death, 89–90, 91, 92
  doubleness of, 77–8
  the Duke seen as emblem of the
    playwright, 106n25
  elements in shaping of, 1
  Engle on, 104n11

equity as concern of, 81
Isabella as ideally 'impure' heroine, 93
Isabella's chastity without charity, 93, 106n26
justice in, 85, 86, 93, 106n29
law in, 84–5, 93
marriages at end of, 93–4, 106n29
paradox in, 82, 91, 105n18, 106n27
perspectivism in, 87
as problem play, 78, 103n6, 106n29
rhetoric in, 83
as romantic comedy, 92–4
sexuality in, 83, 88, 89, 90–2, 93, 94
shiftingness of, 102n4
visual indeterminacy linked to, 104n12
'We Taste Nothing Purely' linked to, 10–11, 82
Menzer, Paul, 72n33
Merchant of Venice (Shakespeare), 32, 163–4
Metamorphoses (Ovid), 54, 145n8
Methodus (Bodin), 81, 104n15
Metrodorus, 79–80
Michel de Montaigne (Hartle), 22n67, 26–7, 147n23
Midsummer Night's Dream, A (Shakespeare), 167n8
Mimesis (Auerbach), 22n64, 39n3
misogyny
　in *Antony and Cleopatra*, 164
　in *Cymbeline*, 160
　in *King Lear*, 116–17
　in 'Of the Affection of Fathers to Their Children', 114, 116, 117
　in *The Winter's Tale*, 160
Mommsen, Tycho, 48, 49, 70n13
monsters, 143–4, 151n52
Montaigne (Friedrich), 17n35
Montaigne, Michel de
　alterity as interest of, 10
　Angelo as anti-Montaignian character, 84
　on being otherwise, 22n65
　Cavell quotes, 126n18
　Collins on Shakespeare and, 16n29
　conservatism of, 34
　as counter-Cartesian, 36
　as cultivating a free self, 39n4
　debate over Shakespeare's connection to, 2–8
　on discontinuous self, 9, 24, 31–4, 36, 41n32, 42n45
　on diversions, 10
　double perspective of, 105n18
　as Epicurean, 72n38
　essaying not resolving, 12, 21n64
　Hamlet compared with, 5–6, 51, 65, 72n38
　on imagination, 22n65
　on intertextuality, 20n57
　knowing and being in, 24–44
　on knowledge of truth, 99
　and (post-)modernity, 34–8
　on multiplicity, 9, 24, 30, 39n4
　naïveté attributed to, 112, 113, 116, 120, 125n4, 131
　as negotiator between Catholics and Protestants, 148n30
　perspectivism of, 9, 24, 39n3, 39n4, 28–9, 31, 37–8
　pessimism of, 11, 113, 120
　on philosophical thought, 157
　post-structuralism and, 43n48
　as quietistic, 30
　reactive reading of texts by, 20n60
　on reading as incorporation and communion, 153n59
　relativism and, 42n44
　retiring to his tower to write, 43n50
　scepticism of, 18n40, 22n67, 23n68, 24–31, 34, 36, 39n5, 40n11, 42n37, 44n56, 106n29, 158–9
　Shakespeare's authorial approach compared with that of, 1–2
　on sitting upon our own tail, 98, 107n34
　on systematic thinking, 21n60
　this study's view of Shakespeare's connection with, 8–10
　on tradition, 23n68
　see also Montaigne's essays; *and essays by name*
'Montaigne and Shakespeare' (Hamlin), 12, 125n4
Montaigne and Shakespeare: The Emergence of Modern Self-Consciousness (Ellrodt), 8, 42n44

'Montaigne and Shakespeare Again' (Hodgen), 7–8
Montaigne and the Origins of Modern Philosophy (Hartle), 44n57
Montaigne and the Quality of Mercy (Quint), 148n24, 148n30
'Montaigne in England and America' (Boutcher), 14n6, 145n1
Montaigne in Motion (Starobinski), 34–5
'Montaigne–Shakespeare and the Deadly Parallel' (Taylor), 17n36
'Montaigne, the New World, and Precolonialisms' (Reiss), 147n16, 147n19, 149n38, 152n57, 152n58
'Montaigne the Writer' (Auerbach), 39n3
Montaigne's English Journey (Hamlin), 8, 69n6
Montaigne's essays
  culture-nature tension in, 165, 166
  Florio's English translation of, 1
  larger thematic and structural parallels with Shakespeare, 12, 21n62
  literary genre created by, 2
  problem plays haunted by, 102
  Shakespeare alters, transforms and confounds, 20n57
  Shakespeare as best reader of, 2, 38, 41n29
  Shakespeare's possible pre-1603 access to, 46–7, 68n5
  Shakespeare's soliloquies linked to, 9–10
  transgress orthodoxy of thought, 12–13
  see also Essayes or morall, politike and millitarie discourses, The (Montaigne)
'Montaignian Moments' (Burrow), 20n60, 21n63
mourning
  in *Hamlet*, 60, 61–2
  Montaigne on, 52–4, 56–7, 58, 59, 60

multiplicity
  Montaigne on, 9, 24, 30, 39n4
  of selves, 156, 157, 166
  Shakespeare on, 9, 24, 39n4, 154
  of truth, 11, 154

Nashe, Thomas, 27, 105n22
nature versus culture *see* culture versus nature
New Oxford Shakespeare, 69n5, 71n29
Nietzsche, Friedrich, 2, 28, 35, 38, 41n29
Notes and Various Readings to Shakespeare (Capell), 2, 3–4, 5, 14n7
Nowotny, Helen, 43n52, 44n56
Nuttall, A. D., 93

O'Brien, John, 1, 10, 108n45, 135, 147n22, 148n26
'Of Coaches' (Montaigne), 153n61
'Of Crueltie' (Montaigne), 17n36, 129
'Of Diverting or Diversion' (Montaigne), 53–60
  on ambition, 56, 66–7
  on death, 55–6
  Hamlet linked to, 45, 60, 62–3, 65–6
  on laments of Ariadne and Dido, 58, 64
  on mourning, 52–4, 56–7, 58, 59, 60
  on revenge, 56, 66–7
  on theatricality, 58–9, 63, 64
'Of Experience' (Montaigne), 29, 77, 98, 103n5, 106n29
'Of Glorie' (Montaigne), 77, 126n18
'Of Repenting' (Montaigne), 21n64
'Of the Affection of Fathers to Their Children' (Montaigne), 110–15
  on economic translation between generations, 112–13, 116
  on fathers, 111–12, 116
  King Lear linked to, 11, 109–10, 112, 116, 117–18, 121, 123
  on Lord of Montluc, 113–14, 117–18, 120
  on mental engenderings, 11, 110, 114–15, 121, 123, 125
  misogyny of, 114, 116, 117

on parent-child relationship as not reciprocal, 110–11
on Pygmalion, 115, 123
'Of the Caniballes' (Montaigne), 132–6
  ambivalence in, 142–3
  binaries complicated in, 141
  on cannibals, 131, 133–6, 138–9, 140–1, 142, 148n24, 149n31, 150n46, 150n47, 153n60
  challenge to vulgar opinions and common report in, 131
  on custom versus nature, 130, 133–4, 140, 144, 152n56, 165
  as essay in the most literal sense, 152n55
  islands in, 136–8, 149n34, 149n36
  key passage of *The Tempest* borrowed from, 129–30
  as literary paradox, 146n11
  on marriage, 141–2, 144
  on Montaigne's encounter with Brazilians, 135–6, 148n27
  music in, 138–9
  on the other, 141, 147n19, 152n57
  polyvalence of 'barbarie' in, 147n22
  on proto-noble savage, 130, 152n58
  on simplicity and truth, 132
  The Tempest linked to, 2, 3–5, 6, 7–8, 11, 16n27, 17n36, 129–32, 144, 145n6, 145n7, 146n13, 146n14, 152n55, 164
  Western equity questioned in, 148n26
'Of the Force of the Imagination' (Montaigne), 22n67
'Of the Inconstancie of Our Actions' (Montaigne), 31, 39n4
'Of the Institution and Education of Children' (Montaigne), 9, 20n57, 28–9
'Of Vanitie' (Montaigne), 31
'On the Meaning of *Ei*' (Plutarch), 33
Orgel, Stephen, 141, 142, 149n37, 150n45
'Originality of Shakespeare, The' (Robertson), 16n28
'Origins and Agents of Q1 *Hamlet*' (Irace), 72n33

Othello (Shakespeare)
  discontinuous self in, 32
  Iago's soliloquies in, 155–6
  Montaigne seen in, 5
  Troilus and Cressida compared with, 104n11
other, the
  Montaigne and Shakespeare as interested in alterity, 10
  'Of the Caniballes' on, 141, 147n19, 152n57
  Shakespeare on cultural, 11, 154, 161, 162–6
Ovid, 54, 115, 145n1, 145n8
Oxford Handbook of Montaigne, 12

Page, Frederic, 17n35
pain, 57, 58, 79–80, 98
painting, 28, 80
Palfrey, Simon, 13n3, 22n65, 127n20, 127n22, 128n25
Panofsky, Erwin, 152n58
Parker, Fred, 9, 105n18, 146n14
Paster, Gail Kern, 145n6, 149n36
Pastor fido, Il (Guarini), 3
perspectivism
  in *Measure for Measure*, 87
  of Montaigne, 9, 24, 39n3, 39n4, 28–9, 31, 37–8
  of Shakespeare, 9, 24, 39n3, 39n4, 28–9, 31, 37–8
pessimism
  of Montaigne, 11, 113, 120
  of the problem plays, 78
  of Shakespeare, 6, 11, 109, 115, 120
  in Shakespeare's later plays, 1
Plato, 4, 24, 80, 81, 104n15, 145n1, 133, 134, 153n59
Plutarch, 33, 153n59
Pollard, Tanya, 74n49
Popkin, Richard, 40n11
post-structuralism, 36, 42n45, 43n48
Problem of 'Hamlet', The (Robertson), 17n34, 51–2
problem plays
  characteristics of, 78–9, 103n6
  doubleness of, 77–8
  Montaigne haunts, 102

problem plays (cont.)
  new strain of brooding attributed to, 104n12
  scepticism in, 103n9
  shiftingness of, 102n4
  as tragi-comedies, 103n9
  Troilus and Cressida, 32, 78, 103n6, 104n11, 106n29
  'We Taste Nothing Purely' compared with, 10–11, 78, 79
  see also *All's Well That Ends Well* (Shakespeare); *Measure for Measure* (Shakespeare)
Prosser, Eleanor, 17n36, 129, 145n6
purity
  absence in *Measure for Measure*, 82–3, 89, 92, 93
  in *All's Well That Ends Well*, 96, 98, 100
  problem plays and, 79
  'We Taste Nothing Purely' on, 11, 78, 81, 82
Pygmalion, 115, 123
Pyrrho of Elis, 25
Pyrrhonism *see* scepticism

Question of Hamlet, The (Levin), 19n52, 73n43
Quiller-Couch, Arthur, 104n12
Quint, David, 11, 132, 134, 135, 148n24, 148n30, 149n31
Quintilian, 57, 59, 62, 64, 74n50

Ramachandran, Ayesha, 24, 152n56
rationality (reason)
  Foucault on history and, 38
  in *King Lear*, 109
  Montaigne and Shakespeare on instrumental, 23n68
  Montaigne on common report versus, 131, 132
  seventeenth-century attitude toward, 37
Reading and Rhetoric in Shakespeare and Montaigne (Mack), 8, 19n52
reason *see* rationality (reason)
Regosin, Richard, 131
Reiss, Timothy J., 147n16, 147n19, 149n38, 152n57, 152n58

relativism, 42n44, 136
revenge, 56, 66–7, 134, 147n23
rhetoric
  Aristotle on, 22n65
  in *King Lear*, 118
  in *Measure for Measure*, 83
  rhetors moved by their own performances, 58–9
  Shakespeare's interest in judicial, 1
Richard II (Shakespeare), 32, 98, 156, 157
Richard III (Shakespeare), 154–5, 166n1
Robertson, J. M.
  on close reading for verbal echoes, 12
  on differences between First and Second Quartos and Montaigne's influence on *Hamlet*, 50, 51
  as disintegrationist, 49
  on looking narrowly to dates, 47
  on magnitude of Shakespeare's debt to Montaigne, 6, 16n28
  on Montaigne as quietistic, 30
  'The Originality of Shakespeare', 16n28
  The Problem of 'Hamlet', 17n34, 51–2
Rossiter, A. P., 23n68, 78, 102n4, 103n9, 106n26, 107n32
Ryan, Kiernan, 22n65, 125n6

Said, Edward, 151n50
Salingar, Leo, 109
scepticism
  in *All's Well That Ends Well*, 29, 98, 99, 107n36
  Cartesian, 40n10
  Cavell on, 126n18
  classical, 25–31
  in *The Comedy of Errors*, 157–8
  critical theory contrasted with, 30
  in *Cymbeline*, 160
  in *King Lear*, 124
  in *Measure for Measure*, 85
  of Montaigne, 18n40, 22n67, 23n68, 24–31, 34, 36, 39n5, 42n37, 44n56, 106n29, 158–9
  in the problem plays, 103n9

Pyrrhonian, 23n67, 26–7, 30, 40n11
sceptical values, 27, 168n10
 of Shakespeare, 18n40, 23n68, 24–31, 34, 39n5, 44n56, 131, 154, 157, 161, 166, 167n8, 168n10
 vulgar, 167n7
 in *The Winter's Tale*, 160–1
Scepticism in Shakespeare's England (Hamlin), 15n12, 40n10, 167n7, 168n10
Sceptick, The (fragment), 27–8
Schlueter, June, 21n62
School of Montaigne, The (Boutcher), 8
Schücking, L. L., 48
Second Quarto (Q2) *Hamlet*
 'A little more then kin, and lesse then kind' in, 71n32
 borrowings from Belleforest in, 71n27
 on death, 65–6
 gains in anger and focus on theatricality compared to Q1, 60, 61, 62, 63
 growing sophistication seen between two Quartos, 70n15
 Montaignian nature of post-Q1 *Hamlet*, 10, 156
 seen as Jacobean, 19n54
 textual history of the play, 47, 48, 49, 50
self
 in *Antony and Cleopatra*, 32–3, 157
 Cartesian versus Montaignian, 37
 'contrarieties' in, 31
 discontinuous, 9, 24, 31–4, 36, 41n32, 42n45, 166
 as double, 126n18
 in flux, 35, 38, 156, 157
 in *Hamlet*, 32, 156–7
 instability of, 1, 2, 36, 155–6, 157
 Montaigne on, 24, 39n4, 157
 multiplicity of selves, 156, 157, 166
 ontological distinction between other and, 152n56
 quest for knowledge and quest for, 35–8
 self-knowledge, 36, 154, 155, 157
 Shakespeare on, 24, 154, 161, 166

soliloquies as gauge of inwardness, 154
 theatricality of the, 31, 32, 157
 uncertainty of, 34
Seneca, 80, 153n59
Sexti Philosophi Pyrrhoniarum hypotyposeon libri III (*Hypotyposes; Outlines of Pyrrhonism*) (Sextus Empiricus), 25–6, 27
Sextus Empiricus, 25–6, 27
sexuality
 in *All's Well That Ends Well*, 99–100
 chastity, 90, 141
 in *Measure for Measure*, 83, 88, 89, 90–2, 93, 94
 in 'Of the Caniballes', 140
 in *The Tempest*, 130
 virginity, 83, 95, 141, 142
 'We Taste Nothing Purely' on, 79, 80
Shakespeare, William
 alterity as interest of, 10
 on being otherwise, 22n65
 as best reader of Montaigne's essays, 2, 38, 41n29
 Collins on Montaigne and, 16n29
 conservatism of, 34
 on cultural other, 11, 154, 161, 162–6
 debate over his connection to Montaigne, 2–8
 on discontinuous self, 9, 24, 31–4
 essaying not resolving, 12
 father's death, 62
 Florio's translation of Montaigne's *Essays* as influence on, 9
 Florio's translation of Montaigne's *Essays* known by, 1, 2, 17n35
 Florio's translation of Montaigne's essays transformed by, 12
 knowing and being in, 24–44
 Montaigne's authorial approach compared with that of, 1–2
 on multiplicity, 9, 24, 39n4, 154
 perspectivism of, 9, 24, 39n3, 39n4, 28–9, 31, 37–8
 pessimism of, 6, 11, 109, 115, 120

Shakespeare, William (*cont.*)
  possible pre-1603 access to
    Montaigne's essays, 46–7, 69n5,
    69n6
  and (post-)modernity, 34–8
  as quietistic, 30
  reactive reading of texts by, 20n60
  on reading as incorporation and
    communion, 153n59
  relativism and, 42n44
  scepticism of, 18n40, 23n68, 24–31,
    34, 39n5, 44n56, 131, 154, 157,
    161, 166, 167n8, 168n10
  on the self, 9, 24, 31–4, 154, 161, 166
  sonnets, 69n5
  on systematic thinking, 21n60
  this study's view of his connection
    with Montaigne, 8–10
  see also Shakespeare's plays
Shakespeare: A Survey (Chambers),
  103n6, 103n9, 105n24
*Shakespeare and Montaigne
  Reconsidered* (Anzai), 14n6, 69n5
'Shakespeare and Ovid' (Bate), 145n8
Shakespeare Association of America, 8
Shakespeare, Court Dramatist
  (Dutton), 19n54
'Shakespeare et Montaigne: Vers
  un Nouvel Humanisme'
  (conference), 8
*Shakespeare, Machiavelli, and
  Montaigne* (Grady), 8, 42n37,
  44n56
'Shakespeare, Montaigne and Classical
  Reason' (Holbrook), 40n5
'Shakespeare, Montaigne, and the
  Rarer Action' (Prosser), 17n36
'Shakespeare–Montaigne–Sextus
  Nexus, The' (Hamlin), 21n60,
  21n61, 38, 39n5
'Shakespeare's Argument with
  Montaigne' (Parker), 9, 105n18,
  146n14
Shakespeare's Debt to Montaigne
  (Taylor), 6–7, 14n8
Shakespeare's plays
  larger thematic and structural
    parallels with Montaigne, 12,
    21n62
  later 'Jacobean' plays, 1
  before Montaigne's *Essays*, 154–68
  multivocal stagings of, 10
  transgress orthodoxy of thought,
    12–13
  wonder as focus of last plays, 159
  see also First Folio (F); First Quarto
    (Q1); problem plays; Second
    Quarto (Q2); soliloquies; *and by
    name*
Shakespeare's Possible Worlds
  (Palfrey), 13n3
Shakespeare's Scepticism (Bradshaw),
  167n8
Shakespeare's Universality (Ryan),
  22n65, 125n6
Shakespeare's Unreformed Fictions
  (Woods), 104n12, 127n19
Shakspere and His Predecessors
  (Boas), 78
Shapiro, James, 75n65
Shaw, George Bernard, 103n6
Sherman, Anita Gilman, 41n24
Simon, David Carroll, 23n68
Six Bookes of a Commonweale, The
  (Bodin), 81
Socrates, 54–5, 65, 66, 79
soliloquies
  in *Antony and Cleopatra*, 157
  of Claudius in *Hamlet*, 19n52
  essays compared with, 9–10, 19n52,
    74n43
  as gauge of inwardness, 154
  for getting in touch with the
    audience, 154–5
  in *Hamlet*, 156–7
  in *Othello*, 155–6
  in *Richard III*, 154–5
Sparrow and the Flea, The (Jourdan),
  18n41, 21n61, 39n5
Starobinski, Jean, 34–5
Sterling, John, 5, 46, 51, 65
Stern, Tiffany, 49, 50
Stoicism, 25, 26, 36, 135, 148n24,
  149n30
Stoll, E. E., 48
Strier, Richard, 158

Tacitus, 80, 81, 93, 104n15
Taylor, Charles, 37
Taylor, Gary, 30

Taylor, George Coffin
  digital methods for confirming work of, 21n62
  Eliot on, 7, 51–2, 53
  on *Hamlet* as Montaignian play, 45–6, 52–3, 68n2
  on linguistic parallels in Shakespeare and Florio's translation of Montaigne, 6–7, 12, 16n27, 62
  'Montaigne–Shakespeare and the Deadly Parallel', 17n36
  reply to Harmon of, 17n36
  Shakespeare's Debt to Montaigne, 6–7, 14n8
  skepticism towards argument of, 17n35
Tempest, The (Shakespeare), 136–45
  ambivalence in, 142–3
  Caliban disturbs the order of things, 143–4, 164
  cannibal in, 11, 129, 131, 136, 142–3
  as cannibalised, 153n59
  culture-nature tension in, 130, 140, 144, 152n56, 165, 166
  discontinuous self in, 33
  doubleness in, 151n48, 152n58
  elements in shaping of, 1
  on ethics of yielding, 11, 132
  Florio's translation of Montaigne linked to, 4, 17n36, 129, 136, 145n6, 145n7, 150n44, 152n55
  hybridity of Caliban, 151n48, 151n50
  key passage borrowed from 'Of the Caniballes', 129–30
  Kirsch on Montaigne's thinking and, 8
  Montaigne's cannibal and Caliban, 142, 150n45
  music in, 138, 139–40, 149n37, 149n39
  'Of Crueltie' linked to, 17n36, 129
  'Of the Caniballes' linked to, 2, 3–5, 6, 7–8, 11, 16n27, 17n36, 129–32, 144, 145n6, 145n7, 146n13, 146n14, 152n55, 164
  Ovid's *Metamorphoses* as source for, 145n8
  Prospero's willingness to forgive in, 151n54
  rape attempt in, 141–2
  reading as an *essai*, 9
  as reversing Montaigne, 11
  setting of, 136–8, 149n34
  wedding masque in, 141–2, 144
'*Tempest, The*, and Cultural Change' (Maguin), 146n13
'That a Man Ought to Meddle with Iudging of Divine Lawes' (Montaigne), 107n35
'That the Taste of Goods or Evilles Doth Greatly Depend on the Opinion We Have of Them' (Montaigne), 67
theatricality
  actors moved by their own performances, 58–9
  actors seen as rogues, 101, 108n42
  in *All's Well That Ends Well*, 101–2
  of being, 24, 32, 34
  diversion linked to, 45, 57
  in *Hamlet*, 10, 53, 60, 62–5
  in *King Lear*, 11, 123, 124–5, 128n24
  mind's engenderings in the theatre, 110
  in 'Of Diverting or Diversion', 58–9, 63, 64
  in *Richard II*, 156
  salutary anxiety of the theatre, 106n25
  of the self, 31, 32, 157
Titus Andronicus (Shakespeare), 161–2
Todorov, Tzvetan, 41n32, 42n44, 147n22
torture, 134
Toulmin, Stephen, 37
Tragedy and Scepticism in Shakespeare's England (Hamlin), 15n12, 40n14
Troilus and Cressida (Shakespeare), 32, 78, 103n6, 104n11, 106n29
truth
  in *Measure for Measure*, 86, 89, 91, 106n29
  Montaigne on, 26, 81, 99
  multiplicity of, 11, 154

truth (*cont.*)
  'Of the Caniballes' on, 132, 133, 134, 145, 149n31
  see also knowledge
Twelfth Night (Shakespeare), 28, 32, 80

uncertainty
  of knowledge, 30, 34
  Montaigne's counter-Cartesianism and, 36
  in science, 43n52, 44n56
  of the self, 34
  sixteenth-century commitment to, 37
Unsettling Montaigne (Guild), 22n65, 148n27, 149n31, 150n46
'Upon Some Verses of Virgil' (Montaigne), 95, 100
Ur-Hamlet, 48, 49, 50, 66
Urkowitz, Steven, 49, 72n35

Vaughan, Alden and Virginia, 143, 151n52
Villey, Pierre, 6, 8
Virgil, 152n56
virginity, 83, 95, 141, 142
Volpone (Jonson), 3

'We Taste Nothing Purely' (Montaigne), 79–81
  All's Well That Ends Well linked to, 10–11, 95, 100, 107n32
  central thesis of, 79
  on law and justice, 80–1, 82
  Measure for Measure linked to, 10–11, 82
  on painting, 80
  on pleasure and pain as mixed, 79–80
  problem plays compared with, 10–11, 78, 79
  'purity cannot fall into our use', 11, 78, 82
  on sexuality, 79, 80
The Tempest linked to, 142
Webster, John, 3
'Weighing the Options in Q1' (Dessen), 72n35
Weimann, Robert, 166n1
'"Well-sayd olde Mole": Burying Three *Hamlet*s in Modern Editions' (Urkowitz), 49
'What Did Montaigne's Skepticism Mean to Shakespeare and His Contemporaries?' (Hamlin), 40n14, 168n10
White, Richard Grant, 70n15
White Devil, The (Webster), 3
'Why Shakespeare is Not Michelangelo' (Burrow), 13n3
Wilson, John Dover, 104n12
Winter's Tale, The (Shakespeare), 104n11, 160–1
Woods, Gillian, 104n12, 127n19
Woolf, Virginia, 35
Worlde of Wordes, A (Florio), 67
Wright, William Aldis, 48, 49

Xenophon, 55

Yachnin, Paul, 153n59
Yates, Frances, 16n28

Zalloua, Zahi, 22n66, 43n48
Zeno, 55–6

EU representative:
Easy Access System Europe
Mustamäe tee 50, 10621 Tallinn, Estonia
Gpsr.requests@easproject.com

www.ingramcontent.com/pod-product-compliance
Lightning Source LLC
Chambersburg PA
CBHW070356240426
43671CB00013BA/2522